HEINEMANN STUDIES IN SOCIOLOGY

General Editor : Donald Gunn MacRae

SOCIAL THEORY AND SOCIAL POLICY

HEINEMANN STUDIES IN SOCIOLOGY

SOCIAL THEORY
& SOCIAL POLICY

Robert Pinker

Head of the Department of Sociology
Goldsmiths' College
University of London

**HEINEMANN EDUCATIONAL
BOOKS LIMITED · LONDON**

Heinemann Educational Books Ltd

LONDON EDINBURGH MELBOURNE TORONTO
SINGAPORE JOHANNESBURG AUCKLAND
IBADAN HONG KONG NAIROBI NEW DELHI

Cased edition ISBN 0 435 82860 8
Paperback edition ISBN 0 435 82681 6

Published by
Heinemann Educational Books Ltd
48 Charles Street, London W1X 8AH
Printed in Great Britain by
Morrison and Gibb Ltd, London and Edinburgh

Foreword

It is customary for teachers in higher education to look for the genealogy of what is called Social Administration in Britain and Social Welfare (not quite the same thing) in North America to two sources. These are the immemorial practice of Christian charity going back to a period long antecedent to the Reformation on the one hand, and the clutch of philosophies and philosophically inspired organizations engaged in doing good in the nineteenth century such as utilitarianism, British Hegelianism, the Social Gospel movement, etc., on the other. Today social administration is a central and major part of the budgeting policy and concern of every civilized society. It is highly bureaucratized. It is highly professionalized, and although many of its practitioners are clearly the great nieces and grandchildren of Lady Bountiful, they tend to be highly trained, rather contemptuous of amateurs, and to pride themselves on their efficiency rather than on their often remarkable virtue.

As parts of a diffuse bureaucracy they find their goals in social policy. By what criteria is that policy made and judged? Usually by standards that are themselves, in no necessarily pejorative sense, based on an ideology of economic efficiency, or a watered-down Freudianism, or some other ingredient in the ideological mix of our time. As the geologist can read the record of past times in the record of the rocks so can the social or intellectual historian discern in contemporary social policy the elements of such factors as I mentioned above and of curious ghosts of *laissez faire*, less eligibility, the Oedipus complex, maternal deprivation, the insurance principle, the deserving poor, and so on and on.

As social policy and social administration have become incorporated into the fabric of higher learning so has there taken place the uneasy alliance with sociology. Often indeed, the two disciplines are confused. Sometimes they are, in research at least, identical. By this I mean that properly conducted research may take its origins in an impulse from the field of social administration, but that if it is properly conducted it will in fact be sociological in its character, and that, of course, sociologists, unconcerned perhaps with a social problem as such, will yet rely for data on problem-oriented researches. What is more, it is increasingly and almost universally the case that students of social administration are turned to a knowledge of some of the methods and ideas of sociology even more than of economics or even psychology.

Now sociology is rich, perhaps some would say, though not this writer, too rich, in ideas. What is the relevance of social theory to social administration? This is but one of the questions to which Robert Pinker directs his attention in these pages. In a way it is his central question. In answering it he gives us a teaching book that is also original in its exploration, its candour, and its ideas. But one cannot confine oneself to the ideas of the old masters, Spencer, Marx, Durkheim, Weber, etc., on such a theme. There are, as has been suggested, other thought worlds involved which lead one into social and economic and ideological history. How these intermesh is another of Robert Pinker's themes. It brings us back to those problems of justice in society which are as old as Plato and which have centrally concerned the makers of sociology as a university discipline in Britain, the late Morris Ginsberg and T. H. Marshall.

And of course the development of sociology as theory and enquiry has not stopped. Many readers will find that the most original and unfamiliar of these pages are concerned with the relevance to social policy of new arrivals, both exciting and often misunderstood, on the sociological scene such as exchange theory, the concept of stigma and the general relevance of phenomenology. As everywhere in the book what we are given here is not mere paraphrase, but interpretation, re-interpretation and something which is new, personal and I believe practically relevant and revolutionary from Robert Pinker. As it should, the end crowns the work. Like all the few really good books for students this one is an addition to all our understanding. From its argument one discovers new problems, new criticism, new standards of judgement. It will be a new misfortune for the unfortunate if their lot is not affected by the concluding contentions of these pages.

For what is at stake is not just the provision of a text for students, however good, or a guide for policy makers and researchers, however novel and cogent. It is the condition of our society and its human compassion. Social policy is not about others; it is about us. I do not agree with everything here, but I have learned and been altered in my attitudes by it. Nor can any of us assume that it will not prove personally relevant either to our own persons or to those who are our kin or whom we hold in our affections. To the contrary: statistically the chances that somewhere, at some time in life, we shall need the relevant help of social administration. That it will be thus relevant and not contemptuous of us as citizens is, as bureaucracy and budgets grow, one of the great issues of our time. Too often is it treated in a grey, a technical, a negligible and mechanical way. The autonomous person must be recovered in social policy. Social theory can help this recovery. This book should do more than instruct; it should open a debate.

DONALD G. MACRAE

Highgate, 1970.

To my Father and Mother

Contents

Introduction

THE purpose of this book is to examine and account for the relationship between sociological theory and the development of social policy and administration. The greater part of the substantive material on social policy relates to England, but the issues raised in this study derive from those problems of a more general nature that arise when we seek to apply social theory to any area of applied study. Furthermore, the current lack of adequate comparative analysis in social policy and administration encourages students of social welfare to over-emphasize the distinctive nature of social welfare problems in each national context. There are, however, a number of common themes that recur in the debate about the aims and consequences of social policies that is taking place today in all advanced industrial societies. Certain of these themes, including the possible uses of sociological theory and research in the resolution of welfare problems, the nature of dependency and stigma, the ordering of social priorities and the factors influencing access to and utilization of social services in industrial societies, are examined in this book.

In the first part we attempt to explain why sociological theory has played a relatively insignificant role in the evolution of English social policy. Each of the four major theorists chosen was concerned with social change and problems created by social change. As the most influential English social theorist of the nineteenth century, Spencer could not be neglected. Marx, Durkheim and Weber were included because of the influence of their work upon the development of sociology in this country. There would be equally valid grounds for including other European sociologists, but this section of the book does not claim to be more than exploratory and provisional in nature. Furthermore, the aim of the book is to point to some possible basis for a closer and more productive relationship in the future between sociology on the one hand and social policy and administration on the other. We may require another and more suitable context in which to undertake a more exhaustive analysis of the failures of the past.

Classical economic theory exercised a more direct and profound influence upon the development of English social policy than did sociological theory during the nineteenth century. In the second part of the book we analyse the legislative consequences of this influence in the context of the new Poor Law. We seek to account for the preoccupation of Poor Law legislators and administrators with the problem of 'able-bodied' pauperism, and also to trace the development of 'blue-book' sociology—both as a challenge to the evaluative criteria of the economic market and as the basis of a new subject area. The Poor Law is interpreted, not simply as an exclusively deterrent service, but as the institutional expression of value conflicts and compromises about the aims of public welfare which were intrinsic in English culture. The second part of the book outlines the historical origins of modern social services as therapeutic and sanctioning agencies. Stigma is described as the commonest and most effective form of sanction.

In the third part we analyse the ways in which the discipline of social policy and administration has suffered from its lack of sociological content. As a subject it has developed an impressive empirical tradition while lacking any substantial body of explanatory theory. The commitment of social administrators to political ends in the attempt to improve levels of social welfare has caused many of them to confuse their own prescriptions with those of the general public, and especially with the expectations of the poor. Some evidence has been collected on the subjective realities of social need, but it offers little encouragement to social reformers. In recent years there has been a revival of neo-Marxist normative theory, which has distracted attention from what seem to be the central theoretical and substantive problems of social welfare. Both normative theories of social welfare and the traditionally administrative and legislative approaches to the problems of social need tend to ignore the subjective realities of everyday life. It is hypothesized that the central dilemma of social welfare arises from the way in which members of industrial societies equate loss of independent economic status with stigma and humiliation. Social and public services are analysed as systems of exchange, and public services are commended as a neglected but potentially valuable means of resolving the dilemma of dependency.

Finally, we consider the contemporary role of positive discrimination programmes in relation to the debate about universalism and selectivity, and the possible effect which the equation of dependency with inferior civic status has had upon the ordering of social priorities.

This book is therefore concerned with the development of an applied social science and its influence on the making of actual social policy, and also with the role which theory has played and might yet fulfil in these processes. A second companion volume is currently in preparation and will be concerned with the comparative analysis of social policy and administration.

Acknowledgments

Authors so often exploit the generosity of relations, friends and colleagues that their acknowledgments are as much a form of apology as an expression of gratitude. I wish to thank Professor Brian Abel-Smith and Dr Josephine Klein for their most valuable comments on the essay from which this book originated. Mr John Carrier and Mr Ian Gulland gave generously of their time and knowledge in reading and commenting on the final draft. I am grateful to Goldsmiths' College for allowing me study-leave in which to write the book. I am especially indebted to Professor Donald MacRae for his wholehearted encouragement and wise advice, which engendered the confidence needed to undertake this work.

My thanks are also due to my aunt, Miss Georgina Winyard, who looked after the children while my wife typed a difficult manuscript with speed, intelligence and forbearance. Miss Sheila Benson helped to prepare the index with great thoroughness. I remain wholly responsible for any deficiencies and omissions in the completed work.

I

SOCIAL THEORY AND THE DEVELOPMENT OF SOCIAL ADMINISTRATION

I

1

A Search for Paternity amongst the Founding Fathers

SOCIOLOGY AND PROBLEMS OF SOCIAL WELFARE

In seeking to understand the rationale of social welfare systems I have usually ended my studies feeling like those provincial ladies of *Middlemarch*, who were 'always wanting in reasons, yet . . . are too ignorant to understand the merits of any question and usually fall back on their moral sense to settle things after their own taste'.[1] Those provincial ladies, of course, lacked the intellectual support of a Mannheimian 'universe of discourse' in which to refine their tastes and achieve even a modest degree of objectivity. None the less, we begin this study of the relationship between social theory, moral philosophy and social policy from what seems, initially at least, to be an identical position.

There is much talk of social improvement by the more intellectual characters of *Middlemarch*, but the talk is to little practical effect. Dr Lydgate contracts a bad marriage, and his dreams of scientific research in his own hospital end in fashionable private practice. Even marriage to a beautiful bluestocking fails to revive the faded scholarship of Mr Casaubon. The town hospital owes its foundation to a hypocritical banker. Will Ladislaw eventually wins his heart's desire and the way to a position of political influence. Mr Farebrother talks little of improving anyone and does good by stealth. The schemes of social improvement so passionately urged by Dorothea Brooke find their closest practical expression in the good 'business' dealings of Caleb Garth, an honest estate manager. George Eliot seems, on balance, to have had modest expectations of intellectuals and zealots when it came to building hospitals and workmen's cottages.

[1] George Eliot, *Middlemarch*, Dent Dutton, 1959, Vol. I, p. 79

3

Hospitals and workmen's cottages figured considerably in the early subject-matter of social policy and administration. The medical needs and housing of the poor were primary concerns of the Victorian sanitary reformers, Chadwick, Farr and Senior. Beatrice Webb began her apprenticeship in social research investigating living conditions in St Katherine's Buildings near Wapping. Whether we start from health, housing, or other areas of need, we are soon led to consider a complex of more or less related contingencies and an equally heterogeneous range of welfare provisions that we term 'social services'. But it is no longer sufficient to itemize these services and their attendant list of social problems when seeking to define the subject-matter of social administration.

Kathleen Jones defines this subject-matter as being 'problem-centred'.

> It starts from the problem end of sociology, in what some sociologists call social pathology; but while sociology is concerned only with the identification and description of social problem areas (suicide, crime, poverty and so on), social administration is concerned with action. It proceeds from social pathology to social legislation and social policy, continues to the study of executive action (what is actually done by administrators, social workers and others—which may not be the same as what is laid on the Statute Book) and ends in consumer research: how the social services affect the ordinary citizen in need.[1]

This definition is of interest because it assumes a remarkable dichotomy between the ends of social administration and sociology. In effect the definition repeats uncritically that traditional distinction between 'pure' and 'applied' social sciences that has characterized these disciplines for so long. The same distinction is pointed to in a more critical way by MacRae who, after describing social administration as 'the training of welfare workers and administrators and the concrete study of individuals suffering social deprivation or disaster[2]

[1] Kathleen Jones, *The Compassionate Society*, and quoted by Muriel Brown, *Introduction to Social Administration in Britain*, Hutchinson University Library, 1969, p. 16

[2] Donald G. MacRae, 'The Crisis of Sociology', in J. H. Plumb (ed.), *Crisis in the Humanities*, Penguin Books, 1964, p. 135

goes on to examine its relationship to sociology. Social administration, we are told, 'is often identified with sociology, draws its ideas from it, and contributes facts and techniques to it. It is, however, above all practical and vocational, concerned actually and excellently to do good, but not concerned primarily with the *ends* of sociology'.[1] MacRae concludes that 'This identification in empirical and pragmatic Britain is almost irresistible, but is intellectually an error and must in time be self-defeating if only because sociology as a living fountain of ideas, images and analyses will dry up'.[2]

We are not told why this cutting off of riches will occur, except that sociology 'should not be the handmaiden of universal virtue'.[3] It may be that the sociological fountain will become blocked with a bric-à-brac of administrative facts and techniques. A second possibility is that social policy and administration has contributed little to sociological theory and is therefore largely parasitic upon that discipline. A third likelihood is that sociological theorists, in their handmaidenly role, have been a little too virginal in relation to their possible involvement in social problems. We would argue that the two disciplines have developed for too long in isolation from each other and that both have suffered in consequence. None the less, MacRae's main argument is incontestable—social administration appears to have failed to generate any substantial body of explanatory theory of its own. It is, however, equally true that sociologists have been oddly diffident about the subject-matter of social administration. This division may have been exacerbated by the fact, or rather the impression, that there are fewer trained sociologists specializing in the field of social administration than in any of the other substantive areas of sociology.

The discipline of social administration lacks that body of theoretical material which might give it a greater intellectual unity and perspective, as well as the means to utilize more effectively the diversity of professional skills which are at the moment concerned with its subject-matter. The current poverty of social administration as a theoretical discipline is indicated by the eagerness with which sociology students begin the study and the speed of their disillusionment as they fail, in company

---

[1] ibid.   [2] ibid.   [3] ibid., pp. 133–4

with their tutors, to relate it to the other sociological components of their courses. It may be, as Titmuss suggests, that there is too much 'over-teaching information and under-teaching the imaginative excitements of unifying perspectives and principles'.[1]

We are offered by Titmuss not a definitive explanation of the subject but an account of its 'interests and perspectives', which include

> the study of a range of social needs and the functioning in conditions of scarcity, of human organizations, traditionally called social services or social welfare systems, to meet these needs. . . . Social administration is thus concerned, for instance, with different types of moral transactions, embodying notions of gift exchange, of reciprocal obligations, which have developed in modern industrial societies in institutional forms to bring about and maintain social and community relations.[2]

The same author suggests in an earlier work that the 'definition, for most purposes, of what is a "social service" should take its stand on aims; not on the administrative methods and institutional devices employed to achieve them'.[3]

In this sense the 'problems' of social policy and administration are identified as being essentially moral rather than technical ones. These moral issues centre upon notions of community and the proper ends of communal action in the alleviation of human needs. We may take this approach further and suggest that in the discipline of social policy and administration most of the central value-problems of general sociology are dramatically heightened and amplified. This observation ought to be a commonplace for social services and the idea of a 'social market', in contrast to an 'economic market', represents the most institutionalized expression of much that we understand by the term 'community'. The history of social policy represents an ongoing endeavour to renew and also restore the social reality of community in the context of advanced industrial societies. Social services are contrived forms of mediation

[1] Richard M. Titmuss, *Commitment to Welfare*, Allen and Unwin, 1968, p. 18
[2] ibid., pp. 20–1
[3] R. M. Titmuss, *Essays on the Welfare State*, Allen and Unwin, 1958, p. 42

between individuals and social groups. The nature of these realities and mediations and their relationship to the development of sociology as a discipline is a central theme in this study.

Every advanced industrial society contains a complex of social welfare agencies, ostensibly concerned with the enhancement of individual and collective wellbeing. Sometimes the policy aims of such systems are so modest that the agencies do little more than prevent an actual lowering of living standards. Social welfare, in one form or another, is the professed aim of most political or economic activities. The subject-matter of social policy and administration includes many of the most intractable and poignant problems of social life. None the less, this material appears to hold less interest for social theorists than the institutional areas of religion, education, industry and deviance. While the influence of religion in industrial societies has gradually declined, the sociology of religion continues to develop as a theoretical enterprise. In the case of education, its growing institutional importance has been matched by a steady increase in the volume of related theoretical enquiry. Paradoxically, the proliferation of welfare agencies and functions in industrial societies has so far evoked little response from theorists. This is especially true of England, which is our main focus of concern.

It may be that even social problems are ranked in a hierarchy of academic esteem and the kinds of problem commonly associated with social policy and administration are not thought to be professionally enhancing to the sociologist. It is undeniable that the subject-matter of social administration frequently includes the needs and dependencies of ordinary people who themselves suffer stigma without retaliation. (Those who do raise the academic status of their need by striking back are taken over by the theorists of social deviance.)

Dahrendorf remarks that 'a scientific discipline that is problem conscious at every stage of its development is very unlikely ever to find itself in the prison of utopian thought or to separate theory and research'.[1] There is certainly little scope for utopianism in unravelling the problems of social security

[1] Ralf Dahrendorf, 'Out of Utopia', in N. J. Demarath III and Richard A. Peterson (eds), *System, Change and Conflict*, Free Press, New York, 1967, p. 475

provision against old age or the institutional care of the mentally handicapped. Much depends, however, on the level at which and the purposes for which the problem is defined. The neglect of social administration by sociological theorists is not a recent phenomenon. The further back in time we go the more evident this neglect becomes. Yet the founding fathers of sociology were by no means indifferent to social problems. It is hardly the case that those who sought to lay the basis of a positivistic social science were disposed to avoid vexatious issues. There were clearly very powerful normative elements present in the work of all the major sociological theorists of the nineteenth century. It will be argued instead that the neglect of those problems specific to social policy and administration was the consequence of a more general concern among sociologists with a more broadly defined problem. Most of the classical texts of nineteenth-century sociological theory represent various aspects of a total response to what appeared at the time to be a completely new kind of social problem.[1]

The origins of classical sociological theory can be seen as an intellectual and emotional response to the emergence of industrial societies in capitalist forms and the popular espousal of the doctrines of the 'Enlightenment'. This response was essentially a critical one, often markedly ideological in nature and in the main conservative. It represented, as Nisbet remarks, an attempt to challenge the Philosophes' conceptualization of society in terms of rational men, motivated by self-interest, entering into 'specified and limited mode[s] of association' on the basis of contract.[2]

Against this view of society was posed the notion of community comprising

all forms of relationship which are characterised by a high degree of personal intimacy, emotional depth, moral commitment, social cohesion and continuity in time. Community is founded on man conceived in his wholeness rather than in one or another of the roles, taken separately, that he may hold in a social order.[3]

---

[1] See also Robert A. Nisbet, *The Sociological Tradition*, Heinemann, 1967. 'The rise of sociology was a direct response to, or reflection of *new* forms of associative life in Western Europe, forms that industrialism and social democracy brought with them,' p. 57

[2] ibid., p. 48   [3] ibid., p. 47

The dominant concern of these social critics was to reinstate the idea and the reality of a moral community. Nisbet describes this continuity of concern in the work of Comte, Le Play, Tönnies, Maine, de Coulanges, Weber, Durkheim, Simmel and, from a radically different perspective, that of Marx.

In their different ways, each of these writers indicts the excessive individualism, impersonality, acquisitiveness and rational calculativeness of capitalist society. The contrast in approach between Marx and these other critics is demonstrated best by comparing his analysis with that of Tönnies. In Marx, it is suggested, 'the loss of community is dealt with as a consequence of capitalism, in Tönnies capitalism is treated as the consequence of the loss of community'.[1] The phenomenon of 'community' is taken by Nisbet as the most fundamental of his five 'essential unit-ideas of sociology, which, form the very warp of the sociological tradition'.[2] Significantly, neither Nisbet, nor the key authors on whose work he draws for illustration, give more than passing reference to issues of social policy. Despite their concern with the idea of 'community', what might have seemed to be one of the potentially substantive lineaments of a new form of social solidarity is either ignored or consigned to a peripheral role. This omission is all the more intriguing when it is recognized that by the last quarter of the nineteenth century all the major industrial societies of Europe had moved or were moving towards some form of collectivist social provision for certain categories of needy people.

The characteristics of nineteenth-century capitalism in its various stages have been very adequately defined and analysed by numerous authorities.[3] For our purposes we focus on the interrelated concepts of 'individualism' and 'the free market', as these were of central and primary concern to those nineteenth-century sociologists we wish to discuss. As a social doctrine or

---

[1] ibid., p. 78   [2] ibid., pp. 6–7

[3] See Max Weber, *General Economic History*, Collier Books, New York, 1961; W. E. Moore, *Industrial Relations and the Social Order*, MacMillan, New York, 1951; J. Schumpeter, *Capitalism, Socialism and Democracy*, Allen and Unwin, 1961; K. Marx, *Capital*, Vols I and II, Dent Dutton, 1946. Our brief discussion relies largely on H. L. Wilensky and C. N. Lebeaux, *Industrial Society and Social Welfare*, Free Press, Glencoe, 1965, which remains the best discussion of the development of social policy in relation to the wider aspects of social change.

ideology the individualist ethic of capitalism stressed the 'moral *duty* to *try* to get ahead' by means of purposive endeavour in a competitive struggle.[1] The institutions of the 'free market' and private property provided the context in which acquisitive forms of self-help could obtain material rewards. Social policy, in the form of a new Poor Law, provided sanctions for reluctant competitors.

As Horton suggests,

> The classical definition [of anomie and alienation] have in common their condemnation of economic individualism and its rationalization in the middle-class doctrines of economic and political liberalism . . . Marx and Durkheim critically describe societies in which . . . economic activities and values had become separated from and commanding over all other spheres of collective life. The most intense social activity in modern industrial societies, economic activity, was the least social.[2]

Fifty years ago a very similar kind of indictment was made by Tawney, namely, that the intrinsic weakness of capitalism was its lack of moral solidarity and identity.[3]

It is necessary to guard against confusing the prescriptions of the classical political economists and utilitarians and the popularized forms of *laissez-faire* doctrine that became part of public debate in the early nineteenth century. Adam Smith and Ricardo were both concerned to allow for some mitigation of the free play of market forces. They were, however, critical of traditional restraints upon competition and of utopian reformists who ignored economic realities such as the 'wages fund'. Ricardo indicted the laxity of the Speenhamland system of poor relief, arguing that any tendency to pay or subsidize wages above the natural or market price of labour could only harm rather than benefit the poor. Additional income of this kind would encourage premature marriages and increases in the birth-rate. The kindest remedy for poverty was a reduction in poor relief and the inculcation of habits of inde-

---

[1] Wilensky and Lebeaux, p. 35

[2] John Horton, 'The Dehumanization of Anomie and Alienation: A Problem in the Ideology of Sociology,' in *British Journal of Sociology*, Vol. XV, No. 4, December 1964, p. 286

[3] R. H. Tawney, *The Acquisitive Society*, Allen and Unwin, 1946

pendence, prudence and forethought amongst the poor. Malthusian doctrines were also gaining strong support in influential quarters. The popularized forms of these theories can be seen as very understandable reactions against what must have seemed at the time to be an alarming *ad hoc* growth of collectivist policies. By 1818 the annual cost of poor relief had reached £18m., while the problem of pauperism remained as intractable as ever.

Utilitarianism, like political economy, also provided a theoretical and ethical apologia for free enterprise and competition. Ford, however, points to the 'internal dichotomy' in the thinking of leading Benthamists 'which would not reveal itself in practice till later; the individual was to be given freedom of enterprise and contract, but the very process of investigation sometimes led to conclusions which involved large-scale interference with that freedom'.[1] The Poor Law Amendment Act of 1834 was the social instrument devised by the practical exponents of these new theories. Its aim was to create the social conditions in which free competition could bring its benefits to all members of the community. The Act epitomized those social values and aims which were to be indicted by nearly all the early major sociological theorists with the exception of Spencer. Similar forms of social policy were developing in France and Germany. Yet in the case of Britain, at least, it is possible for an authority like Ford to give a coherent and convincing account of the development of nineteenth-century social policy with scarcely a reference to sociological theory. Indeed, Ford's title is the only seriously misleading part of his excellent study, which tells us nothing about 'social' theory as the term is understood today.

Our concern is to test the hypothesis that the most influential of the major European sociologists were never greatly involved with the substantive issues of social welfare that later became the defined subject-matter of social policy and administration. In the case of England, with which we are mainly concerned, the pre-eminent social theorist, Spencer, was also an apologist for free competition. During the period in which the theoretical and normative bases of European sociology were being estab-

[1] P. Ford, *Social Theory and Social Practice*, Irish University Press, Shannon, 1969, p. 32

lished, social policy and administration was already beginning to emerge as a separate discipline with radically different traditions. Although confronting the same phenomena, its practitioners asked different questions at an altogether different level of generality.

What later came to be known as the 'blue-book' sociology of the nineteenth century was a largely pragmatic affair, but most significantly it was a pragmatic response, or corrective, to certain kinds of theory. The theories in question were not sociological but economic and ethical. In consequence, social policy and administration developed away from the mainstream of sociological theory, retaining links with that discipline only because it continued to share certain institutional features of a common subject-matter. The legacy of this early divorce has been unfortunate to everyone concerned but it has probably been more damaging to social policy and administration. Various forms of snobbery and obscurantism are practised on both sides, but the real tragedy is that the 'sides' exist or are thought to exist.

In social policy and administration we begin with fact-finding and end in moral rhetoric, still lacking those explanatory theories which might 'show the process as a whole, and reveal the relations of the separate problems to one another'.[1] George Eliot was conscious of the readiness with which reformers leap from evidence to conclusions which they mistake for explanations:

'As to documents,' said Will, 'a two-inch card will hold plenty. A few rows of figures are enough to deduce misery from, and a few more will show the rate at which the political determination of the people is growing.'[2]

Social policy and administration has never really recovered from its own origins—as an empirical corrective to certain forms of normative theory. It is sustained today by the prestige of a few charismatic personalities. The increasing involvement of its practitioners in the actual making of social policy and in the education of social workers tempts us to confuse practical activity with intellectual development. As the discipline becomes more closely involved in political action and policy-making, so it begins to lose even that normative autonomy which was a

[1] ibid., p. 13   [2] *Middlemarch*, Vol. II, p. 27

part of its tradition. A new generation of specialists in social policy and administration is less impressed by the eclecticism in which its established members still rejoice and is more disturbed by its persistent lack of conceptual and theoretical foundations. The question that faces us is whether or not social policy and administration is becoming little more than a motley collection of skills which are applied, on a largely *ad hoc* basis, to a series of problems in the field of social welfare.

There is a tendency amongst some sociologists to look upon social administration as the Caliban of the social sciences. In its time it has certainly served many masters of varying reputation. Rumours about its paternity still give rise to doubt regarding its classification as a species. In the following sections we examine the relationship, or rather lack of relationship, between the work of four major sociological theorists and the origins of social policy and administration. Other nineteenth-century sociologists could equally well have been included, but further enquiry along these lines would be a major study in its own right and, we suggest, a largely negative one.

Durkheim, Spencer, Marx and Weber have been chosen because they represent, by any standards, figures of major influence in the development of sociological theory. Each of these authorities dealt in his own way with a variety of substantive topics which are now part of the subject-matter of social policy and administration. Spencer is of special importance to us, for he played an active role in the debate on the development of British social policy in the nineteenth century. He identified the growing importance of social services in industrial societies with the increasing power of the state—developments which Spencer considered antipathetic to the natural evolution of new types of social organization. Weber was similarly preoccupied with the extension of bureaucratic forms of domination and their effect upon the quality of social life. All of Durkheim's major works were concerned with various aspects of the problem of maintaining social solidarity and the need to improve the quality of moral relationships in industrial societies. In his analysis of these societies Marx attempted to show that such improvement was not possible under capitalist modes of production. At the same time he sought to define and prescribe the conditions under which individuals and societies could realize their full potentialities.

In each case the theoretical work of these writers can be seen as an intellectual response to the impact of social change upon traditional social orders. Each was concerned with those social problems created by social change, and the contribution that social scientists might make towards their resolution. Modern forms of social policy and planning are, in the last resort, practical attempts to modify the new kinds of relationship between economic and social markets that are the product of industrialization. Despite this complementarity of interests, very little of the work of these four theorists was to have any major or lasting influence upon the development of social policy and administration. Only in recent years, as we will attempt to show later in this study, have the potentialities for a closer association between social theory and social policy become more evident. None the less, this part of our study is of a limited nature and permits us to draw no more than tentative conclusions and hypotheses, which more extensive research may later support or invalidate.

DURKHEIM AND MORAL WELFARE

In his first major work, *The Division of Labour in Society*, Durkheim addressed himself to what was to remain his central concern—the forms of social solidarity and the means by which the moral order of modern industrial societies could be preserved and strengthened. Durkheim recognized the structural changes that had weakened and destroyed the traditional corporative associations of craftsmen and workers. In the past such associations served as bureaux of 'indirect assistance' to the needy.[1] And he wastes no sentiment on the complementary decline of the 'provincial spirit' and the 'patriotism of the parish' which he sees as anachronistic forms of local solidarity under conditions of large-scale industrial production.[2] Durkheim is concerned,

[1] Emile Durkheim, *The Division of Labour in Society*, Free Press, Glencoe, p. 11. See also *Professional Ethics and Civic Morals*, Routledge and Kegan Paul, London, 1957, pp. 20–3
[2] Durkheim, *The Division of Labour in Society*, p. 28

however, that other more appropriate forms of intermediary
association should be developed.

In his criticism of social-contract theory, Durkheim argues
that the ethics of the economic market are an insufficient basis
for new forms of social solidarity. Indeed, he accuses the
political economists of encouraging forms of economic behaviour
that are positively antisocial, and chides them for their
'strangely superficial notion' of collective discipline as 'a kind
of rather tyrannous militarism'.[1] While recognizing the necessity
of contracts, Durkheim reminds us that 'When we say contract
we mean concessions or sacrifices made to avoid more serious
ones'.[2] Exclusive reliance upon such restraints is an unsatis-
factory basis for social order which, to be effective, ought to
rest upon morality rather than interest. Durkheim remarks how
'There is nothing less constant than interest. Today it unites
me to you; tomorrow, it will make me your enemy.'[3] The
solution is 'for men to recognize and mutually guarantee rights'
and in order to do this 'they must, first of all, love each other,
they must, for some reason, depend upon each other and on the
same society of which they are a part'.[4]

Durkheim proposes a revived system of occupational guilds
adapted to the structure of large-scale industry. These new
associations would be able to develop mutual-aid functions
parallel to those of the family but exceeding them in their continuity and efficiency. These occupational systems of welfare
might even in a sense be substituted for the family because of
the requirements of trade.[5] As the division of labour becomes
more complex, new opportunities are created for forms of non-
contractual relationships based on occupational groups to
develop. In this way the reciprocities of family life will be
redefined, disputes between parties subjected to more effective

[1] Durkheim, *Professional Ethics and Civic Morals*, p. 29
[2] ibid., p. 208
[3] Durkheim, *The Division of Labour in Society*, p. 204
[4] ibid., p. 121
[5] ibid., p. 18. Durkheim's references to the family are always deferential
and adulatory. In one section he refers to it as 'school of devotion, of
abnegation, the place *par excellence* of morality . . .' (ibid., p. 15) and
alludes to the 'fact that family life has been and still is a centre of morality
and a school of loyalty, of selflessness and moral communing . . .' (*Professional Ethics and Civic Morals*, p. 25)

and sensitive regulation, and legal restraints of a social nature be brought to bear upon contracts. In *The Division of Labour*, Durkheim describes how 'The care of educating the young, of protecting the public health, of presiding over the ways of administering public aid, and of administering the means of transport and communication, little by little move over into the sphere of the central organ'.[1] Industrialization makes more apparent the interdependence between individuals and their society, and new opportunities for co-operation and altruism are created.

This extension of state control in the provision of social welfare does not, however, receive Durkheim's approval. He considers it essential that intermediary associations based on occupation should take the place of declining local agencies and limit the growing power of central authorities. A society in which nothing stands between 'a hypertrophied state' and 'an infinite number of unorganized individuals' is described as 'a veritable sociological monstrosity. For collective activity is always too complex to be able to be expressed through the single and unique organ of the state.'[2] In *Professional Ethics and Civic Morals* Durkheim returns to this issue and argues that the state is 'too far removed from the individual', to undertake such key welfare functions as social security, industrial health and the employment of women and children.[3]

But Durkheim reminds us of the direction and level of his concern with social welfare in his preface to the second edition of *The Division of Labour*, where he draws a distinction between 'the work of the sociologist' and that of the statesman. The sociologist's role is not to present the details of reform but 'to indicate the general principles as they appear from the preceding facts'.[4] Durkheim's treatment of criminality, suicide, mental illness and the provision of education is often detailed and rigorous, but with the exception of education, each of these phenomena is treated as an aspect of a more general problem —as symptoms of social deviance and threats to the moral cohesiveness of society. Proper forms of moral education are

[1] Durkheim, *The Division of Labour in Society*, p. 221
[2] ibid., p. 28
[3] Durkheim, *Professional Ethics and Civic Morals*, p. 40
[4] Durkheim, *The Division of Labour in Society*, p. 23

seen as a remedy for and preservation from these evils rather than changes in social-service provision.

One reason why Durkheim's treatment of these issues did not lead on to a consideration of related social-policy issues may be detected in his approach to the problems of social inequality and social justice. These problems, he argues, only arise under conditions of the abnormal division of labour, for if the division of labour does not, of itself, produce solidarity, it is due 'in part, to the fact that the working classes are not really satisfied with the conditions under which they live'.[1] Where social inequalities do not reflect natural inequalities, as in the case of privileges deriving from birth or inheritance, 'Society is forced to reduce this disparity as far as possible by assisting in various ways those who find themselves in a disadvantageous position and by aiding them to overcome it'.[2] Social inequalities destroy the basis of equivalence and reciprocity in exchange relationships so that 'the task of the most advanced societies is, then, a work of justice'.[3]

Durkheim appears reluctant, however, to specify in any detail the 'various ways' by which social injustice may be remedied. He is more disposed to chide egalitarians with the reminder that 'for centuries men have been content with a much less perfect justice' so that 'one may ask if these aspirations might not perhaps be due to unreasonable impatience.[4] He refers to Saint-Simon's disposition to show 'compassion for the unfortunate, along with a fear of their dangers to the social order.'[5] None the less, the most important requirement

> if social order is to reign, is that the mass of men be content with their lot. But what is needed for them to be content, is not that they have more or less but that they be convinced they have a right to no more. And for this it is absolutely essential that there be an authority whose superiority they acknowledge and which tells them what is right.[6]

It would seem, therefore, that in Durkheim's analysis the claims of social solidarity are to be accorded priority over those of social justice. The amelioration of needs through radical pro-

[1] ibid., p. 356   [2] ibid., p. 379   [3] ibid., p. 387   [4] ibid., p. 387
[5] Emile Durkheim, *Socialism*, Collier Books, 1967, p. 209
[6] ibid., p. 242

grammes of redistribution would not solve a malaise that was in the last resort of a moral rather than economic nature.

It is to moral education rather than social policy to which Durkheim turns. Education must inculcate a spirit of self-discipline and obedience to the social order, so that, para-doxically, the true basis of a genuine personal autonomy is created. Freedom 'is not to do what one pleases; it is to be master of oneself, it is to know how to act with reason and to do one's duty'.[1] What matters is that we should 'choose a definite task and immerse ourselves in it completely, instead of trying to make ourselves a sort of creative masterpiece, quite complete, which contains its worth in itself and not in the services that it renders'.[2] This notion of service is carried over into the work situation where the worker must 'feel that he is serving something. For that he need not embrace vast portions of the social horizon; it is sufficient that he perceive enough of it to understand that his actions have an aim beyond themselves'.[3]

Moral education and the building up of occupational associations rather than egalitarian social policies are com-mended by Durkheim as the new basis of social solidarity in industrial societies. Some reasons for this preference may be inferred from his major works, especially *The Division of Labour* and *Suicide*. Firstly Durkheim is swift to note and applaud the virtues of poverty and the protection that it offers against anomie. Given a true sense of social solidarity, poverty in itself is not a barrier to contentment. By contrast, radical forms of social change such as those which might result from hasty pro-cedures of social reform and redistribution, or the engendering of discontent and envy, may well destroy social contentment. Acceptance of one's lot, even though it be a poor one, is seen almost as a moral safeguard from the worse evils of anomie and social disorganization. We are reminded that poverty by 'forcing us to constant self-discipline prepares us to accept collective discipline with equanimity, while wealth, exalting the individual, may always arouse the spirit of rebellion which is the very source of immorality'.[4]

---

[1] Emile Durkheim, *Education and Sociology*, Free Press, Glencoe, 1956, pp. 89–90.
[2] Durkheim, *The Division of Labour in Society*, p. 401   [3] ibid., pp. 372–3
[4] Emile Durkheim, *Suicide*, Routledge and Kegan Paul, 1963, p. 254

Secondly, although altruism is the essence of organic solidarity, there must be limits to social obligation for 'one cannot give oneself too completely to others without abandoning oneself . . . Morality cannot excessively govern industrial, communal functions, etc. without paralysing them and nevertheless, they are vital'.[1] The claims of social welfare must coexist with those of the economic market although, in the last resort, economic activity must also take account of the wider needs of society.

A third factor that might be taken into account is the place which social policy, especially in its statutory forms, held in the industrial societies of the nineteenth century. We will return to this topic later in our study, but it may be noted now that the characteristic forms of statutory social relief in Britain, France and Germany for the greater part of that century were of stigmatizing and deterrent kinds. The English Poor Law and its continental variants were cultural manifestations of the dominant ethos of capitalism. In times and places where the values of the economic market are dominant, poverty has always been the most frequently and heavily penalised form of deviance. This occurs partly because it is a deviance from the economic norms of individualistic self-help and successful acquisition, and partly because the deviants in question are so frequently compelled from biological necessity to make public declarations of their deviance. In this sense poverty is a unique form of deviance because, even in the most rigorously deterrent systems, a relatively high proportion of offenders will voluntarily confess their guilt—if only to ensure that their innocent dependents will be spared further suffering.

Although the idea of social justice and assistance was upheld as a civic duty by the revolutionaries of 1789, the statutory assistances of the French poor law (*assistance publique*) during the nineteenth century accorded the pauper, *as such*, no legal rights to aid from the community. Not until the beginning of this century were *rights* to relief 'accorded to certain categories of persons: free medical assistance in 1893, assistance to children in 1904, to the old, infirm and the incurable in 1905, to pregnant women and to large families in 1913'.[2] Furthermore, the French

---

[1] Durkheim, *The Division of Labour in Society*, p. 239
[2] Barbara N. Rodgers with John Greve and John S. Morgan, *Comparative Social Administration*, Allen and Unwin, 1968, p. 31

system of *bureaux d'assistance* was not supported by the levy of a local poor rate as in England. Although the local *bureaux* included local representatives the degree of central control seems to have been relatively greater.

Like the English Poor Law, the French system of collectively provided social aid embodied repressive rather than restitutive forms of sanction and would therefore have lacked any obvious affinity with a reformed social order based more exclusively upon organic forms of solidarity. There is a logic in Durkheim's preference for extending mutual aid services on the basis of occupational associations and with an emphasis upon mutuality. In this respect Durkheim anticipated to a considerable degree the contemporary growth of occupational welfare schemes. It is, however, worth noting that between the first and second editions of *The Division of Labour in Society* the sanctioning functions of the French system of statutory social welfare were being ameliorated and complemented by more generous forms of provision, and these changes drew little comment from Durkheim although they might be thought to have had some bearing upon his thesis. It is also significant that Dicey considered the pace of social reform in France at this time to be more rapid and 'socialistic' than was the case in England.[1] The 'social question' for Durkheim, however, was not 'a question of money or force . . . but, much more, the state of our morality'[2] and it was this concern, as Zeitlin observes, that dominated and directed the course of his major sociological enquiries.[3] In one sense the powerful normative and prescriptive elements in Durkheim's theory suggest that social reform through welfare legislation was an insufficiently radical procedure because it would have touched only the economic surface of a moral problem. In another sense socialistic programmes of revolution or major forms of redistribution would have posed too radical a threat to the moral order of society and created new forms of discontent and disaffection.

We are told that Durkheim, although sympathetic to

[1] A. V. Dicey, *Law and Public Opinion in England During the Nineteenth Century*, Macmillan, 1962, pp. lxv–xxvii

[2] Durkheim, *Socialism*, p. 247

[3] Irving M. Zeitlin, *Ideology and the Development of Sociological Theory*, Prentice-Hall Inc., 1968

socialism, never became a socialist.[1] In his study of Saint-Simon and Socialism there are indications of the kind of socialist Durkheim might have become, and these indications are clearest when he is setting forth his intellectual and moral objections to the doctrine. Durkheim points out that although the furtherance of equality in economic relationships is often an aim of socialists, other political doctrines have also shared this goal. He is quick to argue that 'Socialism goes beyond the working man's problem' in its concern to protect the interests of the state as well as the poor.[2] The distinctive feature of socialism is its concern to place economic activity in a direct relationship with the 'conscious agencies of society'.[3] The workers must be brought into a more direct and total relationship with society than the present capitalist system allows, but the 'material changes they hope for are only one form and result of this more complete integration'.[4] Again we are told that

> Socialism does not reduce itself to a question of wages or—as they say—the stomach. It is above all an aspiration for a rearrangement of the social structure, by reallocating the industrial setup in the totality of the social organism . . . summoning it to the light and the control of the conscience.[5]

Durkheim is extremely critical of the central role attributed to economic activities and relationships in socialist doctrines. He makes a distinction between socialism, 'which consists of linking industrial activities to the state' and Communism which 'tends instead to put industrial life outside the state'.[6] The same distinction is drawn in slightly different terms when he suggests that 'the fundamental axiom of socialism is that there are no social interests outside economic interests, whereas the axiom of communism is that economic interests are anti-social . . .'[7] Durkheim never conceived of economic interests and activities as being intrinsically anti-social. He did object to what seemed to be a fundamental inconsistency in socialism, namely, that 'the way to realise social peace is to free economic appetites of all restraint on the one hand, and on the other to satisfy them

---

[1] See Durkheim, *Socialism*, introduction to First Edition by Marcel Mauss, pp. 34–5

[2] ibid., p. 50   [3] ibid., p. 54   [4] ibid., p. 61   [5] ibid.
[6] ibid., p. 67   [7] ibid., p. 237

by fulfilling them'. These appetites, he contends, 'cannot be appeased unless they are limited and they cannot be limited except by something other than themselves'.[1] Only society has the moral force and character to restrain men's restless desires and jealousies. What religion once performed, moral discipline and education must now take care of.

It is almost as if Durkheim equates the extension of ameliorative welfare programmes with the unbridled pursuit of hedonism. He recognizes that philanthropic morality will help curb the material appetites of the wealthy. Durkheim's moral austerity has a socially ubiquitous quality. He is equally anxious that 'the desires of [the poor] should be no less regulated than the needs of the others'.[2] It is intriguing to speculate on the kind of critique Durkheim might have made of the currently popular concept of 'relative poverty'. He would almost certainly have noted the anomic propensities of those drastic falls in income which often accompany retirement or disability. He might also have approved of the view that no individual's or family's resources should be allowed to 'fall seriously short of the resources commanded by the average individual or family in the community in which they live . . .'. It is, however, doubtful whether he would have accepted the last clause in Townsend's definition which extends the notion of community from a local to a 'national or international one . . .'.[3] 'Community' is in the last resort a matter of consciousness, and it is doubtful whether many of the poor, left to themselves, think in national terms, quite apart from international terms. At this stage in the critique we might have encountered that spectre of the 'individual committed only to the pressure of his needs', who 'will never admit he has reached the extreme limits of his rightful portion'—a spectre which appears again and again whenever Durkheim concerns himself with questions of equality and social justice.[4]

---

[1] ibid., p. 242   [2] ibid., p. 245

[3] Peter Townsend, 'The Meaning of Poverty', *British Journal of Sociology*, Vol. XIII, No. 3, September 1962, p. 225

[4] Durkheim, *Socialism*, p. 242. See also *Professional Ethics and Civic Morals*, pp. 10–11, where Durkheim suggests that 'It is not possible for a social function to exist without moral discipline. Otherwise nothing remains but individual appetites, and since they are by nature boundless and insatiable, if there is nothing to control them they will not be able to control themselves'.

It seems probable that Durkheim would have approved of certain developments in social-work practice. Halmos's notion of 'philanthropic' personal service professions such as social work acting as 'moral tutors' to mankind is very much in the Durkheimian tradition.[1] Leonard refers to a 'primary political function' of social workers as that of 'the maintenance of consensus and the management of conflict by helping to alleviate the effects of the unequal distribution of economic power and resources, while leaving intact the basic economic and political structures'.[2] Such an approach reflects Durkheim's ordering of social priorities.

In summary, however, Durkheim's social theory seems to offer little of direct relevance to the discipline of social policy and administration although it offers, indirectly, a great deal that is of value. Apart from the obvious relevance of his major study of suicide to certain areas of social-work practice and community work,[3] the distinctive feature of Durkheim's approach is that it offers so little comfort and encouragement to the collectivist and egalitarian tradition in social policy and administration. He is rigorously critical of those who naïvely assume that the unbridled pursuit of enlightened self-interest will result in the enhancement of collective welfare.

But Durkheim's critique of classical political economy is complemented by a lack of faith in traditional collectivist remedies. He dismisses the panacea of nationalization as a form of 'witchcraft' which would leave the problem of moral regulation unresolved.[4] And there is throughout Durkheim's works a brooding pessimism about the inherently rapacious nature of human desires, which can only be tamed and truly liberated by rigorous moral education. 'Life,' we are told, 'is not all play;

---

[1] See Paul Halmos, 'The Personal Service Society', *British Journal of Sociology*, Vol. XVIII, No. 1, March 1967, and Durkheim, *Professional Ethics and Civic Morals*, esp. pp. 12–13

[2] Peter Leonard, 'The Application of Sociological Analysis to Social Work Training', *British Journal of Sociology*, Vol. XIX, No. 4, December 1968, pp. 379–80

[3] See Erwin Stengel, *Suicide and Attempted Suicide*, Penguin Books, 1964, and P. Sainsbury, *Suicide in London*, Chapman and Hall, 1955, for useful appraisals of this contribution

[4] Durkheim, *Professional Ethics and Civic Morals*, p. 31

the child must prepare himself for pain and effort.'[1] Self-denial
and abstinence are necessary features of a social order. Poverty
is not an unmitigated evil except when heightened awareness
of injustice threatens social stability. There are more important
ends in social life than the satisfaction of material needs. There
is an austerity and logic in Durkheim's social analysis which
points to the conclusion that men's noble instincts can as easily
be debauched by over-generous forms of collectivist welfare
provision as by the restless pursuit of personal gain in the
economic market. Such counsels of restraint and caution could
have little direct or obvious appeal as a normative and theoretical framework for the development of either individualist
or collectivist forms of welfare society. The indirect value of
Durkheim's approach has been largely ignored in the making
of social policy. His emphasis on the need for moral education
has received only a faint and distorted acknowledgment in
public reactions to the use of social services. Even here the
relationship is tenuous and not necessarily of a kind that
Durkheim would have approved. On the right, there are the
traditional anxieties about the 'abuse' of social services and the
need to inculcate habits of restraint amongst the poor. On the
left, there has been much rhetoric about the importance of
heightening the individual's consciousness of citizenship, and
educating him in the use of social services. In practice the role
of moral education in relation to social services has remained
undeveloped; we will return to this subject later in our study.

Spencer and Social Welfare

Like Durkheim, Spencer was much concerned with morality,
but unlike Durkheim he had very explicit views about the use
of statutory social services as instruments of moral instruction.
After years of neglect, there are clear signs of a revival of interest
in Spencer's theoretical sociology, and with this interest a
better understanding of why his approach to social analysis

[1] Quoted by Lewis A. Coser in Kurt H. Wolff, ed. *Emile Durkheim, 1858–
1917, A Collection of Essays*, with translations and bibliography, Ohio State
University Press, Columbus, Ohio, 1960, p. 228. See also Emile Durkheim,
Moral Education, The Free Press, New York, Collier-Macmillan Limited,
London, 1968, p. 160

dominated English sociology for so long.[1] In his excellent study of Victorian social theory, Burrow draws attention to the 'apparently inexplicable' separation that took place in the eighteen-fifties and sixties between the concerns of 'charitable' social science and sociological theory.[2] While the evolutionary orientations of sociological theory drew interest away from analysis of social structure, 'practical' sociology failed to establish any effective theoretical framework for future guidance.

Apart from these differences in subject-matter, there were marked differences of ethical attitude between Spencer—taken by Burrow as exemplifying the school of evolutionary social theory—and Beatrice Webb as being representative of 'practical' sociology.[3] Beatrice Webb bears witness to the 'new consciousness of sin amongst men of intellect and men of property' and the preoccupation of social investigators with the relief of misery. Spencer makes his position equally clear as a moral scientist when he states that it is

> the business of moral science to deduce, from the laws of life and the conditions of existence, what kinds of action necessarily tend to produce happiness, and what kinds to produce unhappiness. Having done this, its deductions are to be recognised as laws of conduct; and are to be conformed to *irrespective of a direct estimation of happiness and misery.*[4]

In his description and analysis of social development and organization, Spencer drew very close analogies with biological organisms. He sought to demonstrate that as social structures become more complex and differentiated, new forms of social integration develop. Spencer conceived of societies as self-regulating systems, exhibiting '*a mutual dependence of parts*'.[5] He argued that '*in proportion as there is to be efficiency, there*

---

[1] See Stanislav Andreski, ed., *Herbert Spencer: Principles of Sociology*, Macmillan, 1969, and Donald MacRae, ed., *Herbert Spencer: The Man versus the State*, Penguin Books, 1970. Both of these collections have excellent editorial introductions

[2] J. W. Burrow, *Evolution and Society*, Cambridge University Press, 1970, pp. 88–90

[3] ibid., pp. 91–2

[4] H. Spencer, *An Autobiography* (2 vols, 1904), II, p. 88, quoted and italicized by Burrow, *op. cit.*, p. 92

[5] Spencer, *The Man versus the State*, p. 282

must be specialization, both of structure and function—specialization which of necessity, implies accompanying limitation.[1] For Spencer this proposition has the status of a 'law', and state intervention is one of the key phenomena that he is most concerned to limit. Spencer wished to impose the most stringent limitations upon the scope of governmental administration, and especially so in the field of social welfare provision, irrespective of the short-run distress that might be caused.

Despite his tendency to equate social evolution with social progress, Spencer remained averse to the idea of the desirability of radical change in his own society, and was especially hostile to the claims of state intervention in furthering social change. He contended that 'though higher institutions will evolve in conformity with general laws, when the nature of citizens permits' this will only take place 'on condition that social units voluntarily act out their natures'.[2] He was not prepared to consider the possibility that state intervention to alleviate poverty might reflect the wishes and nature of the citizenry. Such collectivist policies were, if anything, against nature.

If Durkheim was relatively indifferent to the substantive concerns of social administration, Spencer was preoccupied with such matters. He was dismissive of the claims of 'intellectual' forms of education as a fit object for public subsidy. Like Durkheim, Spencer did believe in the virtues of a moral education, claiming that 'for social welfare, good character is more important than much knowledge'.[3] Good character meant looking after one's own welfare by personal endeavour, thrift and forethought. While Durkheim and Spencer both thought it essential to inculcate social discipline in the minds of the poor, Spencer wished to go further and use social services, or rather the denial of social services, as a disciplinary agent. He denied that he was immune to the claims of charity and fellow feeling and answered his critics with the claim that it was more natural and socially advantageous to rely upon 'parental affection, the regard of relatives, and the spontaneous kindness of friends, and even of strangers' to alleviate suffering and the penalties of immoderate living.[4] It could be argued that Spencer

[1] ibid., p. 308
[2] Herbert Spencer, *The Study of Sociology*, Williams and Norgate, London, 1894, p. 407   [3] ibid., p. 368   [4] ibid., p. 341

fails to follow his logic through to its own ruthless conclusion in these references to voluntary aid. If the state weakens the 'average vitality' of society by intervening to help its weakest members, might not philanthropic kinsfolk, friends and 'even' strangers similarly also cause further evil where they intended only good?

The key distinction for Spencer was between individualist and collectivist forms of aid, the latter being equated with socialism and the curtailment of those personal liberties he prized so highly. Spencer also feared that collectivist forms of social welfare would create a distance between donors and recipients. The effect of such distance was that 'when the miseries of the poor are dilated upon, they are thought of as the deserving poor, instead of . . . the undeserving poor, which in large measure they should be'.[1] The tendency in collectivist provisions of social welfare was always to dissociate misery from the misconduct which caused it. It is significant that Spencer was expounding these views in the eighteen-eighties, at a time when official policy was beginning to favour amelioration of the harsher aspects of poor-law policy. Out-relief was being more generously provided in some unions and certain categories of workhouse inmates were receiving 'extra comforts' as rewards for good behaviour.[2]

These unyielding attitudes towards the easement of distress are related to both Spencer's theory of social development and his theory of politics. He opposed 'maudlin philanthropy' which fostered social inadequates because 'There is no greater curse to posterity than that of bequeathing them an increasing population of imbeciles, idlers and criminals . . .'[3] Spencer proceeds to offer some vivid illustrations of the social dangers of helping the weak and the undeserving at the expense of the stronger and more disciplined members of society. The support of paupers and the mothers of illegitimate children would eventually lead to a deterioration in the biological and moral quality of the nation. We are reminded that

[1] Spencer, *The Man* versus *the State*, p. 82
[2] Medical relief was ceasing to be treated as grounds for disenfranchisement and the central authority was beginning to issue circulars advising more generous treatment of the aged.
[3] Spencer, *The Study of Sociology*, p. 340

If a people who, for a score of generations, had bred from their worst tempered horses and their least sagacious dogs, were then to wonder because their horses were vicious and their dogs stupid, we should think the absurdity of their policy paralleled only by the absurdity of their astonishment.[1]

Such passages give some indication of why, in the current revival of individualist doctrines of social welfare, there is so little explicit reference to the work of Spencer.

Yet Spencer has much to say of relevance to our current dilemmas regarding the financing of adequate welfare provision. He feared that the increasing costs of social welfare would convert the ordinary English workman into a grumbling and disaffected taxpayer, eventually reducing him to pauperism. Spencer also lamented the subversion of the voluntary spirit of mutual aid by the coercive extractions of an insatiable state apparatus. This view of social welfare, repugnant though it may be to many social administrators and sociologists today, remains alive in enough areas of public opinion to count in political terms and act as a check on reforming Ministers of all parties. There is, and always has been, a Spencerian underground in the public debate on social welfare. Spencer's language still has meaning to the marginally respectable who live in fear of imminent pauperization.

This indictment of social philanthropy is complemented by criticisms of both social reformers and bureaucrats. Spencer was impatient of those who made 'so continuous a presentation of injustices, and abuses, and mishaps, and corruptions, as to leave the impression that for securing a wholesome state of things, it needs only to set aside present arrangements . . .'[2] He was equally scornful of those who were 'so habituated to the thought of State control as extending over all social affairs, that they take such control for granted. Everything in their experience being administered, they are scarcely able to entertain the idea that anything can do without administration'.[3] There are Weberian undertones in Spencer's anxious assault on bureaucracy, although he does not credit officialdom with efficiency. Spencer envisaged a future in which the progressive extension of welfare services, both within and without the Poor

[1] ibid., p. 365   [2] ibid., p. 393   [3] ibid., p. 404

Law, would inculcate improvident habits and set new precedents for further welfare provision. The compulsions of charity and the Poor-rate would soon be overtaken by compulsory insurance. Every such extension of welfare would be complemented by an extension of bureaucracy and its powers.[1] With some perception, Spencer notes that the extension of opportunities for bureaucratic careers also constitutes a new form of social welfare for the children of the middle class, so that they recover in salaries for their young what they pay out as taxes for the poor. In Spencer's vision of a welfare future, we eventually reach the stage of a

> despotism of a graduated and centralized officialism, holding in its hands the resources of community, and having behind it whatever amount of force it finds requisite to carry out its decrees and maintain what it calls order. Well may Prince Bismarck display leanings towards State-socialism.[2]

Once again the contemporary appeal of these sentiments goes some way beyond the editorial columns of the *Daily Express*. It is tempting to conclude that the Spencerian tradition has enjoyed a vigorous continuity of existence at the level of everyday life. Spencer's eclipse was perhaps confined to more intellectual circles, and outside these coteries there have been many others who unknowingly claimed him as their own.

In his own time, Spencer's vigorously individualistic doctrines of self-help found expression in the work of the Charity Organization Society, which played a major role in the development of early forms of social-work practice.[3] The Society was formed in 1869 and quickly became well known for its intractable hostility to the extension of statutory welfare provision. Its members gave strong support to the principles of a deterrent and 'orthodox' Poor Law, and attempted to systematize the anarchic variety of voluntary societies that flourished in Victorian England. The purpose of this exercise was to curtail the indiscriminate giving of charity. The central tenet of C.O.S. doctrine was that overgenerous provision of

---

[1] Spencer, *The Man* versus *the State*, pp. 94–5
[2] ibid., p. 107
[3] The best history of the Society is still C. L. Mowat's *The Charity Organization Society, 1869–1913, Its Ideas and Work*, Methuen, 1961

any kind of statutory or voluntary aid damaged rather than mended the moral fabric of society.

The Charity Organization Society was one of the earliest associations to give serious attention to the professional education of social workers. It set up a Committee on Training in 1897 in order to further its aim of engendering self-help amongst the poor. The Society was also influential in the establishment of the School of Social Science in Liverpool in 1904. At the same time it rejected the prospect of co-operation in social-work training at the London School of Economics on 'ethical' grounds and allied itself with a new School of Sociology opened in 1903 under E. J. Urwick.[1] In 1912 the School of Sociology was compelled through lack of funds to merge itself with the London School of Economics as the Department of Social Science and Administration. Thereafter, the distinctive influence and ideology of the Charity Organisation Society lost its identity in a larger Department not notably sympathetic to the Spencerian view of social welfare. Much later the Society, which continued as an independent body, revised its basic doctrines and changed its title, significantly, to the Family Welfare Association. In more informal and unofficial ways the Spencerian tradition can be said to survive in some areas of social work and social administration, but it is no longer explicit because it has ceased to be professionally respectable.

It is difficult to conceive of a theoretical and ideological framework more antipathetic than Spencerian sociology to the development of social policy, either as an academic or a statutory process. Yet there was no other body of sociological theory so well known and influential as the work of Spencer at the time when collectivist doctrines of social welfare were gaining influence in Britain. There was a lack of any normative empathy that might have drawn and held together the theoretical traditions of English sociology and social administration at crucial stages in their respective developments. Paradoxically, Spencer had been 'the household saint and philosopher of the hearth' of Beatrice Webb's youth.[2] The last years of his life coincided with the emergence of Beatrice Webb as an influential figure in the development of English social policy.

[1] ibid., pp. 108–13
[2] Beatrice Webb, *Our Partnership*, Longmans Green, 1948, p. 19n

Spencer's opposition to her conversion to Socialism is described in *Our Partnership*.[1] In their last years of friendship Beatrice's admiration is tinged with regretful disparagement. He is referred to as a 'Poor old man . . . a nature so transparently sincere, so eager to attain the truth, warped by long continued flattery and subordination of others to his whims and fancies into the character of a complete egotist, pedantic and narrow minded—a true Casaubon'.[2]

Spencer was criticized in his own time, as he is today, for an apparent insensitivity to the idea of societies as moral communities. As Nisbet remarks, 'Spencer's argument, reduced to its essentials, stressed the progressive ascendancy of ties based on restitutive sanctions and division of labour over those rooted in tradition and community'.[3] Spencer emphasized the individual rather than the group—despite his organicist analogies —and his ideal individual was the competitive, entrepreneurial person enjoying his citizenship and maximizing his own happiness. The Spencerian model of the just society was one in which 'each shall so live as neither to burden his fellows nor to injure his fellows'.[4] The model expressed a doctrine that was the negation of all those aims and sentiments which 'blue-book' sociology already represented. Spencer moved too easily from theory into rhetoric and, while he occasionally concerned himself with facts about poverty, it remains possible to imagine that he never actually spoke to a real pauper during the whole of his sheltered lifetime.

MARX AND SOCIAL REFORM

Marx's analysis of capitalist society took the form of total critique, but the central focus of this analysis was upon the relationship of men to the means of production, that is, the economic structure of society. Other material and ideological phenomena were features of what Marx termed the 'superstructure'. Any changes in the social structure or in the forms and manifestations of social consciousness were determined by

[1] ibid.
[2] ibid., p. 197
[3] R. A. Nisbet, *The Sociological Tradition*, p. 85
[4] Spencer, *The Study of Sociology*, p. 346

changes in economic structure. Within this framework, social welfare institutions occupy a peripheral role, although Marx noted that at certain times they were often accorded by other social scientists a greater significance than they merited. Antagonistic rather than co-operative relationships were the key features of capitalist societies. Despite massive increases in real wealth, under capitalism the majority of the population lived in poverty. According to Marx's theory of social development, the mass of the labouring poor would experience progressive immiseration. This process would, in time, lead to a heightening of class consciousness and conflict, ending in revolution and the overthrow of the exploiting bourgeoisie by the proletariat. After the revolution, social classes and related inequalities of wealth and income would be abolished and '. . . in place of the old bourgeois society . . . we shall have an association, in which the free development of each is the condition for the free development of all'.[1] Marx's remedy for poverty was a more drastic one than the provision of better social services.

At first acquaintance it may seem paradoxical that a writer so preoccupied with the process of immiseration and the problem of poverty should be relatively indifferent, when not sharply critical, of most contemporaneous forms of social amelioration. In *Capital*, his major work, Marx describes in great detail and with rhetorical force the degraded and cruel living conditions of the labouring and unemployed poor.[2] In the contemporary preoccupation with Marx as a sociological theorist it is often forgotten that his analysis of mid-nineteenth-century capitalist Britain was underpinned with a mass of expertly marshalled empirical data on living conditions in homes and work-places, on income and expenditure and the life chances of the poor. The publication and English translation of *Capital* antedated the empirical researches of Booth, Rowntree and the Webbs. Marx, however, made an exhaustive use of nearly all the major public reports on employment conditions, public health and the housing and dietary of the poor

[1] K. Marx and F. Engels, *Manifesto of the Communist Party*, Foreign Languages Publishing House, Moscow, 1959, p. 74
[2] K. Marx, *Capital*; see esp. Vol. I, ch. 13, pp. 498–543 and Vol. II, ch. 23, pp. 723–89

which were prepared by the great bourgeois social investigators of the early and mid-nineteenth century.

No other major social theorist, before or since, has been as conversant with the English tradition of 'blue-book' sociology as Marx. The great reports for the Privy Council prepared by Sir John Simon and his colleagues, the reports of the Factory Inspectorate and the Registrar General and a vast range of unofficial investigations were all used with expertise and insight. But if Marx gathered together this empirical material as evidence relevant to his theory, there was no comparable response from English social empiricists. As Ford suggests, 'The immediate influence' of Marx and Engels, 'though they gained some followers—on legislation and practice was nil, and on most of contemporary English working-class thinking, limited'.[1]

In *Capital* Marx demonstrated a form of relationship which might have developed between the empirical tradition in English social science and a major theoretical enterprise. Those who collected the evidence, however, were using it to normative ends quite different from those of Marx. The social investigators presented their data as evidence for the urgent need to reform the capitalist system. For Marx the evidence proved that the system itself was corrupt beyond redemption. The normative orientations of Marxist theory were as alien to the ends of practical social administrators and reformers as was Spencerian social theory.

The reasons for this basic antipathy between Marxist social theory, and social policy and administration, merit further analysis. We must take account firstly of Marx's conceptualization of the nature of the state and of administrative processes and aims in democratic capitalist society. Secondly, we have to take note of Marx's tendency to interpret policies of social amelioration as intended or unintended impediments to revolutionary processes. And thirdly consideration must be given to Marx's attitude towards certain sections of the poor.

In the first instance Marx seeks to demonstrate that administration and administrators are nothing more and can be nothing more than the statutory instruments and agents of the ruling class. In *The Eighteenth Brumaire* Marx observes that

[1] P. Ford, *Social Theory and Social Practice*, p. 34

the essential character of social democracy is as follows. Democratic republican institutions are demanded as a means, not for the abolition of the two extremes, Capital and Wage Labour, but for the mitigation of their opposition, and for the transformation of their discord into harmony.[1]

Marx selects the problem of pauperism to illustrate his thesis that nothing of importance can be expected to result from social reforms through existing administrative agencies. Governments cannot 'make *regulations* concerning pauperism *immediately*, without first consulting (their) officials'.[2] The kinds of action taken have never risen above 'the level of *administrative and charitable measures*'[3] and could not be otherwise, since the state itself is the cause of social evils such as pauperism. As we have seen, Marx was to make extensive use of government research material collected by civil servants whose integrity and competence he greatly admired. But he did not question how it had come about that men of the calibre of Senior, Smith and Hunter could reach positions of even limited influence in a bourgeois government. The crucial point for Marx was that under capitalism the efforts of even the best administrators would be negated by factors beyond their control.

Marx derided the tendency of bourgeois governments to explain away social problems such as pauperism as the inevitable consequence of 'natural laws' of population growth, or of innate qualities of private life, or simply as the result of administrative inefficiencies. He identified defective administration as one of the commonest explanations given, and administrative reform as a customary remedy. Such administrative reforms, however, would always founder upon those inherent contradictions of capitalism which were typified in the state. In all capitalist societies there was a contradiction between the professed aims of welfare and available resources, 'between *public* and *private* life; between *general* and *particular* interests'. In consequence the actions of the state could never be more

---

[1] Karl Marx, *The Eighteenth Brumaire of Louis Napoleon*, Allen and Unwin, 1943, p. 58

[2] Quoted in T. B. Bottomore and M. Rubels, *Karl Marx: Selected Writings in Sociology and Social Philosophy*, Penguin Books, 1963, p. 221, from art. 1 (1844) MEGA 1/3, pp. 13-15

[3] ibid., p. 221

than '*formal and negative*'. The norms of bourgeois civil society were those of ruthless exploitation, and it was only possible to end the impotence of statutory administration by abolishing 'the present conditions of *private life* and the state itself.[1]

As a further example of governmental bad faith Marx describes the effect of more stringent factory legislation during the eighteen-sixties. He refers to the tendency of capitalists always to seek compensation in other directions when their selfish pursuit of profits is checked at even 'a few isolated points of the social periphery'.[2] Even these 'paltry measures' in factory reform were implemented with great reluctance and inadequate increases in the inspectorate. There are interesting parallels to be drawn between both Marx's views on the negative functions of the state and those of Spencer, and with Durkheim's analysis of the conflict of interests that characterize the competitive ethos of capitalism.

Our next concern is with Marx's attitude towards social amelioration and social reformers. Both the policies and persons in question evoke some of Marx's best denunciatory rhetoric. In one passage of the *Manifesto* he refers to those 'economists, philanthropists, humanitarians, improvers of the condition of the working class, organisers of charity, members of societies for the prevention of cruelty to animals, temperance fanatics, hole-and-corner reformers of every imaginable kind'.[3] Such programmes of reform, he concedes, are sometimes quite systematic but always require 'that the proletariat should remain within the bounds of existing society'.[4] The reformist Saint-Simonians and Owenites are classed as 'critical-utopian socialists and communists'. Their programmes are dismissed as either premature or 'fantastic' attempts at establishing 'duodecimo editions of the New Jerusalem', based on a 'superstitious belief in the miraculous effects of their social science'.[5] Durkheimian schemes of social reform are anticipated as petty-bourgeois forms of socialism whose 'last words are corporate guilds for manufacture, patriarchal relations in agriculture'.[6] Marx had

---

[1] ibid., pp. 222–3
[2] Marx, *Capital*, Vol. I, pp. 529 *passim*
[3] Marx and Engels, *Manifesto of the Communist Party*, p. 83
[4] ibid.   [5] ibid., p. 87   [6] ibid., p. 79

good reason to indict social amelioration and reform in such a ferocious manner.

There can be no positive role for ameliorative programmes of social reform in Marx's theory of social development. In this theory the concept of 'increasing misery' has considerable importance,[1] for it is the experience by which class consciousness and conflict are intensified. Proletarianization and pauperization are stages in an inexorable process that will end by destroying capitalism. Marx, as we have seen, was convinced that programmes of social amelioration such as housing reform and shorter working hours could not bring permanent benefits to the poor under capitalism. Time, and the necessary research, would show that the worker had been swindled or deceived when he least expected to be. Again, there are interesting similarities of view between Spencer and Marx on the advisability and efficacy of 'philanthropic' social policies. We have noted Spencer's anxiety that the rising cost of rates and taxes can only have a pauperizing effect upon independent and industrious workers. And Marx also wryly points out that 'Pauperism constitutes one of the incidental expenses of capitalist production; but capital knows how to shift this burden, for the most part, from its own shoulders to those of the working class and the lower middle class'.[2]

Marx did not deny that some temporary benefits might accrue to the poor in the process of social reform. He welcomed attempts to improve educational opportunities for working children and efforts to stop the vicious system of 'gang' labour in rural areas. But less than forty years after Marx's death, bourgeois and social democrat political parties were introducing schemes of social insurance and medical aid specifically designed to check and even reverse the downward mobility of lower-middle and working-class families and to alleviate the living conditions of the very poor.

---

[1] Freedman reminds us of the continuing uncertainty about what Marx meant by his term 'increasing misery'. It can mean either 'that the *absolute* volume of goods and services available per worker would decline or . . . that the labourer's *share* of a rising national income would be smaller'. Robert Freedman (ed.), *Marx on Economics*, Penguin Books, 1961, p. 61. For our purposes this uncertainty is not important, for the poor may become or be made conscious of deprivation whether they have been affected by changes of an absolute or a relative nature.   [2] Marx, *Capital*, p. 712

We can argue, as Marx did, that ameliorative social policies are bound to fail in the long run, or alternatively that they have succeeded to the extent that collectivist forms of welfare provision have been the salvation of capitalism. In either sense, the discipline and practice of social policy and administration can only be seen, in the logic of Marxist theory, as a snare and a delusion or as a heresy. Programmes of social amelioration are either an irrelevance, momentarily snatching the workers' wives and children from 'beneath the Juggernaut wheels of capital's car'[1] and ministering to the unlucky victims, or they are a dangerous subversion of revolutionary processes because they demonstrate the possibility of improving the life chances of the poor and satisfying the claims of social justice without revolutionary change.

Marx's interest in social welfare and social justice was, however, supplementary to his commitment to the overthrow of the existing social order, because he considered that these social aims could not be achieved under capitalism. As Aron suggests, 'The centre of Marxist thought is the contradictory character of capitalist industrial society'.[2] These contradictions were unresolvable. The dimensions of social change envisaged by Marx went far beyond schemes for the immediate enhancement of social welfare; his normative theory pointed towards the creation of an entirely new social order and a new kind of humanity. Marx's diagnosis and description of inhuman working conditions and brutally low living standards is more than a sociological exercise or a plea for urgent social remedy—it is the empirical fuel for the ideological fire of a revolutionary movement. If we follow the logic of Marx's argument we are driven to the conclusion that poverty, at least for the duration of capitalism, is good for the poor because it is good for revolution. The less we intervene to ameliorate social evils the shorter will be the lifetime of capitalism and the shorter, if more profound, will be the misery of the poor. If Durkheim was disposed to leave the poor alone for their moral good, the logic of Marxist social theory suggests equally that we should do likewise on behalf of their revolutionary future. Both Spencer and Marx

[1] ibid., p. 714
[2] Raymond Aron, *Main Currents in Sociological Thought*, Penguin Books, 1968, p. 143

opposed social ameliorations which would prevent the survival of the fittest. They differed over which social groups were fittest and most likely to survive. Each of these total forms of analysis and prescription is characterized by its own special kind of dehumanization, detachment and abstraction. The poor and the unfortunate always seem to end up as creatures serving ends external to themselves and irrelevant to their own present condition.

Sometimes it seems very difficult for any kind of normative theory to wear a human face. This can be especially true when certain kinds of humanity act in ways likely to jeopardize the theory. We referred earlier to the need to take some account of Marx's attitudes towards the poor. Despite the moral fervour which inspires Marx's description of life amongst the very poor, the general impression left is one of indignation rather than compassion. There is an almost Spencerian quality in Marx's descriptions of what today would be euphemistically described as 'families with multiple problems' or members of the 'underclass'.

Marx describes such groups as 'the "dangerous" class, the social scum, that passively rotting mass thrown off by the lowest layers of old society . . .' Such a class is dangerous because 'its conditions of life . . . prepare it far more for the part of a bribed tool of reactionary intrigue'.[1] Elsewhere this stratum is described as 'the tatterdemalion or slum proletariat' who are made up of three social elements. There are the able-bodied paupers and the orphans and pauper children, and both these categories form the 'industrial reserve army'. And thirdly 'we have the demoralised, the degenerate, the unemployable', those who have given up, the aged and the victims of industrial accidents with their dependents. 'Pauperism', we are told, 'constitutes the infirmary of the active labour army and the dead weight which has to be carried by the industrial reserve army'.[2] The poor attract moral censure for different reasons. During most of the nineteenth century they were usually evaluated in terms of their propensity for self-help. In the work of Marx they are evaluated in terms of their propensity for revolution.

We have been concerned to understand why a highly general form of sociological and economic analysis, deeply concerned

[1] Marx and Engels, *Manifesto of the Communist Party*, p. 59
[2] K. Marx, *Capital*, Dent Dutton, 1942, pp. 711–12

with the nature of social progress and the causes of poverty, failed to make any direct theoretical contribution to the growth of social policy and administration as a discipline and in its institutional forms. We have seen that in his own lifetime Marx greatly underestimated the improvements that could be permanently effected in the quality of life of the poor by the provision of better social services. It is, however, quite pointless to criticize Marx for failing to imagine forms of social institutions and activities that did not exist in his day; we can be grateful that his imagination was so fertile in other respects. The real reason for this failure to connect in any sociologically meaningful way is that the political consequences of successful social reform are far more disastrous to Marxism than effectively rigorous social policies based on deterrence and repression.[1] Marxism is a social theory only in peripheral terms, peripheral, that is, to its central political objectives.

Marx's ultimate concern was human welfare, but he laid down very stringent and onerous conditions for its realization. He is vague about the actual forms of social life and relationships that will characterize the classless society. Today's political manifestos always make some specific references to improvements in social welfare. The Communist Manifesto includes a brief list of social measures that are likely to follow the revolution. They are almost all coercive measures, and necessarily so, until public power has lost its 'political character'. The tenth and final prescription is 'Free education for all children in public schools. Abolition of children's factory labour in its present form. Combination of education with industrial production, &c., &c'.[2] On specific proposals for social welfare the

---

[1] One contemporary neo-Marxist advances the thesis that British sociology has been overshadowed and usurped by those 'dispirited descendants of Victorian charity', social work and social administration. One of the reasons for the failure of our national culture to produce 'theories of society as totalities' has been the tradition of piecemeal reformism nurtured by the discipline of social administration. Perry Anderson, 'Components of the National Culture', *New Left Review*, No. 50, July-August 1968, pp. 8 and 13. In Anderson's cultural melodrama, social administration seems to be cast in the role of a seedy Victorian villain, shuffling on and off stage and at every climactic point, reducing the plot to bathos with a distracting monologue on food adulteration and the state of the drains.

[2] Marx and Engels, *Manifesto of the Communist Party*, p. 74

eloquence and rhetoric of Marx end in the ambiguities and silence of an ampersand.

WEBER AND STATE WELFARE

Weber's concern with the relationship between sociology and social policy arose in part because of his interests in the wider problem of values in social science and in the phenomenon of bureaucratization. The part played by Weber in the debating of these issues has been described and analysed by a number of authorities.[1] Weber contended that it was not the task of sociology 'to provide binding norms and ideals from which directives for immediate practical activity can be derived'.[2] He did not claim that the canons of scientific objectivity precluded moral commitment but insisted that sociologists ought to make their value orientations explicit.

In the debates which took place in the Association for Social Policy, Weber argued against the kinds of involvement in policy-making which committed the sociologist to sponsorship or support of special interest groups or government departments. At this time the German government, under Bismarck's chancellorship, had been implementing an extensive programme of welfare legislation.[3] Although Weber's political

[1] J. P. Mayer, *Max Weber and German Politics*, Faber and Faber, 1956; Reinhard Bendix, *Max Weber, An Intellectual Portrait*, Doubleday Anchor, 1962; and T. S. Simey, *Social Science and Social Purpose*, Constable, 1968, are amongst the most notable contributions to this subject.

[2] Quoted by Simey, *op. cit.*, p. 72, from Edward Shils and Henry A. Finch (eds), *Max Weber on the Methodology of the Social Sciences*, Free Press, Glencoe, 1949, p. 83

[3] By the end of the nineteenth century the range of German social legislation was the most impressive and extensive in Europe. In 1881 Bismarck introduced the first part of his compulsory social insurance scheme covering accidents. This scheme was withdrawn after bitter criticism from the liberal members of the Reichstag. Bismarck put forward a second and modified scheme in the following year, which made provision against accidents and sickness, but only the sickness scheme became law. The aims, principles and administration of this scheme were later to provide the model for the British legislation of 1911. Membership of Bismarck's scheme was compulsory, but the state used friendly societies and other private agencies to administer the system under state control. A modified scheme of accident insurance was passed by the Reichstag in 1884, excluding state and workmen's contributions. Its scope was limited to certain industries, and the

position was on the radical left, the essence of his criticism of these policies was that these new schemes of provision for the sick, the aged and the unemployed were excessively paternalistic and bureaucratic.

Weber was profoundly pessimistic regarding what seemed to him to be the inexorable process of bureaucratization. And he believed, like Spencer, that bureaucratization and the extension of welfare legislation were processes inextricably related to each other. Weber argued that

> among other factors, primarily the manifold tasks of the so-called 'policy of social welfare' operate in the direction of bureaucratization, for these tasks are, in part, saddled upon the state by interest groups and, in part, the state usurps them, either for reasons of power policy or for ideological motives.[1]

Weber had in mind Bismarck's dual policy of checking the spread of socialism by both electoral and welfare legislation.[2]

---

initial costs of accident were met from the sick fund. Employers were therefore only liable to pay in cases of serious injury where recovery was delayed for more than thirteen weeks.

Bismarck's greatest triumph however was the implementation of compulsory insurance against old age in 1889. Premiums were divided equally between employer and employee, and the age of eligibility for pension fixed at 70. The scope of this social insurance legislation was gradually extended by amending laws until, by 1903, the great majority of the population were accorded rights to assistance in the cases of sickness, accident, incapacity, widowhood and orphanhood. The total coverage of these schemes exceeded ten million workers, and the levels of provision were very generous by the standards of the time. The effect of these compulsory insurance laws was to greatly reduce the claims upon poor relief. The rules of administration and eligibility in the insurance schemes were highly complex, but the state was not directly involved either in levying premiums or dispensing benefits. This brief account gives some idea of the radical extensions of welfare provision that occurred in Germany during Weber's working lifetime.

[1] H. H. Gerth and C. Wright Mills, *From Max Weber*, Routledge and Kegan Paul, 1961, p. 213

[2] These social reforms were a part of Bismarck's policy of combating social democracy and socialism. A temporary law of 1878, which forbade the propagation of socialist doctrines, was enforced with some severity throughout the country. A new and permanent antisocialist law was introduced to the Reichstag in 1889, and its defeat was a contributory factor in the downfall of Bismarck in the following year. The influence of the

Although bureaucracy comes to power under conditions of mass democracy its extension represented a growing threat to individual freedom. Weber feared bureaucracy not because of its inefficiencies but because it seemed to him to be *the* most efficient form of domination. It was inescapable and virtually indestructible, declining only with the culture of which it was a part.[1] Bureaucracy was also '*the* means of carrying "community action" over into rationally ordered "social action". Therefore, as an instrument for "societalizing" relations of power, bureaucracy has been and is a power instrument of the first order—for the one who controls the bureaucratic apparatus.[2] The most effective constraint upon bureaucratic power was the strengthening of parliamentary authority in the policy-making process.

Weber shared Durkheim's reservations about socialism as an alternative to capitalism, but his objections were based on the view that it was more likely to lead to a 'dictatorship of the bureaucrats' than a 'dictatorship of the proletariat'.[3] Similarly the extension of welfare provision by employers would end in a new kind of industrial serfdom, comparable to the 'new feudalism' of welfare capitalism indicted by Titmuss in his pamphlet *The Irresponsible Society*.[4] Bureaucracy was a potential threat both to capitalism and socialism, and policies of social welfare were of supplementary importance in his social analysis. As Bendix has observed, 'Weber was preoccupied with the problem of individual autonomy in a world that was increasingly subjected to the inexorable machinery of bureaucratic administration'.[5] Social-welfare legislation, far from constituting a basis for new freedoms, had already become a part of the

socialists continued to grow despite this legislation. In 1890 the Social Democrats won 35 seats and by 1912 their representation in the Reichstag had increased to 110 out of a total of 393 seats. In this last election before the First World War the Social Democrats polled 35 per cent of the total votes registered.

[1] M. Weber, *Theory of Social and Economic Organization*, Free Press, Glencoe, 1964, pp. 337–41; and Gerth and Mills, *From Max Weber*, pp. 228–30

[2] Gerth and Mills, *From Max Weber*, p. 228

[3] Quoted in Bendix, *op. cit.*, p. 459

[4] R. M. Titmuss, *The Irresponsible Society*, Fabian Tract 323, 1960

[5] Bendix, *op. cit.*, p. 464

insidious domination of formal organizations over the human spirit. At the end of the vigorous critique of bureaucracy which he delivered to the Vienna meeting of the Association for Social Policy in 1909, Weber refers to 'This "corrupt" civil service of France, this "corrupt" civil service of America, this much abused "night watchman's government" of England', and asks, 'How, in point of fact, do these nations fare? . . .' He answers that 'Democratically governed nations with an undoubtedly partly corrupt officialdom have gained far more success in the world than our highly moral bureaucracy . . .'[1]

We can infer from this last sentence something of Weber's overriding patriotic concern for Germany's national standing and security in the world. In his early study of the land question and the problem of rural migration in eastern Germany, Weber confesses that for him the primary interest of the survey was 'not a question of the land workers; I am not asking do they live well or badly, or how can we help them'.[2] Weber's concern was to see the causes of rural migration resolved in order that the replacement of German peasantry in frontier areas by Poles and Russians might cease.

Although Weber's wife, Marianne, was a writer on problems of social welfare, his own involvement in such matters appears to have been limited to his part in the intense and prolonged debate amongst the members of the Association for Social Policy. The issue that preoccupied Weber, however, was the broader question of objectivity in the social sciences and the position that he took up on this matter remains of considerable relevance to social scientists involved in welfare policy-making today. The other problem of relevance to social policy that concerned Weber was that of bureaucratization, to which the extension of social services was again a supplementary issue. Social welfare was an inevitable component of the debates, because Germany had already established the basis of a highly bureaucratized system of social welfare, and other members of the Association were involved in this development as specialist advisers and investigators. For Weber the social gains from improved forms of welfare provision had to be set against what he believed were the inevitable and more serious dangers to personal liberty.

[1] Mayer, *op. cit.*, p. 130   [2] ibid., quoted by Mayer, p. 33

SUMMARY

We have considered four major nineteenth-century sociologists who formulated general theories about society. Each of these writers, in their different ways, was either hostile towards specific and reformist remedies for social problems, or not greatly interested in such issues. Both Spencer and Marx were highly critical of programmes of social amelioration. For Spencer, 'philanthropic' programmes of social reform amounted to little more than meddlesome attempts at subverting the laws of social evolution. For Marx, social reform was a bourgeois deceit, subverting or delaying the process of social revolution. Durkheim interpreted the problem of social reform in moral rather than political or economic terms and shared with Spencer an attitude towards poverty that was intrinsically fatalistic. Weber's interest in the issue of social reform was incidental to his concern with the more general problems of the value question in the social sciences, and the process of bureaucratization in industrial societies.

Spencer's work is an apologia for all that he considered to be best in *laissez-faire* capitalism. The tenor of Marx's and Durkheim's sociologies amount to radical critiques of capitalist society. Durkheim rejects the dominant value and normative orientations of capitalism and looks forward to its moral transformation. Marx looks unequivocally towards its destruction. Weber looked to the future with doubt and pessimism and saw very little of which he could approve.

It is Spencer's social theory that appears to have had the most direct influence on the development of social policy and administration, and that influence was largely negative. MacRae comments that in his studies of the teaching of sociology in the U.S.A. before 1912, he found Spencer was 'the single most widely recommended author'.[1] In England the influence of Spencer on social-work theory and practice was effective for a certain period of time, after which it declined in popularity. Spencer would not have approved of the gradual break-up of the Poor Law and the extension of the role of the state in social welfare.

[1] Spencer, *The Man* versus *the State*, p. 48

This, however, is not the end of the matter. As we have implied, Spencer's views on what ought to be the aims of social policy represent one of the continuing and enduring traditions of English culture. We must take account of those recurring shifts in both specialist and lay opinion, which lead to revivals in individualist and deterrent policies and sentiments. In recent years the more radical policy statements of the Institute of Economic Affairs represent, in modified and euphemistic forms, many features of Spencerian doctrine. There remain, however, subtler and more pervasive Spencerian influences in contemporary social policies that should be noted. It is in the existing and official ordering of social welfare priorities that we can still observe Spencer's principle of the survival of the socially fittest being put into effect.

This subject will be examined at greater depth later in our study, where it will be argued that the allocation of welfare resources in Britain still reflects a hierarchy of social evaluation in which those persons deemed to be the least fit and capable of surviving are placed in the lowest categories of provision and esteem. Our purpose will be to examine how and why the evaluative criteria of competitive individualism survive in the practice of English social policy. These values are no longer explicitly stated, as they once were in Spencer's more polemical essays, in the official Poor Law policy directives, and in the tracts of the Charity Organization Society. The values are often put into practice, none the less, partly by default, partly by intent, but never with explicit official approval or with acknowledgment to their theoretical origins. The ideas of collectivist intervention and the planned alleviation of social needs are now so much a part of the established political consensus that uncompromising counter-doctrines could not find expression in any other way.

Spencer was important in the development of social policy and administration as a discipline, because the normative content of his theory epitomized that which was hostile and alien to the political aims of 'blue-book' sociology. After the demise of the Charity Organization Society, the discipline of social policy and administration was directed towards predominantly collectivist ends by the Webbs and other specialists in the subject. But it was also, as we shall attempt to show, directed away from contact with those subsequent developments in the main areas of sociological theory which took place both in Britain and on the continent of Europe. There are also indications that the subject-matter and central concerns of Durkheim, Weber and Marx were, for different reasons, not easily relatable to the main concerns of English social administrators. In England the discipline of social policy and administration appears to have little claim to parentage amongst the founding fathers of sociological theory.

With the passage of years, all academic disciplines acquire their myths and legends, their fables of a time when giants bestrode their landscape. Sociology has always been much concerned about its parentage and the stature of its progenitors. Merton consoles us with the thought that pygmy children standing on the shoulders of giants can see far enough for most purposes. Real giants are always immortal; they have stature in time as well as height. The test of such stature is whether they survive being denigrated, deemed no longer fit for service by disrespectful pygmies and put out to grass. Some of them may later be recalled to service, but there is always the danger that over-exposure of the old giants reduces the market value of the younger ones. Dickens describes the problem with great delicacy in *The Old Curiosity Shop* in his account of the gathering at a wayside tavern of travelling showmen, one of whom was the proprietor of a giant.

> 'How's the Giant?' said Short, when they all sat smoking round the fire.
>
> 'Rather weak upon his legs,' returned Mr Vuffin. 'I begin to be afraid he's going at the knees . . .'
>
> 'What becomes of the old giants?' said Short, turning to him again after a little reflection.
>
> 'They're usually kept in caravans to wait upon the dwarfs,' said Mr Vuffin.
>
> 'The maintaining of 'em must come expensive when they can't be shown, eh?' remarked Short, eying him doubtfully.
>
> 'It's better that than letting 'em go upon the parish or about the streets,' said Mr Vuffin. 'Once make a giant common and giants will never draw again.'[1]

---

[1] Charles Dickens, *The Old Curiosity Shop*, Chapman and Hall, p. 193

So far as our limited enquiries go, it would not seem that social administration is keeping any sociological giants in its 'carawans'. It is ironic that our discipline has played so little part in such a picturesque form of community care. One possible consolation is that we have not been involved in the considerable costs of maintenance. Certainly we would never have cast any of them on the academic parish or the streets, as our excellent care of Booth, Rowntree and the Webbs bear witness.

2

The Origins of Social Administration

THE PROBLEM OF POVERTY: EARLY THEORETICAL PERSPECTIVES

The focus of this study will now be almost exclusively centred upon the English experience of social policy and administration. It is hoped, none the less, that our methods of procedure and presentation will provide a basis for future comparative studies.[1] Any analytical treatment of social policy and administration must first of all seek to unravel and identify the growth of those ideas, concepts, doctrines and theories which have helped to form the intellectual basis of an academic discipline, and which have also contributed to the making of social policy and the practice of administration. Social Policy and Administration exists as a field of specialized knowledge and as a social activity. It is a part of the cultural history of ideas and a component part of the social structure. Thus there is an important distinction to be drawn between the intellectual and the institutional aspects of our subject-matter.

This distinction is exceedingly difficult to make in practice, because some social administrators have also been involved in social investigation and have been formal contributors to the academic study of policymaking and the administrative process. Furthermore, the administrative process has been strongly

[1] The lack of basic and reliable empirical material on the development of social policy and administration in other countries is the most serious obstacle to a comparative approach. As a discipline, the study of comparative social administration scarcely exists, although in recent years a useful start has been made at the level of national case-studies. See Barbara N. Rodgers with John Greve and John S. Morgan, *Comparative Social Administration, op. cit.*; see also R. Mendelsohn, *Social Security in the British Commonwealth*, 1954; and G. R. Nelson (ed.) *Freedom and Welfare: Social Patterns in the Northern Countires of Europe*, 1953. In many ways the discipline has remained stubbornly resistant to comparative treatment.

influenced by theories and doctrines originating from a wide
range of other disciplines, notably political economy, as well
as the everyday influence of lay common sense and obscurantism. Despite these difficulties, social policy and administration
provides an intriguing context in which to observe the complexity and subtlety of the relationships between thought and
action.

We have, therefore, to take account of the range of theories,
of normative prescriptions and empirical investigations which
influenced the development of social policy and administration
—and also of the roles played by policymakers and administrators in this process. These phenomena will be considered
initially in the historical context of nineteenth-century England
and the administrative context of the Poor Law after 1834.
The origins of the discipline and all the great normative disputes about social policy which are still pertinent today derive
from the new Poor Law of 1834. Despite the ritual attention
given to the Victorian Poor Law in so many texts on social
administration, the impression remains that this subject-matter
is little more than a historical prologue to nobler and more
important matters. It is this failure of imagination and analysis
that contributes to the present theoretical poverty of the
discipline.

Our hypothesis will be that the history of social policy and
administration starts as a makeshift rearguard action against
the authoritative prescriptions of certain forms of normative
theory, which sought to explain and justify a new kind of competitive and industrial social order. The reformed Poor Law
was the statutory and practical expression of these theories. In
the years following 1834, a growing number of social investigations led to the accumulation of a body of evidence about
social conditions. This evidence provided the substantive basis
of what we now term 'blue-book' sociology. Only the subject-
matter happened to be sociological, but from this evidence,
inferences were drawn and principles formulated. This combination of evidence and principles went to make up the discipline of social policy and administration.

In the world of practical affairs an *ad hoc* policy of contain-
ment was gradually complemented by a policy of cautious
revisionism and reform. Seen in historical perspective this pro-

cess may be described as a counter-attack against the principles
of 1834 and the social and economic doctrines represented by
those principles. Conflict was a feature of this process of inter-
action, but it was conflict of a kind resolved by compromises
rather than victories. The spirit of the discipline of social policy
and administration has been, at any rate until quite recently,
empirical and sceptical in quality rather than ideological and
authoritative. It is tempting to conclude that the continuing
resistance of the discipline to theory is explicable in terms of its
own history, a history which is the record of an arduous campaign against the social consequences of theory, and especially
the normative theory of political economy. The early development of sociology was also, in part, a critical response to the
social order of capitalism. It is often forgotten that there was
another major and critical response in the social sciences to
these phenomena, but it was a response at very close quarters,
which precluded any overall appraisal or total critique. The
almost separate development of the two disciplines reflects the
difference in perspective between men looking at the problem
and men living with a variety of problems.

The development of new forms of industry in early nineteenth-
century England required the creation of a mobile supply of
labour and the conversion of large numbers of agricultural
labourers into factory workers. These migrations of labour
helped to speed up the disintegration of traditionally rural
communities. The factory system made new kinds of demands
upon its labour force. Factory work required regularity of
attendance and disciplined application to routinized tasks. The
requirements of mass production led to greater specialization
in work roles and increased the risks of skill obsolescence. This
new economic system placed a premium on geographical
mobility and changed the quality of contractual relationships
between employers and employees. Finally, greater reliance
came to be placed on the criteria of ability rather than ascription and inheritance in the assignment of work roles.

The nature of these social changes has been very adequately
documented and analysed by the writers referred to above.[1]
The effect of these changes on the structure and quality of

[1] See pp. 9–10, and also H. Perkin, *The Origins of Modern English
Society 1780–1880*, Routledge and Kegan Paul, 1969

family life is still a subject of considerable debate. It may be that in certain parts of England the nuclear family antedated industrialization, and the weakness of extended family systems amongst the rural poor accounts for the relative ease and speed with which industrialization occurred in certain areas.[1]

Families in the new manufacturing towns were exposed to both greater risks and greater opportunities, which were expressed through radical changes in class structure and patterns of social mobility. Perkin concludes from the available evidence that

> Industrial production, itself, on which everything else hinged, achieved its maximum rate of growth, at 3·5 per cent per annum ... from the 1810's to the late 1840's, and though from then until the early 1870's it was only slightly lower, at 3·2 per cent per annum, in the last few years of the period it slumped to 1·7 per cent per annum, only half the peak rate of the Industrial Revolution.[2]

The same writer suggests that 'Contrary to contemporary opinion', the overall effect of these changes on living standards was 'not only that the rich were getting richer at a faster rate than the poor, but that the whole scale of income distribution was being stretched, so that inequalities were increasing within as well as between classes, from top to bottom of society'.[3]

The available statistics on the incidence of pauperism imply a decline in the need for poor relief. But Perkin rightly points out that although the proportion of paupers fell from 1 in 9 of the population in 1803 to 1 in 23 in 1870, allowance must be made for the effect of deterrent poor-law policies and the growth in the volume of alternative forms of voluntary provision. By the end of the century 'with industrial opportunities declining on the one side and educational opportunities disappearing on the other, upward mobility for the working class was probably at its nadir, and could scarcely provide adequate compensation

---

[1] See P. Laslett, *The World We Have Lost*, Methuen, 1965; E. A. Wrigley, *Population and History*, Weidenfeld and Nicolson, 1969; and J. Hajnal, 'European Marriage Patterns in Perspective', in D. V. Glass and D. E. C. Eversley, *Population in History*, Edward Arnold, 1965

[2] Perkin, *The Origins of Modern English Society*, p. 411

[3] ibid., p. 417

for the poverty and inequality of entrepreneurial society'.[1] The massive and complex nature of these social changes posed organizational problems and moral dilemmas in welfare policy of similarly formidable dimensions. How these problems were at least partially resolved is our present concern.

In some sections of his *Law and Public Opinion*, Dicey refers to three major stages in legislative response to these problems. He starts with a period of relative legislative quiescence between 1800 and 1830, which is overlapped and succeeded from 1825 to 1870 by a period in which Benthamist individualism and popularized *laissez-faire* doctrines dominated public opinion and legislation. Towards the end of this second phase, collectivist doctrines begin to exert a radical influence on policy-making. The eighteen-sixties are, for Dicey, a turning point in the history of English social legislation, marking the stage at which collectivism begins to gain an ideological ascendancy.

Some critics have drawn attention to inconsistencies in Dicey's analysis. Parris reminds us of the range of collectivist acts that Dicey refers to, all of which were passed during the supposed period of *laissez-faire* influence. The first state education grant, the introduction and extension of factory and mines legislation, and, in strictly administrative terms, the Poor Law Amendment Act of 1834 can all be taken as indications of collectivist influence.[2] Parris also refers to Brebner's analysis of the relationship between *laissez-faire* doctrines and state intervention, and concurs with his view that Dicey greatly exaggerated the degree to which *laissez-faire* ever dominated public opinion and policymaking.[3]

Any characterization of nineteenth-century social legislation as the outcome of conflict between two major and distinct sets of doctrine, each of which enjoyed a period of dominance, would be seriously misleading. It would also oversimplify the influence of Utilitarianism on the making of social policy. In fairness to Dicey, however, we must remember that he does

[1] ibid., pp. 426–7

[2] Henry Parris, *Constitutional Bureaucracy, The Development of British Central Administration Since the Eighteenth Century*, Allen and Unwin, 1969, pp. 260–1 and 265

[3] ibid., p. 286. See also J. B. Brebner, 'Laissez-faire and State Intervention in Nineteenth-Century Britain', *Journal of Economic History*, Supplement, viii, 1948

also refer to the subtlety of the interplay between individualist and collectivist doctrines. He begins his seventh lecture by noting that

> With the passing of the Reform Act began the reign of liberalism, and the utilitarianism of common sense acquired, in appearance at least, despotic power, but this appearance was to a certain extent delusive. At the moment of the Benthamite triumph there were to be found thinkers who, while insisting on the need for thorough-going reforms, denied the moral authority of individualism and denounced the dogma of *laissez-faire*.[1]

In one sense Dicey uses the individualist elements in Bentham's writings in the same way in which Weber employed certain features of Calvinist teaching. He was concerned not so much with 'the dogmas to be found in Bentham's works as ideas due in the main to Bentham, which were ultimately, though often in a very modified form, accepted by the reformers or legislators who practically applied utilitarian conceptions to the amendment of the law of England'.[2] This analogy cannot, of course, be consistently drawn, for it is difficult to talk of the secularization of a Benthamist doctrine!

Dicey was equally aware of the debt which collectivism owed to Benthamism. He refers to the failure of statesmen in 1830 to note 'the despotic or authoritarian element latent in utilitarianism'.[3] Many of those who sought to promote the principle of utility in legislation were soon drawn to favour the extension of state intervention in order to combat vested interests and cope with the new problems of industrial and urban growth. Leading public figures such as Senior, J. S. Mill and Chadwick, who were to varying degrees of utilitarian outlook, did not hesitate to modify their individualism in response to practical considerations. Parris refers to Senior's pragmatic observation that 'The only rational foundation of government . . . is expediency—the general benefit of the community. It is the duty of a government to do whatever is conducive to the welfare of the governed'.[4]

---

[1] A. V. Dicey, *Law and Public Opinion in England During the Nineteenth Century*, op. cit., p. 211
[2] ibid., p. 134   [3] ibid., p. 308
[4] Quoted by Parris, p. 258

A philosophical doctrine which is also committed to research offers its principles as hostages to fortune. (Only Bentham could have referred to research as 'a positive addition to the stock of national felicity.')[1] This development of 'blue-book' social research in the nineteenth century played an important part in the progressive modification of the individualist tenets of Utilitarian doctrine, and in various attempts to resolve a basic conflict in the theory of philosophical radicalism. Benthamist economic theory, deriving from Adam Smith, postulated a natural identity of interests in the economic market, where collective harmony would be the consequence of each man freely following his own personal interests. In the sphere of social relationships, however, Benthamist legal theory rested on the principle of an achieved identity of interests, 'artificially' secured by collectivist intervention.

The occasional obscurities and inconsistencies in Dicey's analysis seem to arise, firstly, from his failure to define 'collectivism' with any precision and, secondly, from his tendency to imply an invariable relationship between the extension of public social services and the spread of collectivist or socialist doctrines. In the later part of his study Dicey fails to attempt any systematic distinction between these two phenomena. Collectivism may imply various degrees of state intervention for a number of social and political ends. Statutory powers can be used in *laissez-faire* economies to enhance social welfare by increasing the freedom of market forces. In Bismarck's Germany, statutory social services were extended in order to check the spread of socialist doctrines. Generous forms of statutory welfare provision may be institutional features of extreme right-wing totalitarian regimes, as in the case of Nazi Germany. In both of these instances the collectivist doctrines were antipathetic to socialism, and this was also the case throughout the greater part of the English experience of social reform. Socialism employs state intervention in order to achieve a wider range of political ends than the enhancement of social welfare through better social services. It also rejects the notion that collective welfare is no more than a summation of the efforts of individuals pursuing their own interests in enlightened competition with others.

[1] Bowring, xi, 133n; and quoted by Parris, p. 276

The history of social policy and administration, like the history of its subject-matter, is a record of conflict and compromise between normative theories and the crucially important changes that evidence effects on those theories in the context of social welfare and human need.

Three major confrontations between policy makers stand out in the history of the Victorian Poor Law. The first of these occurred in 1834, with the passing of the Poor Law Amendment Act;[1] the second and most neglected occurred in the 1860s, a period of re-appraisal and reform;[2] the third took place in 1905 when a Royal Commission was appointed to sit in judgment on the welfare policies of Victorian England.[3]

The Poor Law Amendment Act of 1834 created a central authority—the Poor Law Commissioners—and provided this authority with a small paid inspectorate. At local level the Act entailed the combination of 3,000 separate Boards of Guardians into 630 unions. The Guardians of each Union were required to build a workhouse. Outdoor relief, provision for the destitute in their own homes, was to be abolished. Any person asking for relief would be offered assistance only if he consented to enter the workhouse. Inside the workhouse, the pauper's condition would be rendered less eligible, or more unpleasant, than that of the poorest paid independent labourer outside. In this way, the workhouse test would separate the genuinely destitute from the work-shy.

The status of the pauper was an intentionally debased one. The pauper lost his freedom and was deprived of his personal reputation in the workhouse, although he could leave whenever he wished. If the pauper happened to be enfranchised he also lost the right to vote. He wore distinctive garb and was compelled to perform degrading and tedious tasks of work in return for a minimum subsistence. Pauperdom was a familial as well as a personal status. The pauper's wife and children entered the workhouse with him and shared his lot. Classification meant the separation of family members in the workhouse, and only infants under the age of three were allowed access to their mothers.

[1] 4 & 5 William IV, c. 76   [2] 30 Victoria, c. 6
[3] *Report of the Royal Commission on the Poor Laws and Relief of Distress* (1909), Cd 6425

The urgent problem to be solved was that of able-bodied pauperism and, in practice, this definition was all-inclusive. The normative doctrines of political economy defined work roles as the central human activity. All other activities, sentiments and needs were supplementary to the status of work. The best and only way of meeting these supplementary needs was to engender a desire to work in slothful and demoralized able-bodied men.

The principles of 1834 were designed to redeem the pauper from his own moral baseness. The provision of deterrent workhouses marked the proper limit of state intervention, but such intervention as occurred was to take place in an orderly, purposive and supervised manner. Supervision required the setting up of an inspectorate answerable to the central authority. This collectivist innovation aroused the hostility of both economy-minded Guardians and philanthropic reformers. The considerable powers newly vested in the central authority were in practice inhibited by parliament and the prevailing mood of certain sectors of public opinion.[1]

A large number of new workhouses was built, but most of the Guardians were too mean or poor to build anything other than new general mixed workhouses. The families of able-bodied men were segregated, but classification rarely went further than this. Other special cases of need, the sick, new-born babies, the old, the insane, and the feeble-minded, continued to be housed in institutions functionally designed to deter the able-bodied. And many Unions failed to abolish out-relief, preferring to offer inadequate levels of aid to the poor in the privacy of their own homes. A few Unions used out-relief to practise generosity by stealth. Thus the most important of the collectivist innovations embodied in the Act was inhibited by circumstance and sloth, but it still represented the establishment of an important precedent.

The new Poor Law carried Malthusian principles as far as common sense and common humanity permitted. Malthus himself held that the only effective remedy for social misery was moral restraint. As Durkheim was to argue later in the century, moral rather than political reformation was the best remedy

[1] See David Roberts, *Victorian Origins of the British Welfare State*, New Haven, Yale University Press, 1960, pp. 69–70 and pp. 318–19

for most social ills. An uncompromisingly Malthusian Poor
Law would have meant no Poor Law at all, and very little
private charity except in the most extreme cases of distress.[1]
The Act was therefore an ethical compromise between Malthusian abolitionism and the collectivist view that the state was
obliged to succour its weakest members.

The administrative and conceptual devices by which these
compromises were effected owe their origins to Bentham. The
idea of a central inspectorate, the policy of strict 'classification'
and the concept of 'less eligibility' made a modified form of
Malthusian poor law workable—and tolerable to all but sensitive minds. Poynter has attempted to trace the influence of
Bentham's teachings on the investigators who produced the 1834
Act. He concludes that 'the Commissioners offered the same
middle way between prodigality and starvation which Bentham
had propounded four decades earlier' in his complex and
ambitious Pauper Plan.[2] Little of Bentham's writings on pauperism were published in his lifetime, but it is probable that some
of these documents were privately circulated in influential
quarters.[3] Chadwick was Benthamist in his insistence upon the
need to make a sharp distinction between indoor and outdoor
relief, in his belief in the efficacy of a workhouse test and the
less-eligibility principle and in his arguments for the establishment of a central and incorruptible inspectorate. As Poynter
concludes, 'The general principles on which it [Bentham's
Poor Plan] was based bear so many resemblances to the principles of 1834 that the onus of proof is surely on those who would
deny Bentham's influence on the Act which created the new
Poor Law'.[4] In more general terms, Dicey refers to 'Liberalism
of the Benthamite type' as being 'the political faith of the time'[5]
although the sustained opposition to the 1834 principles shows
that other faiths and theories had their supporters.

The Utilitarian test of an effective social policy was whether
it was conducive to the greatest happiness of the greatest
number. State intervention was justified if it could be shown
to further this end. It is this quality of opportunism in Utili-

---

[1] J. R. Poynter, *Society and Pauperism*, Routledge and Kegan Paul, 1969,
pp. 156–8

[2] ibid., p. 320   [3] ibid., p. 107   [4] ibid., p. 327

[5] Dicey, *op. cit.*, p. 32

tarian thought which explains why 'there is a Utilitarian socialism as well as a Utilitarian individualism'.[1] At the same time, the appeal of individualistic political economy to many Utilitarians has been attributed by Burrow to the way in which the notion of competition provided a 'numerical index of relative wants'.[2] 'The price mechanism,' he suggests, 'offered in the objective sphere of social life what the Benthamite calculus failed to do in the subjective and inscrutable area of psychology.'[3] This relationship between political economy and Utilitarian doctrine could hold good so long as the definition of pleasure was restricted to material goods and services.

The concept of 'less eligibility' was a psychological device which, in the non-market context of a workhouse, reminded individuals in a forceful way of what they did *not* want. Since the economic market, in most instances, had never offered these paupers much more than marginally superior material rewards, the sanction of less eligibility took a necessarily psychological form. It imposed the pain of humiliation and stigma. In another sense the concept of 'less eligibility' mitigated the full rigours of a totally Malthusian Poor Law by substituting psychological sanctions for the physical sanction of being offered no material help whatever. In this sense, Benthamism had a moderating influence upon the extreme forms of Malthusian abolitionism.

Neither the Benthamist nor the Malthusian reformers of 1834 were content to rely exclusively upon sanctions in eliminating able-bodied pauperism. Apart from the surfeit of neo-Malthusian tracts commending the virtues of restraint and chastity to the poor, the authors of the 1834 Report refer to the need to follow reform with 'measures to promote the religious and moral education of the labouring classes'.[4]

The Poor Law Amendment Act of 1834 was more than 'an attempt to rule the poor by the principles of political economy'.[5]

[1] Morris Ginsberg, 'The Growth of Social Responsibility', in Morris Ginsberg (ed.), *Law and Opinion in England in the Twentieth Century*, Stevens and Sons Ltd, 1959, p. 16

[2] J. W. Burrow, *Evolution and Society*, pp. 72–3

[3] ibid.

[4] *Report from the Commissioners for Inquiry into the Administration and Practical Operation of the Poor Laws*, 1834, XXVII, p. 362

[5] Asa Briggs, 'The Welfare State in Historical Perspective', *European Journal of Sociology*, Vol. II, 1961, No. 2, p. 234

The Act was a major landmark in social legislation because it represented a fusion of both collectivist and individualist policies. Collectivist means were used to achieve individualist ends. The central authority was to intervene in social affairs in order to enforce the free play of market forces. A seemingly cruel procedure would result in the greatest kindness if able-bodied paupers could be driven back onto the labour market where, according to the laws of political economy, employment and the recovery of personal dignity were awaiting them. Those who drafted and administered the Act had no wish 'to rule the poor'. They wished to direct them, harshly if necessary, along the only true path to freedom.

To this end the Act embodied positive economic functions and negative welfare functions, for it was based on the proposition that men could and ought to find their true welfare only in the economic market. This proposition derived logically from the confident definition of the problem as that of able-bodied pauperism. Both problem and solution were conceived of in economic terms, and the cause of the problem was again confidently identified as a moral one, rendered more acute by charitable laxity and an indifference to economic laws. The new Poor Law became an institutional expression of the normative doctrines of political economy.

The distinction between able-bodied and non-able-bodied pauperism would have been impossible to draw in many instances. All the major Poor Law returns were based on the assumption that such definitions were possible, and the effective operation of the Act required the maintenance of this fiction. Yet the state of medical knowledge alone precluded any finesse or consistency in classification. Indoor paupers could be classified as 'able-bodied', 'temporarily disabled' and 'non-able-bodied'. 'Lunatics and idiots' were also separately classified. But none of these terms was carefully defined or uniformly applied. Children were classed according to the physical condition of their parents, and we are not told what procedure was followed when one parent was classed as able-bodied and the other as non-able-bodied. In some Unions the majority of paupers were returned as non-able-bodied and in others almost all but a few aged paupers would be classed as able-bodied.

A great deal depended on the severity with which the workhouse test was applied. We have found from a study of later returns that 'in particular, fit old people would frequently be classified as sick while sick younger people would be frequently classified as able-bodied'.[1]

The Poor Law Amendment Act of 1834 constitutes a prime example of normative theory finding legislative expression in defiance of the empirical evidence. As McGregor has observed, 'Of all the empirical investigations before the fifties that which preceded the Act of 1834 was the least open-minded, the most concerned to validate the presuppositions of political economy'.[2]

The subsequent history of the Poor Law is a record of the gradual rectification of errors committed in the name of normative economic theory. Relatively little is known about the medical condition of paupers during the years immediately following the Act of 1834. There is, however, one major return for the last quarter of 1839 which reported that out of 260,000 recipients of outdoor relief, 87,000 were *partially* able to work.[3] The Poor Law Commissioners had warned the Home Secretary in an earlier report of the need for new forms of provision to care for the growing numbers of the contagious sick. They argued that it would be 'good economy on the part of the administrators of the poor laws to incur the charges for preventing the evils, where they are ascribable to physical causes, which there are no other means of removing'.[4] The lay commissioners, however, remained equally alive to the need to 'prevent medical relief from generating or encouraging pauperism'.[5] Even the most rudimentary collection of evidence was beginning to call into question the principles of 1834—one of

[1] B. Abel-Smith and R. Pinker, 'Changes in the Use of Institutions in England and Wales between 1911 and 1951', *Transactions of the Manchester Statistical Society*, 1960, p. 22. This paper contains further information and references on the classification of paupers at the beginning of the twentieth century. It seems probable that the general tendency was towards severity in classification, and the majority of paupers grouped as able-bodied would not have been fit to undertake a day's work when called upon to do so.

[2] O. R. McGregor, 'Social Research and Social Policy in the Nineteenth Century', *British Journal of Sociology*, Vol. VIII, No. 1, March 1957, p. 148

[3] *Sixth Annual Report, Poor Law Board, 1839–40* (1836), pp. 17–18, HMSO, 1840

[4] Quoted by McGregor, p. 149, from *Fourth Annual Report of the Poor Law Commissioners for England and Wales* (1838), p. 94

[5] Continuation Report, 1840, p. 74

the few occasions in the history of English social policy on which theory was allowed to take normative wings and find a legislative perch.

'BLUE-BOOK' SOCIOLOGY AND THE EMPIRICAL RESPONSE TO THEORY

Able-bodied pauperism had been diagnosed as *the* social problem of the eighteen-thirties. Poor Law statistics for this period are unreliable, but it seems clear that the application of the principles did reduce the proportion of the able-bodied in the workhouses. At the same time, the free play of market forces filled the empty workhouse beds with other kinds of inmate. By the 1850s the Poor Law Board was facing other and more serious problems than able-bodied pauperism. The trojan horse of the English workhouses was being filled, not with militant labourers, but old sick people and babes and sucklings. Their numbers slowly grew in every workhouse until, by 1861, at least 50,000 of the 130,000 pauper inmates of workhouses were sick or infirm patients.[1] As many Guardians neglected to enforce the workhouse test, roughly twice that number were receiving medical relief in their own homes.

The sick poor who lacked adequate housing or home care had only the workhouse for refuge. There were but 15,000 voluntary hospital beds in the whole of England and Wales.[2] Although it was still necessary for Florence Nightingale to remind doctors that 'The very first requirement in a hospital [is] that it should do the sick no harm',[3] major advances in medical knowledge and expertise were changing the function of hospitals. Voluntary hospitals were becoming centres of curative medicine, of teaching and research. As the status and competence of the medical profession increased, doctors were able to take away from their voluntary boards of governors and lay administrators the control of admission procedures.[4]

[1] Robert Pinker, *English Hospital Statistics*, Heinemann, 1964, p. 75 and pp. 91–5
[2] ibid., pp. 60–1
[3] Florence Nightingale, *Notes on Hospitals* (3rd Ed.), p. iii, London, 1863
[4] Brian Abel-Smith, *The Hospitals 1800–1948. A Study in Social Administration in England and Wales*, Heinemann, 1964, pp. 33 *passim*

This development meant the exclusion from voluntary hospitals of those chronic sick for whom little could be done. It also meant the exclusion of infectious cases because of their danger to other patients.[1] As children were recognized as being prone to infectious diseases, they too were excluded. This was one of the main reasons behind the establishment of a few special voluntary children's hospitals in the 1850s.[2] In addition, the voluntary hospital governors excluded paupers, partly because they were not deserving poor, and partly because the sick pauper could not provide against the cost of his own burial if he were to die.[3] Thus it came about that the workhouses received an increasing number of the medical and social casualties of the industrial revolution—sick children, the tuberculous, those with venereal diseases, the chronic sick, the maimed and the infirm aged.[4]

Children, sick or well, were the second major problem in the workhouses. There were orphans, abandoned children, and especially illegitimate babies and their mothers, who again were debarred from most voluntary lying-in hospitals. The Webbs estimate that between 1834 and 1908 roughly 1 in 3 of all the indoor and outdoor paupers relieved on any one day were under 16 years of age. This gives a figure of seldom less than 200,000 and sometimes more than 300,000.[5] Had the volume and scope of Victorian charity been less generous, these numbers would have been even larger.

The Poor Law Board bureaucracy showed little interest in the rapidly changing functions of their workhouses. The form of the official statistical returns still reflected what the Board thought the Guardians were doing rather than the new functions which were actually being fulfilled by the workhouses. Indeed, the central authority was scarcely equipped to collect any kind of specialized material. Between 1834 and 1854—a period during which at least a hundred new workhouses were built— the Central Board failed to employ a single architect of its own.

---

[1] ibid., p. 38 and p. 45
[2] ibid., pp. 24–5 and p. 38
[3] ibid., pp. 11–12
[4] Pinker, *English Hospital Statistics*, pp. 91–5
[5] Sidney and Beatrice Webb, *English Local Government, Vol. 8, English Poor Law History*, Part II, Vol. I, Cass, 1963, pp. 246–7

During the same period the Guardians were employing about 2,000 doctors, mostly on part-time contracts. Yet it was not until 1865 that the central authority appointed its own medical inspector.[1]

Even those narrowly defined and cautiously exercised responsibilities accepted by the central authority required a competent bureaucracy. The majority of the Poor Law Inspectors came from reasonably prosperous rural gentry or urban middle-class backgrounds. Few had attended a university, but most of them had studied either law or political economy.[2] They believed that the means existed 'for the absorption of surplus labour, when the natural process is not interfered with by the administration of the poor laws',[3] and they were opposed to those 'humanity mongers who corrupted paupers with easy relief'.[4] As a group, both the senior poor-law administrators and their inspectorate were suspicious of professional experts such as doctors, engineers and architects. Exceptional individuals in each calling enjoyed very high personal status throughout the community and even attained high public office in other government departments. None the less, from the earliest days, within the newly reorganized poor law, experts were treated as subordinates. For example, the duties of the first poor law medical inspector were 'only to answer in particular cases on such particular points as might be required of him'.[5]

The 'closed' mind and the 'smug layman's arrogance'[6] of the senior administrators was, however, still superior to the incompetence and ignorance of those working at local levels of authority. The 650 local Unions were managed by 25,000 Guardians, who were mostly semi-literate small farmers and shopkeepers answerable to a rate-paying franchise. Such men had scarcely any idea 'that there was such a thing as a qualification for an appointment'.[7] Medical officerships were customarily put out for the lowest tender and were often taken

---

[1] ibid., p. 220

[2] David Roberts, *Victorian Origins of the British Welfare State*, pp. 152–4

[3] ibid., p. 171

[4] ibid.

[5] S. and B. Webb, p. 221

[6] Royston Lambert, *Sir John Simon—1861–1904—and English Social Administration*, MacGibbon and Kee, 1963, p. 523

[7] S. and B. Webb, p. 236

up by local doctors at a financial loss simply to prevent a potential competitor in private practice from setting up his plate in the locality.[1]

In the wider community, however, the influence and prestige of the medical profession was increasing. The Medical Act of 1858 set up a General Medical Council to regulate entry and standards of minimum qualification laid down by the profession itself. The later development of antiseptic and aseptic techniques did even more to make hospitals safe for the sick and to raise the status of doctors. In the 1860s doctors were the only highly qualified personnel employed by Guardians, but few of these were foolish enough to give up private practice and enter into full-time public service. It was the shortage of private patients that forced so many doctors into Poor Law work.[2]

English society in the mid-nineteenth century was not able to provide enough educated persons to fill the growing number of intermediate posts in which specialized skills were required.[3] None the less, advances of a radical nature were taking place. McGregor refers to the remarkable improvement in administrative talent which occurred during the decades following the Reform Act. He describes these new public officials as 'the architects of the new, industrial civilization, professional public servants who formulated the social and administrative principles on which it was to develop'.[4] The growing prestige and competence of the medical profession was a part of this development, and the profession itself provided an increasing number

[1] Abel-Smith, *The Hospitals*, pp. 56–8. The same lack of interest in qualifications and expertise, applied to all other important posts at local level—relieving officers, masters, matrons and overseers. At Greenwich workhouse the overseer was a pensioned NCO, and the attendant of male lunatics was a former naval man with the dual qualification of ex-bandsman and Master at Arms. L.C.C. Archives, Greenwich Union, Letters from Government Departments, 25-11-73

[2] Abel-Smith, *The Hospitals*, pp. 101–2

[3] The extent to which 'late nineteenth-century England was still educationally a very underdeveloped society' is indicated very clearly by D. V. Glass, 'Education and Social Change in Modern England', in A. H. Halsey, Jean Floud and C. Arnold Anderson (eds), *Education, Economy and Society*, Free Press, Glencoe, pp. 391–413

[4] O. R. McGregor, 'Social Research and Social Policy in the Nineteenth Century', p. 150

of senior public officers and investigators of social problems. Unfortunately, the English Poor Law was one of the last government departments to be affected by these developments.

The middle years of the nineteenth century also saw the establishment of the National Association for the Promotion of Social Science (1857) and the continuing growth in number and activity of smaller local statistical societies.[1] The first of these associations typified the empirical tradition in English social science. It was problem-orientated, eclectic in its choice of problems and relatively unconcerned with theory. The research of men like Chadwick, Senior, Farr, Ashley and Simon was part of its subject-matter. (None of these social investigators would be directly eligible for membership of the British Sociological Association today although several were Fellows of the Royal Society in their lifetimes.) The traditions of the National Association were to be continued in the work of Booth, Rowntree, the Webbs and Bowley.

A number of these leading social investigators were public officials who used the statistical societies to publicize their findings and stimulate informed discussion on a variety of social problems. As Perkin observes, 'Civil servants not only contributed many of the most valuable papers: they used the societies as a platform for urging their own policies, and even as pressure groups to bring public opinion to bear upon their own political chiefs'.[2] Both Simon and Chadwick employed these tactics in their campaigns for public health reform.[3] This growing body of empirical data, and the debates that followed their publication, were establishing the foundations of modern social administration and challenging the normative tenets of political economy. Chadwick's great Report on the Sanitary Condition of the Labouring Population of Great Britain in 1842 can be seen as an attempt to rectify the theoretical errors that underlay his own original diagnosis of the problem of pauperism only ten years earlier. The initial failure of Chadwick's public health campaign was only a temporary triumph for *laissez-faire* economic theory. The advance of empirical investigation

---

[1] H. Perkin, *The Origins of Modern English Society 1780–1880*, pp. 326–8
[2] ibid., p. 328
[3] Lambert, pp. 299 and 307; and S. E. Finer, *The Life and Times of Sir Edwin Chadwick*, Methuen, 1952, pp. 488–91

continued with the transformation of the Census into an effective instrument of social analysis and such reports as those of the Privy Council's Medical Department.[1]

By the end of the eighteen-fifties a significant number of administrators and 'open-minded' scientific experts like Senior and Simon had been won over to the collectivist alternative, which was implicit in Benthamism. None the less, this conversion was a modified and cautious one, and always imbued with a professional empiricism. Even the Poor Law Board was not safe from what Perkin describes as the gradual professionalization of government. The resistances to change within the Poor Law bureaucracy were so powerful because the Poor Law itself represented the social instrument by which *laissez-faire* could be made to work. The Inspectors and their supporters interpreted pauperism as a moral problem. Salvation lay in the moral education of the poor and the sternly merciful policy of compelling the pauper to support himself. The causes of his debasement were a failure of will and the positive encouragement of slothful habits by charity-mongers. Doctors, sanitarians and educationists introduced new kinds of criteria, based on new kinds of evidence, by which need and desert could be evaluated. They offered new explanations of poverty. Those still committed to a doctrinaire *laissez-faire* morality could only respond to this evidence with stricter prescriptions and sanctions. If disease was a major cause of poverty then such a contingency should be anticipated. Men could always save and insure against illness and, if they failed to do so, then they must suffer at least some of the consequences.[2] The market could offer its rewards and incentives only if its sanctions and penalties were allowed to take effect. The Poor Law was as essential to the industrial prosperity of Britain as its factories, mills, coal-mines and ports.

[1] See Lambert, *op. cit.*, esp. ch. XV

[2] A contemporary restatement of this view is given by Milton Friedman in *Capitalism and Freedom*, University of Chicago Press, 1968. 'Those of us who believe in freedom must believe also in the freedom of individuals to make their own mistakes. If a man knowingly prefers to live for today, to use his resources for current enjoyment, deliberately choosing a penurious old age, by what right do we prevent him from doing so? . . . Why restrict the freedom of 99 per cent to avoid the costs that the other 1 per cent would impose on the country?' p. 188

The campaign to improve medical and welfare services was not an attack on capitalism and the market economy. It was a more limited attempt to prove that prevention rather than proof of indigence was both more economical and humane, and that some curtailment of the right to do as one wished with one's own was necessary for collective well-being. A major focus of this critique was the health of the poor for, as Dicey remarks, 'A collectivist never holds a stronger position than when he advocates the enforcement of the best ascertained laws of health'.[1]

It was this kind of development—the challenge of new evidence revealing persistent and worsening social evils and the inability of *laissez-faire* doctrines to offer remedies—that persuaded J. S. Mill of the need for stronger collectivist policies. By the 1860s Mill was convinced that adequate standards of public social service were necessary and could not be attained so long as real power remained in the hands of inefficient, corrupt and parsimonious Poor Law Guardians.

It was J. S. Mill who developed and made explicit the collectivist ethic in Utilitarianism. Mill drew a clearer distinction between the concepts of happiness and pleasure, and recognized that pleasure was not the only desirable good. He extended the notion of pleasure to include promoting the welfare of others, and was willing to countenance a more positive intervention of the state to regulate market forces in the interests of social and individual welfare.[2] Twenty-five years earlier Mill had drawn attention to those 'disturbing causes' neglected by political economists and not explicable in terms of political economy. In doing so he was 'to exercise a profound influence on the development of sociological theory. The science of the laws of these disturbing causes J. S. Mill called "social economy" . . . this was in 1836—but it is obviously sociology to which he is referring'.[3]

If J. S. Mill was to make a major contribution to the development of English sociology, he was at the same time establishing one of the various traditions in that amalgam of doctrines that

[1] A. V. Dicey, *Law and Public Opinion in England During the Nineteenth Century*, p. lxxiv

[2] See Morris Ginsberg, 'The Growth of Social Responsibility', p. 9

[3] J. W. Burrow, *Evolution and Society*, p. 75

made up English socialism. As Lichtheim suggests, Mill was a key link between the earlier continental socialists and liberal reformers and the development of reformist Fabian labour politics.[1] Mill's contribution to social administration was expressed in his attempt to resolve the basic contradiction in Benthamist thinking about social welfare. While Benthamist doctrine required that 'the individual was to be given freedom of enterprise and contract', the very process of investigation led to conclusions which involved large-scale interference with that freedom'.[2] Mill accepted the conclusions and revised his views on individual liberty. In doing so, he weakened the philosophical affinities of utilitarianism with the doctrines of political economy.

The pressure for social reform was inspired by lay philanthropists moved by compassion, specialists of various kinds influenced or converted by the findings of empirical social science, enlightened public administrators and members of professions asserting their new-found authority. The movement was part of a general questioning and uncertainty about the course of social development in mid-Victorian society. The dominant and indigenous school of social theory was a response to, but not a part of, this process.

Burrow describes evolutionary social theory as a response to an acutely felt need for reassurance and certainty at a time when so many of the central and guiding doctrines of Victorian society appeared to be coming under question and attack. Evolutionary social theory represented 'a reaction against the collapse of systematic utilitarianism and the weakening of traditional religious belief'.[3] The researches of the empirical social scientists had been one of the factors hastening that collapse. Evolutionary social theory seemed to meet, to some extent, 'the need for a definition of progress which must itself be normative if it is to have normative consequences'.[4] It represented at least the hope that 'Mankind was one not because it was everywhere the same, but because the differences

[1] George Lichtheim, *The Origins of Socialism*, Weidenfeld and Nicolson, 1969, p. 139

[2] P. Ford, *Social Theory and Social Practice*, p. 32

[3] Burrow, *op. cit.*, p. 97

[4] ibid.

represented different stages in the same process. And by agreeing to call the process progress one could convert the social theory into a moral and political one'.[1] The explanation offered by Spencer, however, allowed no role to social amelioration through collectivist forms of welfare. As we have seen already, such policies were, in Spencerian terms, positively subversive of true social progress.

J. S. Mill left the issue more open by referring to the 'fundamental problem' of the social sciences as being that of finding 'the laws according to which any state of society produces the state which succeeds it and takes its place. This opens the great and vexed question of the progressiveness of man and society; *an idea involved in every just conception of social phenomena as the subject of science*'.[2] But J. S. Mill's major contribution to social science was to be in the field of methodology rather than theory, and his sociology derived from Utilitarianism rather than social evolution. Once he had adopted a more collectivist position on social welfare issues, he used his influence to practical effect. In Dicey's view, J. S. Mill transformed 'the greatest happiness principle, which was taken to be a maxim of self-interest' into a 'precept of self-sacrifice' and service to others.[3] One practical consequence of this conversion was J. S. Mill's involvement in the campaign for workhouse reform and the support he gave in Parliament to the Metropolitan Poor Bill. This Bill, which became law in 1867, was a major collectivist addition to the Victorian statute book.

The campaign for Poor Law reform began to build up slowly in the 1850s and it was initially led by middle-class ladies like Louisa Twining and Florence Nightingale with a special interest in nursing reform, by members of the medical profession, and by sections of informed lay opinion. Miss Twining founded the Workhouse Visiting Society in 1858, the first group of middle-class ladies to undertake voluntary social work in the workhouses.[4] The membership of this Society included some formidable women, who were well able to stand up to workhouse masters and Guardians. They were disgusted by the

[1] ibid., pp. 98–9
[2] Quoted by Burrow, *op. cit.*, pp. 107–8
[3] Dicey, *op. cit.*, p. 430
[4] Abel-Smith, *The Hospitals*, p. 70

conditions they found in the workhouses and especially in the sick wards.

A number of sick ward scandals[1] forced the Poor Law Board to set up their own committee of enquiry, which failed to collect any relevant evidence and reported after several years, in 1864, that it 'found no grounds for interfering in the present system'.[2] The publication of this report was immediately followed by two more scandals in which sick paupers died of gross neglect at Holborn and St Giles. The Poor Law Board at last appointed its own medical officer and prepared to undertake its own systematic investigations.

Eighteen-sixty-five was a crisis year. A group of doctors under the sponsorship of James Wakley, the editor of *The Lancet*, carried out an investigation of all the London workhouses and published a horrifying account of the conditions they found. Eminent laymen and doctors such as Charles Dickens, J. S. Mill, and the President of the Royal College of Physicians, founded an association for the Improvement of London Workhouse Infirmaries. Dr Rogers, a workhouse medical officer, formed the Poor Law Medical Officers' Association.[3]

The Poor Law Board, however, initiated its own enquiries. Two of the Board's inspectors, Dr Smith and Mr Farnell, carried out separate enquiries during 1866 into workhouse medical care and recommended radical improvements in the quality of provision.[4] Two more inspectors, Mr Corbett and Dr Markham, conducted further investigations at the end of 1866 and tried to estimate the number of sick paupers.[5] Standard Poor Law returns showed a figure of only 11 per cent of the total workhouse population as being 'able-bodied'—a proportion very similar to that found by Dr Smith and the Lancet Commissioners.[6] By rigorously excluding elderly paupers, whom they considered fit for work, Corbett and Markham

[1] ibid., p. 72

[2] H of C Sessional Paper 349, BPP Vol. IX, 1864 (*Report from the Select Committee on Poor Relief*)

[3] *The Hospitals*, p. 71

[4] H of C Sessional Paper 372, 1866, BPP Vol. LXI, 1866; and H of C Sessional Paper 387, 1866, BPP Vol. LXI, 1866

[5] H of C Sessional Paper 18, 1867, BPP Vol. LX, 1867

[6] Pinker, *English Hospital Statistics*, p. 14

reduced the proportion of non-able-bodied indoor paupers to 44 per cent of the total. Comparable official investigations of provincial workhouses indicated that about 38 per cent of the inmates were 'sick'.[1] Our own appraisal of the contemporary evidence suggests that approximately 40 per cent of the London workhouse inmates and 33 per cent of the provincial work-house inmates were sick by any reasonable definition. Allowing for the stringency of the classification and the exclusion of many children, it seems highly probable that the proportion of non-able-bodied paupers was significantly higher than these figures suggest. It was quite clear from these and other findings that able-bodied pauperism was only one of the Poor Law's many problems.

DETERRENCE AND THERAPY—THE ADMINISTRATIVE COMPROMISE

The growing body of evidence about the plight of the non-able-bodied pauper, particularly with regard to the infectious sick, strengthened the case for building separate hospitals for the poor, to supplement those of the voluntary sector. The Sanitary Act of 1866 empowered local sanitary authorities to build fever hospitals. This Act, however, was permissive and clearly very little was expected of its provisions at the time.[2] The major official response to pressures for reform came in the Metro-politan Poor Bill, introduced to Parliament on 8 February 1867. This Bill was guided through Parliament by Gathorne-Hardy with great skill and aided on its way by a fortuitous outbreak of scarlet fever in London and the recent memory of the previous year's cholera epidemic. It was one of the most important health measures passed in the nineteenth century.[3] The new Act was a 'carefully balanced compromise between central direction and local autonomy with some measure of rate equalization built into it'.[4] It was limited to London but

[1] ibid., pp. 14–17 and pp. 91–5
[2] 'The power for these authorities to provide hospitals was repeated and widened by the Public Health Act of 1875, so that general hospitals could be provided. This power was, however, very seldom used . . .' Brian Abel-Smith, *The Hospitals*, p. 124
[3] ibid. See chs 5 and 6 for a more detailed account of these developments.
[4] ibid., p. 79

extended in size the areas of administration and checked, without destroying, the influence of local Guardians. J. S. Mill supported the Bill in Parliament on the grounds that 'The denial of it would be a far greater step towards centralization'.[1] The Bill was, in fact, passed by a minority Government with support from both sides of the House. It represented a practical remedy for an urgent social problem and a compromise between individualist and collectivist doctrines.

The Act was limited to London but it provided for the setting up of separate fever and smallpox hospitals, general infirmaries, and the extension of dispensaries. Control of these fever hospitals was vested in a Metropolitan Asylums Board which, although still under the aegis of the Poor Law, would not be directly accountable to ratepayers. Two-thirds of its members were nominated Guardians and one-third ordinary rate-paying citizens. All the London Unions were now combined into one district with regard to smallpox, fever and insane patients.

The cost of building and running these new hospitals was to be met from a new Metropolitan Common Poor Fund, control of which gave the President of the Poor Law Board considerable power over local Guardians. Any Board of Guardians refusing to build separate infirmaries and dispensaries for the non-infectious sick would not be able to draw on the Common Fund for payment of the salaries of their own medical officers. In 1869 another Poor Law Amendment Act was passed which empowered provincial authorities to build separate infirmaries, but without the financial inducements of a Common Poor Fund.

A major period of hospital building began in England and Wales and continued without interruption until 1914. Every year between 1861 and 1891 an average of 1,100 infirmary beds were added to public hospital provision. By 1891, 3 in every 4 hospital beds in England and Wales were in Poor Law institutions.[2] These Acts had laid the statutory basis for the largest public hospital service in Europe. Yet the new service was contained and nurtured within the institutional context of a deterrent Poor Law, and the defenders as well as the critics of the principles were from the start seeking to use it for their own purposes.

[1] ibid.   [2] Robert Pinker, *English Hospital Statistics*, p. 50

The genius behind the drafting of the Metropolitan Poor Bill was John Lambert, a senior official of the Poor Law Board and a former Poor Law inspector. Lambert was 'a mysterious spring-mover'[1] on all departmental committees, who was quietly gathering power to himself until, by 1871, he was virtually supreme within the central authority. Lambert disliked specialists, especially medical ones, and firmly believed that policy-making was the layman's prerogative. Above all else he believed in the principles of 1834.

Lambert did not begin to reveal his grand design until after the merging of the Poor Law Board and two other Public Health departments into one new central authority—the Local Government Board, an amalgamation which took place in 1871. In return for services rendered, Gladstone made Lambert Joint Permanent Secretary with Henry Flemming, an ageing 'civil servant of the old type'. The famous sanitary reformer Sir John Simon was passed over for this appointment and had to be content with the post of Medical Officer.[2]

During the following year Lambert made himself indispensable to his new political masters while he isolated and subordinated the medical experts, who were largely hostile to the 'principles'. Having imprinted the spirit of the old Poor Law Board throughout the new department, Lambert launched a massive campaign against out-relief. A greatly strengthened inspectorate went forth to call upon the Guardians to return to the Principles of 1834.

The establishment of free hospitals for infectious paupers was not in itself a serious threat to the principle of less eligibility. Most infectious diseases could be readily diagnosed, and determined malingerers were unlikely to find daily contact with smallpox victims a condition preferable to employment. Furthermore, Lambert and the inspectors recognized that once the genuinely sick paupers were removed to real hospitals, there could be truly deterrent workhouses for the able-bodied without risk of scandal and cruelty. The initial effect of the Board's own investigations seemed to have discredited its own belief that able-bodied pauperism was the central problem.

---

[1] Royston Lambert, *Sir John Simon 1861–1904*, p. 524
[2] The best account of these departmental intrigues is given in Lambert ch. XXII.

The new evidence could, however, be used in a number of ways. The twenty-six Inspectors now possessed some of the statistical knowledge required for effective planning and classification.

This hardening of attitude on the part of the inspectorate found support from the recently established Charity Organization Society. Sampson Low's survey of Metropolitan charities in 1857 shows that in London alone the total income of charities was £2½m. while the total Poor Law expenditure was only £1½m.[1] Most of this philanthropy was disbursed in an unsystematic way. Many of the leading members of the Charity Organization Society became Poor Law Guardians and enforced the principles of an 'orthodox' destitution authority. In this way, the applicant who was refused by the Guardians was now very likely to meet the same unsympathetic listeners when he turned to a voluntary aid society.

The new inspectorate in 1871 were inexorably driven back in terms of their own logic to admit that the customary test of work in workhouse stone-yards failed to deter. In times of unemployment, men queued at the workhouse gates for the right to any kind of paid work. Consequently, Chief Inspector J. S. Longley and his staff decided to create a new kind of Test House exclusively reserved for the able-bodied. They chose the Poplar Board of Guardians—one of the sternest Boards in London—to implement a new policy based on rigorously deterrent principles and a renewed attempt to achieve strict classification.[2]

The sick were rehoused in a separate infirmary, children were consigned to a Poor Law school and the aged and infirm sent off to a small workhouse in Bromley. The main workhouse at Poplar was converted into a 'House of Industry', organized into 'such a system of labour, discipline and restraint as shall be sufficient to outweigh the advantages of an assumed subsistence'.[3] Men were required to pick 5 lb and women 3 lb of unbeaten oakum a day, and failure to complete the task meant either being charged before a magistrate the following morning

[1] Sampson Low Junior, *The Charities of London*, 1861, p. 26
[2] Sidney and Beatrice Webb, *English Local Government*, p. 378 *passim*
[3] ibid.

or consignment to a bread-and-water diet in the refractory ward.[1]

The services of the Poplar test house were available to the other Metropolitan Unions, and soon an 'Order for Poplar' became the terror of the London poor. By 1873, the Test House, with a capacity of 788 places, contained only 166 inmates. Most of the new inmates left as soon as possible, only to be as swiftly driven back again through lack of work. There were never less than 100 inmates on bread-and-water diet. At first the local magistrates supported the Guardians and, where necessary, imposed sentence on refractory paupers of anything up to twelve months' hard labour, but in 1879 the Test House policy received a major setback when local magistrates stopped convicting the paupers brought before them.[2]

Similar schemes were, however, started at Kensington and Birmingham. The Birmingham Guardians went so far as to substitute sloping wooden shelves for beds.[3] Both of these schemes ended in failure and for the same reasons. The ultimate measure of success was an empty test house. Guardians reared in small-scale ways of money-making and saving could scarcely be relied upon to possess the ideological fervour necessary to keep empty a 700-bedded institution built at considerable cost. At Poplar, the numbers of sick and aged paupers continued to increase until every other building in the Union was overcrowded. In 1882 the sick were allowed back into part of the Poplar Test House, and the 'Crusade' began to lose both momentum and credibility. The other reason for failure was that in many areas work simply was not available at any wage. The realities of the economic market were making a nonsense of the normative theories of political economy. None the less, the inspectors claimed success in forcing down the number of persons receiving out-relief. They were equally confident that they could contain within a single Poor Law system both therapeutic services for the sick and deterrent policies for

---

[1] Oakum is made from old tar-saturated ropes which have to be laboriously and painfully unpicked. The severity of the task imposed on these paupers can be measured by noting that even male hard-labour prisoners were only required to pick a daily quota of 3½ lb., ibid.

[2] Sidney and Beatrice Webb, p. 381

[3] ibid., pp. 385-6

the able-bodied. Now that social research had revealed the variety of needs facing the Guardians, efficient classification became essential if outright cruelty was to be avoided. The inspectors reported in 1884 that 'By the removal of the sick to distinct buildings it became possible to restore due discipline amongst the able-bodied . . .'[1]

Chief Inspector Longley also went to some trouble to explain how even improved medical services could be contained within a deterrent system by offering 'none but indoor relief to the patient where it is possible to do so', and insisting that 'where opportunities of providing against sickness have been manifestly neglected', it should be obligatory for the patient's family to enter the workhouse while he or she recovered in the infirmary.[2] At Birmingham, the Charity Organization Society Guardians insisted that sick paupers be carried from the ambulance to the infirmary through the workhouse gates.[3] Those receiving domiciliary medical care were also stigmatized. Longley advised that 'the stamp of pauperism [be] plainly marked upon all relief given'. The words 'Dispensary' and 'Infirmary' were never to be used in forms, advertisements and addresses without the prefix 'Pauper' or 'Poor Law' or 'Workhouse' being added.[4]

At the same time, many more new Poor Law hospitals were being built. By 1882, six fever hospitals and four Imbecile Asylums had been erected, and there were twenty infirmaries in London alone, accommodating nearly 9,000 patients.[5] By 1896 every London Union had a modern purpose-built infirmary. In the space of 25 years the Poor Law inspectors and their senior officials had bullied and cajoled the Guardians into creating the biggest hospital service in the country.[6] Dis-

---

[1] ibid., p. 461

[2] Fourth Annual Report of the Local Government Board, 1874–5, C 1328, Appendix 12; H. Longley, Report to the Local Government Board on Poor Law Administration in the Metropolis, HMSO, 1875, pp. 59–60

[3] Report of the House of Lords Select Committee on Poor Relief 1888 (239), p. viii, HMSO, 1888, p. vii

[4] Longley, op. cit., pp. 59–60

[5] Twelfth Annual Report of the Local Government Board, 1882–3, C 3778, HMSO, 1875, p. xxxv

[6] As early as 1891 there were 12,133 beds in separate Poor Law Infirmaries, excluding a further 60,778 beds in workhouse sick wards, compared with 29,520 beds in voluntary hospitals. By 1911, the number of beds in separate

graceful institutions remained, but the best of the Poor Law hospitals stood comparison with any medical institutions in the world.[1]

Longley and the inspectors had based their campaign on two forms of deterrence—'the Test House' for the able-bodied and the 'Infirmary Test' for the sick. It soon became clear, however, that a modern infirmary was intrinsically a therapeutic rather than a deterrent institution. Whatever petty restrictions Guardians and inspectors might impose on the sick, nothing could obscure the fact that hospitals were safer and better places to be treated in than the patient's own home. This truism was recognized most extensively not amongst the pauper class but amongst artisans and the lower middle classes. As early as 1872, 82 per cent of the patients in Metropolitan Asylums Board hospitals were gainfully employed before admission. Because there were no paying hospitals for the infectious sick and it was signally impossible to make the non-pauper fever cases 'less eligible' than the pauper ones by turning them away at the hospital gates, there was no alternative but to admit them. Furthermore, the lay Relieving Officer or Guardian could only challenge the authority of the medical superintendent at the risk of causing unnecessary death. Although the doctors were excluded from power at the senior levels of the Poor Law, they could be authoritative in their own hospitals.

The Royal Commission on Small Pox and Fever Hospitals recommended, in 1882, that infectious diseases hospitals ought to be open and free to all classes.[2] By this date, however, lower middle-class citizens were already using the general infirmaries as well as the fever hospitals. But any recipient of medical relief was *ipso facto* a pauper and as such he became disenfranchised. As the Third Reform Act of 1884 greatly extended the franchise, many of this new electorate were now exposed to the same risk of humiliation as any pauper. In the following year, another

---

Poor Law Infirmaries had risen to 40,901, with a further 80,260 beds in workhouse sick wards, compared with 43,221 voluntary hospital beds. See Pinker, *English Hospital Statistics*, pp. 75 and 49

[1] Abel-Smith, *The Hospitals*, pp. 202–4

[2] *Report of the Royal Commission on Smallpox and Fever Hospitals, 1882*, C 3314, p. vii

Act was passed, excluding recipients of medical relief from disenfranchisement.[1] In 1891, the London Unions were forbidden by a further Act to levy charges on the infectious sick.[2]

Thus it came about that, long before Beveridge and the Labour Party, a free public hospital service for one type of patient was established, within a deterrent Poor Law. By 1890 even the poor were losing their fear of hospitals and, in 1906, evidence was presented to the Royal Commission on the Poor Laws, showing that in some infirmaries, Guardians had started to provide pay-bed facilities for the 'better-off' patients, who wanted extra privacy and care.[3] The rising middle class would not be denied access to public social services of a quality such as this.

During the 1880s the Local Government Board was controlled by a series of liberally minded presidents. John Lambert retired in 1882. His successor, Hugh Owen Junior, did much to raise the calibre of Poor Law administration, encouraged by Sir Charles Dilke, an outstandingly able President of the Board. A whole series of ameliorative orders was issued by the Board during the 1880s and 1890s. Deserving paupers, especially the aged, were to be allowed private supplies of tea, tobacco and sweets.[4] Sterner policies were still directed at the able-bodied. Those in Whitechapel Workhouse were read to, every evening from 6.30 to 8.00, by 'mental instructors' on subjects 'touching labour, immigration, providence, temperance and kindred subjects'.[5] And for every aged pauper there still remained the final indignity of a pauper's funeral.[6]

There were still many bad workhouses, and in the provinces a large number of Unions continued to lack adequate infirmary

[1] Medical Relief Disqualification Removal Act, 1885, 48 8 49 Vict., C 46, S2

[2] Public Health (London) Act, 54 & 55 Vict., C 76

[3] *Report of the Royal Commission on Poor Laws, 1905–9* (Majority), pp. 244–5; see also Vol. II Qs 23387

[4] Even these new concessions had their uses. We learn that at Billericay, Essex, in 1896, 'an ill behaved man of 78 applied [for a weekly ounce of tobacco] but was told that if he was good he might ask again in six weeks . . . In 1906 the same old man . . . was allowed an extra ounce'. George Cuttle, *The Legacy of the Rural Guardians*, Heffer, 1934, p. 96

[5] *Report of the House of Lords Select Committee on Poor Relief, 1888* (239), para. 4506, HMSO, 1888

[6] Cuttle, *op. cit.*

accommodation. When the new editor of *The Lancet*, Ernest Hart, carried out a second survey in 1895 he found many provincial workhouses as bad as those he had visited in 1865.[1] At the same time, the best efforts of the local Guardians stood comparison with contemporary standards of modern welfare building. What is now Grove Park Hospital was opened as Greenwich Workhouse in 1903. A showpiece model of this institution had won a Diploma of Merit for the Local Government Board at the Paris Exhibition of 1900. In the souvenir brochure issued to commemorate its opening, the building was described as the 'new Paupers' Palace at Lee'.[2] Photographs of the wooden benches made to seat hundreds at a time in the bare dining-hall suggest that the claims of the Guardians that it was 'suited for the English home of an American millionaire' were somewhat exaggerated. None the less, they were no doubt entitled to claim that the central heating and the 'neat little lavatories' were amenities which 'any undergraduate at Oxford would be only too glad to have'.[3] Unfortunately, this excellent institution stood empty for several years while the Guardians quarrelled over which category of pauper should use it.[4]

The massive programme of capital investment in new public hospitals, complemented by a vigorous campaign against out-relief, illustrates the uneasy compromise which prevailed within the Poor Law during the last quarter of the nineteenth century. Social investigation in the eighteen-sixties, the improvement in medical skills and the pressure of informed public opinion forced the Poor Law bureaucracy to make classification effective. A factor of major importance in these changes was the role of new professional associations, challenging the authority of lay administrators. But the calibre of public administration was also improving rapidly. Collectivists interpreted the growth of the Poor Law hospital service as an attack on the principles of 1834. Those who held firm to the principles of political economy accepted and developed these new services as a tactical

---

[1] E. Hart, 'The Sick Poor in Workhouses' (Reports on the Nursing and Administration of Provincial Workhouses by a Special Commission of the *British Medical Journal*), 1st Series, p. 36, London, 1894

[2] Souvenir of the New Greenwich Union Workhouse, Grove Park

[3] ibid.

[4] *Municipal Journal*, 3 April 1903, pp. 341–4

accommodation in the face of new evidence. Only by pre-serving the concept of able-bodied pauperism could the normative basis of the Poor Law retain meaning and legitimacy. The removal of the sick to classified institutions might serve to make that meaning plain once more and silence the criticisms of reformers and philanthropists.

SOCIAL POLICY AND THE ECONOMIC MARKET

The English Poor Law, however, did not recover a unitary sense of purpose, and its critics were not silenced. In 1905 a Royal Commission was set up to investigate the working of the Poor Law and to advise on administrative reform. The Com-mission, under the chairmanship of Lord George Hamilton, a former Tory Cabinet Minister, had a membership representing a range of views on poor relief. The overall composition, how-ever, was biased towards those who might be expected to support 'orthodox' and deterrent principles.[1] Mrs Webb, George Lansbury and Francis Chandler were known critics of the Poor Law.

Significantly, the proposal that non-able-bodied paupers should be removed altogether from the Poor Law came from its own Inspectorate. The new Chief Inspector to the Local Government Board, James Davy, advised the Commissioners at the start of their enquiries that the Metropolitan Poor Act of 1867 had subverted the principle of 'less eligibility' by making the treatment of the sick pauper the envy of the poorest self-supporting patient.[2] Davy conceded that it was no longer possible for a deterrent Poor Law and a therapeutic medical service to co-exist. Better classification separated the able-bodied from the non-able-bodied but did not make it any easier to distinguish the destitute from the non-destitute sick.

[1] The membership of the Commission included three Permanent Heads and one Senior Medical Inspector of the Local Government Board; five poor law Guardians, including two Charity Organization Society members, and another four members of that Society. There was also a political economist, Professor Smart, who had written in support of a deterrent poor law; two Church ministers; Charles Booth; and Mrs Beatrice Webb. The only known and active critics of the Poor Law were George Lansbury and Francis Chandler, who were socialists and Guardians, and Mrs Webb.

[2] *Royal Commission on the Poor Laws 1905–9*, Vol. I, Cd 4625, para. 3290

With great reluctance Davy proposed that one possible solution of the dilemma 'may be found in the abandonment of the whole problem as one which is outside the scope of the ordinary poor relief . . .'. He was 'frankly admitting that in a populous urban community there is a class for whom charity cannot provide, and for whom perhaps the state should provide'.[1] Davy was therefore prepared to allow all the sick poor, whether or not they were also destitute, to be removed from the Poor Law, so that it would once again be possible to follow a vigorously deterrent policy against the able-bodied. Other inspectors supported their chief in his recommendation.

The Royal Commission spent a further four years collecting over thirty large volumes of evidence. During the course of the enquiry, Mrs Webb found herself in conflict with the majority of her colleagues 'on the crucial question of a Poor Law statutory committee of the county council *versus* a distribution of services between the education committee, the health committee etc.', and having been out-voted on this issue decided to prepare 'a great report of (her) own'.[2] Consequently, in 1909, two separate reports were published. The Majority Report advised against the removal of Poor Law medical services from the destitution authority. The signatories found it difficult to understand how a public medical service, established in its own right, would be able to limit its scope of provision to the poor, or how the medical profession would be able to preserve its freedom from the 'excessive socialism' that would be implicit in such a system. They were also fearful of the costs of such a service.[3] The compromise suggested by the Majority Report was that those applying for medical relief should be treated before being investigated as to their means. The sick poor ought also to be accommodated separately and not be required to suffer disenfranchisement.[4]

The Majority Report based its hopes for the future not on the extension of collectivist health services but upon the growth of provident dispensaries and the extension of the principle of

[1] ibid., paras 2866 and 2891
[2] B. Webb, *Our Partnership*, pp. 397–8
[3] *Report of the Royal Commission on the Poor Laws 1905–9* (Majority), pp. 290–1
[4] ibid., p. 368 and p. 298

voluntary insurance. Its signatories retained enough of the
individualist tradition to remain wary of making 'medical
assistance so attractive that it may become a species of honourable and gratuitous self indulgence, instead of a somewhat
unpleasant necessity resorted to because restoration of health
is otherwise impossible'.[1] By implication, something of dis-
honour and stigma *ought* to be retained in public systems of
social welfare.

The signatories to the Minority Report claimed that they
wanted nothing less than the break-up of the Poor Law, rather
than modifications and improvements which left its basic
structure and doctrines intact. It is questionable, however,
whether the alternative system proposed by the Minority would
have resulted in a more liberal and humane system than the
Poor Law it sought to replace.[2]

Parris refers to 'that current of thought which arises in
Bentham at the beginning of the century and flows into
Fabianism at its end'.[3] The same linkage is imputed by Perkin
when he describes the Fabians as 'the intellectual grandchildren of the Benthamites', who completed the separation of
the radical Utilitarian tradition from its entrepreneurial ideals.[4]
The Fabian tradition, as exemplified in the Minority Report,
certainly had little affinity with Benthamist notions of freedom.
The Webbs, who wrote the Report, wanted a unified medical
service outside the Poor Law, but they were opposed both to
free choice of doctor and the adoption of an insurance principle, because either of these arrangements implied that
patients had rights. They also considered it to be the duty of
doctors 'to insist on the necessity of greater regularity of
conduct' and the abandonment of 'the evil courses which may

---

[1] ibid., pp. 294–5

[2] McBriar argues that although an element of 'deterrence' remained in
the Minority Report, its basic assumption was that 'vagrants and habitual
idlers were rather exceptional people and could be dealt with by the
ordinary judicial powers which the state already possessed'. A. M. McBriar,
Fabian Socialism and English Politics, 1884–1918, Cambridge University Press,
1962, p. 268. Our concern is with the draconian measures that the Webbs
were willing to contemplate in the elimination of disease.

[3] Parris, quoted from R. A. Lewis, *Edwin Chadwick and the Public Health
Movement 1832–54*, Longmans, 1952, p. 188

[4] Perkin, *op. cit.*, p. 262

have led to [the patient's] ill-health'.[1] In place of the sanctions of the price-mechanism, the Webbs wished to introduce the sanctions and directives of 'Public Registrars' and other experts in health and welfare provision.

The Majority Report was little more than a well-intentioned muddle—an attempt at reconciling the doctrinal anomalies that had for so long characterized the English Poor Law. It is questionable whether any such resolution was possible and doubtful whether the kinds of change proposed by the Majority would have been worth the trouble involved. The Minority Report was autocratic in its prescriptions and insensitive to the realities of everyday life for ordinary people. It was, however, based on a coherent and logical administrative structure and firmly committed to the idea of prevention. Both Reports were prepared to impose rigorous sanctions upon 'malingerers', but in one sense the Minority document was more generally committed to the idea of compulsion and direction. While the Majority Report was prepared to limit sanctions to those who came within the Poor Law, the Minority Report favoured a vigorous campaign to improve the health of the poor, if necessary, without their consent.[2] In many ways the Minority Report was a disappointing farewell to the collectivist traditions of the nineteenth century.

The government's response to the publication of the two Reports was largely negative. The Poor Law was left alone, and the programme of reform that had begun several years earlier outside the destitution authority was continued. The passing of measures like the Old Age Pensions Act of 1908 and the National Health Insurance Act of 1911 indicates the way in which the Poor Law was being supplemented and by-passed in the making of social policy.

None the less, the Poor Law had survived into the twentieth century as a major form of collective welfare provision, and its hospital services continued to expand until the outbreak of the First World War. The Poor Law survived because it exemplified the normative doctrines of political economy. It was the necessary social complement to the free play of com-

[1] Minority Report, p. 853
[2] Abel-Smith, *The Hospitals*, p. 230

petitive market forces. The Poor Law also constituted the theology of political economy, for it presumed to offer both an explanation of, and a treatment for, a problem defined very much in terms of original sin. The price mechanism punished the wrong-doer in the market. The workhouse test took care of the recalcitrant who was too idle to enter the market and receive whatever rewards and punishments were due to him.

Those who held firmly to the principles of 1834 responded to criticism and change by redefining and narrowing their terms of reference. Their response to the gradual accumulation of evidence about poverty was belated and reluctant. For the sternly orthodox administrators like J. S. Davy, the able-bodied poor remained the most important, if no longer the largest, category under Poor Law jurisdiction. The spirit of less eligibility inevitably affected other needy groups remaining within that jurisdiction, but there was neither pattern nor consistency in this relationship. The survival of the Poor Law also provided a reassuring counterpoint to the extension of collectivist forms of social service based on preventive rather than deterrent principles.

Dicey was preoccupied with the steady growth of collectivist influence and social legislation, but he exaggerated both the extent and finality of this encroachment. The formulators of social policy rejected all the total critiques of the existing social order. The dominant ethos of the economic market was never radically undermined, though it was at times challenged and modified. After 1834, the history of philanthropy and ameliorative social reform was that of a rearguard action against the imperatives of human psychology, formed in a competitive economy. The economic market remained the nexus for the most authentic and general social experiences of the citizenry. It was the source of those central norms and values towards which all effective socialization was directed.

In their dialogue with the value premises of political economy and the individualist traditions of utilitarianism, collectivist exponents of social welfare never adopted a coherent and systematic counter-ideology.

By contrast, the principles of political economy, in their popularized forms, defined the most meaningful and crucial areas of human experience. The essential quality of those principles was expressed in exaggerated but explicit form by Dickens in *Hard Times*:

> It was a fundamental principle of the Gradgrind philosophy that everything was to be paid for. Nobody was ever on any account to give anybody anything, or render anybody help without purchase. Gratitude was to be abolished, and the virtues springing from it were not to be. Every inch of the existence of mankind, from birth to death, was to be a bargain across a counter. And if we didn't get to Heaven that way, it was not a politico-economical place, and we had no business there.[1]

Social-welfare policies in capitalist societies have always had to make their compromises and accommodations with this philosophy. Similarly, in all known socialist societies, welfare principles have had to take account of the economic imperatives of work and productivity. The Minority Report anticipated such societies simply by extending the notion of compulsion from a residue of the poor to most of the population. The aims of this new form of compulsion were extended from deterrence to prevention and treatment. Its scope was widened from a concern with able-bodied pauperism to all forms of deviance that constituted a threat to collective well-being. The imperatives of collective welfare are as potentially coercive as those of self-help.

In the vigorous capitalism of nineteenth-century England, self-help was the ultimate expression of economic virtue, and poverty the most reprehensible form of deviance. Poverty which led to dependency and dependencies which led to poverty were phenomena to be penalized. The claims of human sensibility and civilization restricted many of these penalties to a psychological form. It is ironic that the most effective critics of the Gradgrind philosophy used a Gradgrind methodology to gain their ends, namely, the inexorable pursuit of 'facts'. The difference was that these critics interpreted the 'facts' in different ways and used them to different ends.

Between 1900 and 1914 collectivist doctrines of social welfare were gaining popularity and influence, and reached the dimensions of a counter-attack upon the principles of 1834. These pressures for reform, however, found expression in both

[1] Dickens, *Hard Times*, Chapman and Hall, p. 286

major political parties. During the nineteenth century, the Conservative as well as the Liberal Party had played its part in initiating major collectivist welfare measures.[1] Conservative administrations were responsible for the Metropolitan Poor Act, 1867 and the Public Health Act, 1875; the Education Acts of 1876, 1891 and 1902; the Workmen's Compensation Act, 1897 and the Local Government Act of 1888. The role of the Liberal Party in social reform is better known, but its major and most dramatic contribution was to occur between 1905 and 1914. In retrospect, the history of social reform in Britain during the latter part of the nineteenth century seems remarkable for its continuity and degree of success. It was sufficient to keep social influence to a minimum and to keep alive the hope that more radical reforms could be achieved without drastic social upheavals.

Socialist doctrines exercised very little direct influence upon the making of social policy at the turn of the century. Movements like Hyndman's Social Democratic Federation were of minor importance and gained scarcely any support amongst the poor. Ford refers to the 'English radical socialism' of the first decade of the twentieth century as 'a curious compound of the class consciousness of many trade unionists who were not socialist, Ruskin, the Bible, the administrator's hatred of waste and injustices, gas and water socialism, and claims to the national ownership of some of the major means of production'.[2] The Conservative Party had been much the most effective agent of social reform during the greater part of the nineteenth century. Thereafter, and for a relatively brief period, the Liberal Party took over this role.

As McCallum points out, the traditional ideology and class structure of the Liberal Party imposed definite limits on its

[1] The following major Acts affecting the development of social policy were passed under Conservative administrations between 1867 and 1905. Master and Servant Act, 1867; Metropolitan Poor Act, 1867; Factory Act, 1874; Public Health Act, 1875; Employers' and Workmen's Act, 1875; Artisans' Dwellings Act, 1875; Education Act, 1876; Mines Regulations Act, 1887; Local Government Act, 1888; Housing of the Working Classes Act, 1890; Education Act, 1891; Workmen's Compensation Act, 1897; Factories and Workshop Act, 1901; Education Act, 1902; Unemployed Workmen's Act, 1905

[2] Ford, *Social Theory and Social Practice*, pp. 115–16

collectivist aims. 'They might socialise pragmatically, but they would not impose full-blooded socialism'.[1] The Liberal Party came to represent an uneasy compromise between individualist and collectivist principles. Both major parties were affected by these doctrinal cross-currents and it was the consequent ambiguities in informed public opinion that preoccupied Dicey. All the absolute precepts of Blackstonian constitutionalism, of utilitarianism and of Christianity itself seemed to be reduced to 'a question of probability and degree . . . euphemisms adapted to maintain the fiction of universal principles . . .'[2] Dicey failed to observe, however, that the same process of qualification and compromise was at work amongst what he referred to as socialist and collectivist doctrines.

In his biography of Seebohm Rowntree, Briggs refers to the way in which 'the practical implications of "sociology" were pondered by many people who did not call themselves "socialists". Indeed for some people "sociology" was an acceptable alternative to "socialism".'[3] From a Marxist perspective, the collectivist inclinations of English empirical sociology added up to a very modest form of socialism indeed. The development of social investigation and the use of social statistics to discredit the logic of political economy had been largely an amateur affair, conducted by public administrators and private researchers, working outside the universities. Booth, Rowntree, the young Beveridge, Masterman and the Webbs were notable amongst those who carried forward this tradition to the end of the nineteenth century. The most politically involved and committed of these empirical sociologists were Sidney and Beatrice Webb. Their primary object of attack in the first decade of the twentieth century was the Poor Law.

It is difficult to do justice to the contribution which the Webbs made both in the development of social-welfare policies and the establishment of social policy and administration as an academic discipline. Beatrice Webb was not yet a socialist when she joined the Fabian Society in 1893. English Fabianism

---

[1] R. B. McCallum, 'The Liberal Outlook', in Ginsberg, *Law and Opinion*, p. 67. See also Asa Briggs, *Seebohm Rowntree 1871–1954*, Longmans Green, 1961, ch. III

[2] Jevons, quoted by Dicey, p. 446

[3] Briggs, p. 52

derived its theoretical origins from classical political economy
and utilitarianism as well as socialism. Sidney Webb had been
a Society member since 1885 and is credited by McBriar, at
that stage in his career, with 'just beginning to find his way as a
Socialist'.[1] By 1886 the Society had broken with revolutionary
socialist doctrines and in its 1887 Manifesto committed itself
to parliamentary action, campaigning 'for Government action
to promote equality through education and through taxation'.[2]
In the Society's debates about Marxist theory, the Webbs
described Marx's theory of history as 'merely one hypothesis
amongst many . . . which appears to describe some of the
phenomena of social evolution . . . but not others'.[3]

At the time of the Royal Commission, Beatrice Webb was
far more preoccupied with immediate problems of social welfare
than with the transformation of capitalist society. In 1909, on
the eve of the great campaign to break up the Poor Law, she
was still debating the relative merits and demerits of the
Liberals and the Tories as agencies of reform. All she asked
was that they should be '*progressive*', which meant that they
should be sympathetic to the Minority Report.'[4] Reluctantly
she concluded, 'So I really don't know from what party we
shall get the most. We may have, in the end, to establish a real
Socialist Party if we want rapid progress'.[5] Although both
Sidney and Beatrice took care to avoid being identified with
extremist political factions, they were treated with great caution
and suspicion by those Liberal ministers concerned with social
questions.[6] The Minority Report has been criticized both for
its lack of radicalism and for being such an uncompromisingly
radical document that it destroyed the chance for immediate
reforms of a moderate nature. It would hardly be fair to indict
the Webbs on both counts, but the fate of the Minority Report
indicates the narrow range for political manoeuvre that was
open to them at the time.

The major contribution of Beatrice Webb to the campaign

---

[1] A. M. McBriar, *Fabian Socialism and English Politics, 1884–1918*, Cambridge University Press, 1962, p. 14
[2] ibid., p. 27
[3] Quoted by McBriar, *op. cit.*, p. 63
[4] B. Webb, *Our Partnership*, p. 462
[5] ibid.   [6] McBriar, *op. cit.*, pp. 258–9

for Poor Law reform was in providing the kind of sociological data without which informed debate would have been impossible. Beatrice Webb's work in cajoling and compelling the Local Government Board to collect meaningful statistical data for the Commission, and her own collection of relevant material, constitutes a monumental achievement by any standard. She raised the debate from the level of armchair moralizing to a new standard of intellectual integrity and coherence. Like Chadwick, however, Beatrice Webb's ruthless empiricism often gave the impression of lacking any normative enthusiasm beyond an overriding commitment to efficiency and the avoidance of waste.

The intellectual disposition of the Webbs was to study 'the history of social institutions as they actually exist, not in any assumed perfection of development, but in all the changing phases of "health or disease" that they have actually passed through'.[1] This empirical approach to the study of social institutions never acquired any significant theoretical basis and the broad range of their work reveals an 'incapacity for general ideas about social structure'.[2]

The failure of the Webbs, and other contemporary empirical sociologists, to formulate a distinctive body of normative theory helps to explain why the objectives of collectivist reformers at the beginning of this century were so ill-defined and limited. Factors of political expediency were also important, for the reformist lobbies cut across formal party allegiances. None the less, it remains true that out of the great period of social legislation between 1905 and 1914 no clearly formulated principle or set of principles emerged that was in any way comparable, in terms of clarity and conviction, with the principles of 1834.

'Less eligibility' and the 'workhouse test' normatively complemented the social structure of the early nineteenth century. It was left to Lloyd George and his colleagues to find a formula of compromise for their own time, and that formula was expressed in the notion of 'insurance'. The National Health Insurance Act of 1911 was the most important piece of social legislation of the pre-war period. This Act owed nothing to the Webbs and was indeed the antithesis of their Minority recom-

---

[1] Quoted by McBriar, *op. cit.*, pp. 51–2
[2] D. G. MacRae, *Ideology and Society*, Heinemann, 1961, p. 176

mendations, for the insurance principle defined the recipient of social benefit as a contributor with a consumer's right to make claims and choices. These rights, however, were in no way related to the claimant's status as a citizen but derived exclusively from his status as a wage-earner in the economic market. The exact limit of these claims was made clear with regard to unemployment benefit when the insurance 'fund' was exhausted in 1934 and replaced by a 'dole'.

The insurance principle was based on the ethic of an economic rather than a social market. Under the Poor Law the state did not recognize any claims from applicants as rights. The 1911 Act made private insurance companies co-partners in collective welfare provision, and by doing so introduced the economic criteria of social and personal worth into a public social service. Women and children, for example, were excluded from the scheme because they were, in actuarial terms, 'bad risks'. Yet the scheme was popular with the middle classes because it was a means by which the poor could learn to practise thrift. The scheme was also popular with the poor because it gave them rights of a truly authentic nature. The authenticity of these rights derived from the criteria of the economic market and the citizen's experience of life, in which he had learned to equate reciprocal exchanges of money over time with the preservation of public and personal esteem.

The subsequent history of the insurance principle exemplifies the continuing dominance of market criteria in those major English social services concerned with income maintenance. In a later volume we hope to explore this development down to the present day. The Beveridge Report and the social legislation of the nineteen-forties was a brief and very limited revival of collectivist principles, which attempted to draw a clearer distinction between the evaluative criteria of the economic and the social market. The State took over the functions which had been discharged by private insurance companies under the 1911 Act. The deterrent Poor Law had been based on a trusting faith in the efficiency of market mechanisms, and it failed because the offer of work could never be guaranteed. Further developments in economic theory and the official adoption of Keynesian policies led to the wartime Coalition Government's publication in 1944 of a White Paper on Employment policy.

In this White Paper the Government accepted responsibility for seeking to ensure a high and stable level of employment after the war.

This new commitment was an attempt to make the market economy more efficient, and was the essential prelude to the extension of social services based on an insurance principle. In this way the traditional obsession of the Poor Law with the concept of able-bodied pauperism was subtly reinterpreted. The State would now play a more active role in preventing unemployment, so that the notion of entitlement to benefit could still derive primarily from proof of past economic performance rather than social need. Proof of desert was established by the purchase of insurance stamps. Increases in national prosperity and marginal redistribution of wealth and income were, thereafter, sufficient to support and encourage a further extension of the criteria of the economic market in the field of social security. The Beveridge scheme collapsed because the range of benefits provided by flat-rate social insurance no longer reflected the widening range of aspirations and expectations amongst the general public. Private occupational schemes developed rapidly to fill this need for large sections of the public.

The recent National Superannuation Scheme exemplifies the continuing extension of market criteria of social evaluation in services concerned with income maintenance. The scheme retains a significant element of redistribution, but its overall effect is to legitimate a hierarchy of economic esteem rather than social need. This ordering may well be in accordance with the most widely held views about the nature of social justice. The new scheme extends forward from retirement to death the economic valuation that each citizen has been accorded in the market during his working lifetime. There are many other important areas of social provision where market criteria have been significantly modified and restricted in their application. The essential point, however, is that the new superannuation scheme does nothing for those who fail for one reason or another to qualify for membership at even the lowest level. By contrast, this group of people, which includes the most tragic examples of human need and distress, receives relatively inadequate forms of public provision. The moral

would seem to be that the more closely a social service reflects
the values of the economic market the more efficient and
generous it should become.

The field of social security, however, provides the most
sensitive index of official and popular attitudes towards social
welfare, for it is concerned with the actual giving and receiving
of money and hence involves the most crucial definitions of
personal and public esteem. And it is in this area of human
experience that the aims of social welfare can be seen to remain
subordinate to the normative doctrines of political economy.
In effect, it is the principles of the Majority rather than the
Minority Report that have dominated the history of social
policy in this century.

The State now undertakes the role which the Majority
Report recommended should be left to voluntary schemes of
insurance. The ethical claims of the social market have not
secured any significant measure of autonomy since 1911. Since
the abolition of the Poor Law, these social claims have simply
found an easier and less brutal accommodation with the requirements of a market economy. And the dominant notions of
'welfare' and 'citizenship', which derive from the characteristic
forms of social consciousness, still have closer affinities with the
ethics of the economic market than those of the social market.

SUMMARY

Dicey was preoccupied by what he diagnosed as the erosion
of traditional values and beliefs in Victorian society under the
impact of industrialization. He argued that collectivist and
socialist doctrines were in part a response to, and in part the
cause of, this doctrine. More recently Burrow has suggested
that evolutionary social theory was a response to the intellectual
and emotional need of middle-class Victorian society for order
and a belief in progress. The development of empirical social
science was a major part of the challenge to the claims of
political economy and the doctrines of *laissez-faire* competition
and self-help. The concern for social welfare—and the attempt
to further it by laying bare the statistics of social misery—was
ethically and logically incompatible with the main tenets of
evolutionary social theory.

It is appropriate to end this chapter with a summary in the form of a footnote on the Webbs. They played a central role in the campaign to abolish the Poor Law and redefine the aims of social welfare. They also did more than anyone else to make popular and give repute to the academic study of welfare institutions. In their concern to trace the development of social institutions, the work of the Webbs acquired a historical rather than a sociological perspective. By setting out to build a social science 'upon the precise observation of actual facts'[1] they bent the small twig of a new discipline in the way that it was to grow. The Webbs played a major role in ensuring that the London School of Economics would provide a 'centre for teaching a kind of down-to-earth sociological economics very different from the theoretical and philosophical economics taught at the older centres of learning'.[2] The formation of the Sociological Society in 1903 preceded the establishment of the Department of Social Science. The Society was composed of 'a body of Neo-Darwinians' who included MacKinder, Hobhouse, Wallas and Westermarck.[3] The first sociology courses were offered in 1904–5. The origins of a separate Department of Social Science in 1912 are described by Titmuss,[4] and a fuller account of the establishment of the School is given by Hayek.[5] It would be intriguing to know more of the reasons why two separate Departments were established, thus giving institutional expression to the distinction between 'theoretical' and 'practical' social science.

Towards the end of her life, Beatrice Webb regretted her earlier disposition to 'leave the future to take care of itself',[6] and concluded that 'where we went hopelessly wrong was in ignoring Karl Marx's forecast of the eventual breakdown of the Capitalist system as the one and only way of maximizing the wealth of nations'.[7] The First World War and the trade depressions which followed it, combined with the establishment of the Soviet Union, had shaken her belief in the virtues of

[1] McBriar, *op. cit.*, p. 54   [2] McBriar, ibid., p. 219

[3] Janet Beveridge, *An Epic of Clare Market*, Bell and Sons, 1960, p. 61

[4] R. M. Titmuss, *Essays on the Welfare State*, pp. 14–18

[5] F. A. Hayek, 'The London School of Economics, 1895–1945', in *Economics*, New Series, Vol. XIII, No. 49, February 1946

[6] B. Webb, *Our Partnership*, p. 482

[7] ibid., p. 488

working within the given political system and achieving the ends of social welfare by gradual reform. This late conversion to Marxism came too late to influence the course of English social policy or to invalidate the claim that 'It is to the Webbs that we owe our debt of not requiring massive social change in every detail of society as a pre-requisite of reform . . .'[1] If the Webbs failed in many of their practical aims, it was not so much because they failed 'fully to appreciate the importance of politics'[2] as that they failed to understand politicians. The discipline of social administration owes more of its present empirical strengths and theoretical deficiencies to the Webbs than to any other authority. And the contemporary practitioners of the discipline, benefiting by the errors of the Webbs, have learned how to live and prosper better amongst politicians.

Beatrice Webb claimed that she had 'never read a word' of Bentham, but acknowledged his influence through the work of Spencer and accepted much of the utilitarian ethic as it had been reformulated by J. S. Mill.[3] Her central criticism of 'the Benthamites' was that they never attempted 'to verify and correct their hypothesis, and by this verification to discover other premises'.[4] Unlike Bentham, or Mill, she had few qualms about the right of those who know best to compel improvement in those who are presumed to know least. Both of the Webbs shared Bentham's commitment to administrative efficiency and the suppression of waste. Their empirical contribution to the development of social policy and administration was and remains unrivalled. But their sociological perspective was never more than institutional in scope and did not look beyond Spencer for other more accommodating theoretical orientations. Such theory as they wanted was taken from social and moral sciences other than sociology. The final commitment to the Soviet form of Communism came too late to influence, through their work, the development of English social policy. And it would exaggerate their undoubted importance to suggest that the course of events would have been significantly changed. In the last analysis, the influence of the Webbs seems to have been more strongly felt in the making of a new branch of social science than in the making of actual social policy.

---

[1] MacRae, *Ideology and Society*, p. 173   [2] ibid., p. 175
[3] B. Webb, *Our Partnership*, p. 210   [4] ibid., p. 211

II

THE USES OF SOCIAL THEORY

3

Ideology, Rhetoric and Evidence

NORMATIVE MODELS OF SOCIAL WELFARE

Collectivist forms of welfare provision have remained central features of the programmes of the major political parties. The rise of the Labour Party and the eclipse of the Liberals has not led to any dramatic heightening of conflict over welfare aims between the Labour and the Conservative parties. The commitment of the Labour Party to socialism is no more wholehearted than that of the Conservative Party to *laissez-faire* individualism. The academic debate about social policy has, however, become more sharply polarized in recent years. On both sides those who occupy extreme positions have grown more isolated from parliamentary processes. It is arguable that this isolation has come about because the academic debate is more imbued with ideological imperatives than its parliamentary counterpart.

The main theme of this chapter is to explore the role of value judgments today in the making of social policy and the examination of welfare problems. In the past it was relatively easy to identify the value component in debates about social welfare. This component is no longer as clearly distinguishable. In recent years, problems such as poverty and the persistence of social inequality have become of general interest to certain kinds of sociological theorist. In those areas of applied social science where social problems are the subject of analysis, what is termed normative social theory appears to have usurped the traditional role of social philosophy. It is hypothesized that the intended or unintended effect of this displacement has been to endow old-fashioned value judgments with scientific pretensions.

The distinction between non-normative and normative social theory was very clearly drawn by Durkheim. He observed that

Social theories separate themselves at once into two large categories. One seeks only to express what is or what has been;

97

it is purely speculative and scientific. Others on the contrary, aim to modify what exists; they propose, not laws, but reforms. They are practical doctrines.[1]

It may be difficult in practice to make and maintain this distinction, but it is dangerous to the status of a science if we forget that such a distinction exists. It is arguable also that 'prescriptive' would be a more appropriate term than 'practical' in this context, for normative theories differ greatly in the degree of their practicability. Durkheim goes on to suggest that 'Individualism, like socialism, is above all a ferment which affirms itself, although it may eventually ask Reason for reasons with which to justify itself'.[2] It is the way in which Reason is courted, or seduced, that concerns us in this essay.

Normative theory has been described by Homans as theory which seeks to explain 'how men ought to behave if they are to accomplish certain results'.[3] Horton argues that any attempt to explain social problems 'invariably involve[s] normative theory, values, ideologies, or whatever one may care to call the subjective categories of our thinking about society'.[4] It is of some importance, however, to establish whose 'thinking' is under discussion—that of sociologists and other experts, or the subjective reactions of ordinary citizens who use social services. Ordinary citizens may also think about social services—and social problems generally—without sociological expertise or strong ideological commitment. The danger in all forms of theorizing and model-building in social policy is that sociologists may confuse their own constructs with the subjective reality of ordinary users. This danger is especially strong when the models in question contain strongly prescriptive and moral elements.

In one sense this is exactly what most forms of theorizing have done in this field of social enquiry, although we shall argue that, in the main, these theories have been philosophical rather than sociological in origin, and that these origins have

---

[1] Emile Durkheim, *Socialism*, pp. 51–2   [2] ibid., p. 41
[3] G. C. Homans, 'Structural Functional and Psychological Theories', in Demarath III and Peterson (eds), *System, Change and Conflict*, p. 347
[4] John Horton, 'Order and Conflict Theories of Social Problems as Competing Ideologies', in *American Journal of Sociology*, Vol. LXXI, No. 6, May 1966, p. 713

been openly acknowledged. They can be broadly grouped into two types—the 'institutional' and the 'residual'—which are then developed in similar ways. These types of approach can be distinguished in terms of their model constructs, both of which contain highly normative elements. The protagonists of each model then proceed to justify it by the selective presentation of evidence from recent history and contemporary events. In this way both kinds of model are related to differing interpretations of processes of structural change.

The residual model of social welfare is closely linked to 'optimistic' theories of economic growth, of 'embourgeoisement' and 'convergence'. It is argued that with increasing and more diversified prosperity, the incidence of such problems as poverty is declining. The aim of social welfare under these circumstances should be to focus selectively upon a residual and declining minority of needy groups. In this way, scarce resources will be used more efficiently and, in appropriate cases, provided at a level sufficiently generous to bring about a marked improvement in social circumstances. This claim is not easily reconciled with the accompanying argument that universalist services are wasteful because they permit abuse, whilst selectivist services deter all but the genuinely needy.[1]

The 'institutional' model of social welfare is closely related to differing interpretations of the effects of economic growth, and the extent to which either 'convergence' or 'embourgeoisement' have occurred. The evidence of a persisting and increasing incidence of poverty is stressed rather than the growth of affluence. Demographic trends, such as the increasing proportion of dependents in industrial societies, are given greater emphasis. Much importance is attached to the definition of poverty as a relative concept. The inability of the market to achieve anything remotely akin to a 'just' allocation of goods and services renders it necessary for social services to be established as major institutions rather than residual agencies in industrial societies. The effect of industrialization is so to

---

[1] A useful summary of the present state of debate about selectivity is given in P. R. Kaim-Caudle, 'Selectivity and the Social Services', in *Lloyds Bank Review*, April 1969, No. 92, p. 45: also in Arthur Seldon, 'Which Way to Welfare?', *Lloyds Bank Review*, October 1966. See also Milton Friedman, *Capitalism and Freedom*, University of Chicago, Chicago, 1968

heighten the risks and consequences of contingencies like unemployment, poverty, illiteracy, disease and homelessness, that these services must be provided on a universal basis, expanding rather than contracting in scope.[1]

Thus, both models are established in order to make possible more accurate predictions about the effect and efficacy of forms of welfare provision. Both models draw on historical and sociological evidence to predict the likely course of developments in social policy. The residualist model rests on moral assumptions about the self-evident virtues of competition and self-help. The universalist model rests its moral claim on the ethics of co-operation and mutual aid. In both cases psychological assumptions are made about the attitudes of individuals towards welfare provision and about their social expectations of welfare.

Commitment to an institutional view of social welfare services is not necessarily the same as an unqualified commitment to universalist social policies. Significantly, the most effective— and trenchant—critic of the residual model is by no means an out-and-out universalist. In his most recent work, Titmuss concedes that 'there is no escaping the conclusion that if we are effectively to reach the poor we must differentiate and discriminate'.[2] For Titmuss,

> the challenge that faces us is not the choice between universalist and selective social services. The real challenge resides in the question: what particular infrastructure of universalist services is needed in order to provide a framework of values and opportunity bases within and around which can be developed socially acceptable selective services aiming to discriminate positively, with the minimum risk of stigma, in favour of those whose needs are greatest[3].

The normative element pervades Titmuss's approach, but it derives from ethical rather than sociological theory and it is made very explicit. He draws our attention to 'the consequence of undefinable causality' when seeking to justify

---

[1] See especially Richard M. Titmuss, *Commitment to Welfare*; H. L. Wilensky and C. N. Lebeaux, *Industrial Society and Social Welfare*; and David C. Marsh, *The Future of the Welfare State*, Penguin Books, London, 1964

[2] Titmuss, *Commitment to Welfare*, p. 159   [3] ibid., p. 135

the 'infrastructure of universalist services'.[1] And his pre-occupation with the causes and consequences of stigma seems to be the diamond point on which his argument turns. The exponents of the residual model of welfare, he argues, over-estimate 'the potentiality of the poor, without help, to understand and manipulate an increasingly *ad hoc* society . . .' At the same time, residualists also fail 'to understand the indignities of expecting the poor to identify themselves as poor people and to declare, in effect, "I am an unequal person".'[2] More than any other theoretician in the field, Titmuss is able to evoke the subjective realities of everyday life for the poor.

Titmuss's conception of social welfare is focused in its objectives 'rather than the particular administrative method or institutional device employed to obtain objectives . . .'[3] A central concern of social policy is with 'questions of identity and alienation, for alienation threatens or destroys the system of unilateral transfer.' Thus, its 'primary areas of unifying interest are centred in those social institutions that foster integration and discourage alienation'.[4] In this way a sharp distinction is drawn between the values and ends of social policy and the values and ends of the competitive market.

Wedderburn has no doubts about which values predominate in Britain and the United States.[5] She argues that little more than a residue is left of the universalist framework of the British welfare state. That residue is neither particularly socialist nor radical in its aims and amounts to little more than a tempering of the prevailing winds of competition and acquisitiveness. Wedderburn goes on to criticize the lack of any serious attempt to relate the notion of class conflict to the way in which social priorities are ordered. The preoccupations of writers like Marshall with the concept of citizenship are interpreted as attempts to explain how social services can ensure a basic equality of civic status and thereby compensate for persisting structural inequalities. Wedderburn summarizes her central concern by stating that 'a Socialist cannot be simply concerned to perpetuate and to emphasise in state legislation the values

---

[1] ibid., p. 134   [2] ibid., p. 163
[3] ibid., p. 21   [4] Ibid., p. 22
[5] Dorothy Wedderburn, 'Facts and Theories of the Welfare State', in R. Miliband and J. Saville (eds), *The Socialist Register*, Merlin Press, 1965

of the market; he must be involved with the ideological struggle against these very values'.[1]

Thus, in their different ways, Titmuss and Wedderburn put forward normative models of social welfare that imply an unambiguous conflict between the aims and values of social policy and the dominant ethos of capitalism. 'We may interpret the "enemy" in this case,' writes Titmuss, 'as those who support the prevailing system of values in society and their attendant social provisions and policies.'[2]

From a different set of premises and a different interpretation of evidence, however, it is possible to argue that the aims and values of social policy now dominate those of the market and capitalism with equally deleterious consequences. A middle position, less ideologically committed either way but still normatively orientated, would be to argue that there is no intrinsic conflict between social and economic policy.

Conceived of in this way, social-welfare agencies and social-policy structures in their totality would seem to show a wide range of systemic features. It can be argued that an ideal construct such as Britain's 'welfare state' displays a group of interrelated social processes that are to a high degree self-maintaining. In relation to the wider social system, welfare systems contribute in very real terms to the maintenance of stability and consensus. They are, *par excellence*, adaptive mechanisms for social survival and tension management. In this sense, social welfare becomes a 'major force in denying the prediction that capitalism would collapse into anarchy'.[3] In functionalist terms, social services are one of the more civilized ways in which societies maintain themselves and survive. Social services receive and reallocate resources in order to ameliorate social conflict and strengthen the bonds of social solidarity.[4]

The implicit assumption beneath this form of analysis is that of a 'reciprocity of interest satisfactions' between the various participants.[5] It can be argued, however, that any exchange

---

[1] ibid., p. 144

[2] Titmuss, *Commitment to Welfare*, p. 46

[3] R. M. Titmuss, 'The Welfare State: Images and Realities', in Charles I. Schottland (ed.), *The Welfare State*, Harper Torchbooks, New York, 1967, p. 100

[4] W. W. Isajiw, *Causation and Functionalism in Sociology*, Routledge and Kegan Paul, London, 1968, p. 89   [5] ibid., p. 95

media, whether monetary or in the form of goods and services, are designed to 'make possible smooth utilisation of resources but have nothing to do with the question of whether the resources would be utilised at all'.[1] As in other areas of social life, such an analytical framework fails to take into account the variety of ends held by groups in different social situations and the varying propensity of these social groups to use power in pursuit of these ends.[2]

A similar point is made by Goldthorpe, who criticizes those who interpret the making of social policy as a pragmatic and necessary response to social crisis. These explanations, he argues, are essentially 'functionalist' and neglect certain key issues. Any attempt at explaining the development of social policy in Britain must analyse the situation in terms of the ends involved and the groups in conflict with each other, rather than in terms of the 'needs' of society, considered as a whole.[3] Such an approach permits one to ask whether or not it was a 'particular kind of society' whose survival depended upon the extension of welfare provision and whether alternative modes of action might have been incompatible with the interests of decision-takers. Functionalist explanations of power tend to neglect 'the shifting balance of power between rival factions' and hence do not provide adequate reasons for any given ordering of social priorities. Questions of this kind, Goldthorpe suggests, can best be asked within 'an action frame of reference'.

At this stage in the argument it is worth noting how difficult it is to proceed beyond normative model-building and theorizing in the field of social policy once one has begun. In examining these postulates about the relationship between social and economic policy, one hears two conflicting reports of who is being raped. The less dramatic news that the two have been cohabiting for some time now in relative harmony is not believed by anyone.

[1] ibid., p. 99

[2] See John Rex, *Key Problems of Sociological Theory*, Routledge and Kegan Paul, London, 1961, ch. VI, p. 96 *passim*

[3] John Goldthorpe, 'The Development of Social Policy in England, 1800–1914, Notes on a Sociological Approach to a Problem in Historical Explanation', *Transactions of the Fifth World Congress of Sociology*, Washington D.C., 2–8 September 1962, Vol. IV, International Sociological Association, 1964, pp. 41–56

The institutional and residualist models we have reviewed do not purport to be other than normative, and they are effective in setting out certain ends of social policy to which, it is argued, men *ought* to aspire. They also attempt to describe what are the consequences of failing to live up to these ideals. The evidence selected is interpreted in often conflicting ways, and this seems to be unavoidable in the field of social policy, where the facts so often only attain meaning in the light of value.[1]

A problem arises from the fact that all the normative models discussed represent distinctive constructions and interpretations of social reality. They are a part of the knowledge of intellectuals and other specialists. Titmuss makes a very similar point in discussing the influence of the Charity Organization Society's concept of welfare on social policy in the eighteen-seventies.[2] The point remains, however, that the danger of confusing the subjective interpretations of specialists with those of other minority—or majority—groups is present at all times and all points on the ideological spectrum. One might expect those with the best access to evidence to be most open-minded, as was Canon Barnett, who defected from the Charity Organization Society because he could no longer accept that the evidence of poverty justified the aims of the Society. The question we must then ask is the extent to which these models (and for that matter any normative models in sociology) actually take account of the experience and subjective reality of the everyday life of ordinary people. As yet, we have little reliable evidence about the citizenry's attitudes towards social services, or their expectations of welfare policy and workers.[3]

RELATIVE DEFINITIONS OF SOCIAL NEED

Neither the 'institutional' nor the 'residual' models derive naturally from any major school of social theory. They are

[1] D. V. Donnison and V. Chapman, *Social Policy and Administration*, Allen and Unwin, London, 1965, p. 28

[2] Titmuss, *Commitment to Welfare*, p. 39

[3] Among the more useful studies in this field are Political and Economic Planning, *Family Needs and the Social Services*, Allen and Unwin, London, 1961; Noel Timms, 'The Public and the Social Worker', and Jean S.

strongly and explicitly normative, but not markedly theoretical in a sociological sense. Both models seem to derive from assumptions of principle about what ought to constitute the moral order of a 'good' society. In brief, the discipline of social policy and administration appears to have retained closer affinities with moral philosophy than with sociological theory, apart from those kinds of theory which are so highly normative that they are indistinguishable from ideology. None the less, this powerful tradition of moral commitment that we have already noted in our review of the origins of social policy and administration has always been complemented by an equally strong commitment to democratic principles, rational discourse and a respect for evidence. A moral concern to do the 'best' thing for the most people with the least delay has also made this tradition a highly pragmatic one in the last resort. In these types of normative approach, the value elements are made very explicit.

As a subject, social policy and administration has attracted an impressive range of empirical investigation. It would be reasonable to expect, therefore, that, in sociological terms, the dominant theoretical orientations of the discipline would be positivistic. In practice, however, relatively few specialists in the field were, until very recently, trained in sociology. Furthermore, the very nature of this empirical material—in large part an inventory of human want and misery—makes it equally likely that any related body of theory will be strongly normative —that is, it will contain powerful prescriptive overtones. We have noted some of the historical reasons for this absence of significant and complementary involvement of theoretical sociologists in this subject-matter. Specialists in social policy and administration have remained committed to moral philo- sophy and political science rather than the other social sciences in their search for frameworks of theory and principle.

The relationship between social research and the making of social policy bears the signs of this combined heritage of prag- matism and moral conviction. Social surveys of the changing patterns of human need led to an accumulation of empirical

Heywood, 'The Public Understanding of Casework', in *Social Work*, Vol. 19, No. 1, January 1962; and Institute of Economic Affairs, R. Harris and A. Seldon, *Choice in Welfare*, 1965

evidence about the extent and nature of social injustice. This evidence has been related to both claims and counter-claims of a moral kind, and their translation into political programmes of action and ideology. The arguments have always tended to become moral and political rather than sociological.

One consequence of this relative neglect of sociological theory —and neglect by theoretical sociologists—has been that we still lack adequate explanations of the causes of social need, why individuals define their needs as they do, and why these definitions so often appear to be at variance with those of the social scientists.

A further consequence has been the development of an even closer and more productive relationship between social research and the making of social policy. The effect of these limited successes has perhaps led to a sharper division between the pragmatic and ameliorative traditions of social policy and administration and the more revolutionary forms of normative social theory. It is therefore possible to make two markedly opposed interpretations of the relationship between social science and social policy. In one sense we can talk of the achievement of social research in terms of its practical consequences for human betterment. From another perspective we can lament an apparent 'loss of principle' or moral direction in the discipline as a whole. The discipline, it can now be argued, lacks any distinctive kind of normative orientation.

It is arguable that if a discipline is to play any effective part in the short-term amelioration of social problems, its practitioners must be prepared to compromise on issues of principle. At the same time, the moral commitment must and will survive so long as the practitioners themselves differ over the means and ends of social-welfare provision. The most generalized and clearly articulated forms of these ideological differences over ends are expressed in the 'institutional' and 'residual' models of social welfare. As means of achieving these ends, universalism and selectivity are more interchangeable procedures than is often supposed.

The key conceptual distinction may therefore lie between 'institutional' and 'residual' models of social welfare rather than 'universalism' and 'selectivity' as methods of allocation. In these ideal forms, the 'institutional' model of social welfare is one in which there is a powerful value commitment to universalist forms of welfare provision, supplemented where necessary by selectivist services. Allocation takes the form of positive discrimination programmes rather than means tests. In practice, however, means tests tend to proliferate on an *ad hoc* basis because positive discrimination programmes are unable to differentiate between individuals and groups with sufficient finesse.

Residualist models of social welfare display a strong value commitment to selectivist form of welfare provision, supplemented where necessary by universalist services. Allocation takes the form of means tests, which in practice often affect receivers as negative acts of discrimination. Again, in practical terms, some minimum framework of universalist services tends to emerge and become institutionalized, usually for reasons of administrative convenience.

So long as conditions of scarcity prevail and demand potentially exceeds the supply of social services, forms of rationing prevail. The institutionist begins with generosity and is driven reluctantly towards stringency in allocation. The residualist starts with stringency and is driven reluctantly towards generosity. The overall effect on the recipient is a more uniform one than ideologists of either the left or the right will care to admit. Only if one group ceases to press its case will the balance shift markedly.

We can therefore identify the 'institutional' and 'residual' models of social welfare as the two major value-orientations amongst specialists in social administration. In the actual context of policy-making and administration, compromises of one kind or another are the rule. The persistence of scarcity, the existence of many different kinds of claim upon national resources and the desire to do the best for those in greatest need combine to weaken the appeal of uncompromising universalism or selectivism to policy-makers. None the less, radical minorities still attempt to influence policy and to negate the real or imagined influence of their rivals. The radical right favours selectivity in order to prevent waste, encourage thrift and give effective aid to the social groups in greatest need. In order to achieve these ends, forms of statutory intervention such as a 'reverse income tax' are proposed. (Such schemes would have been interpreted by Dicey as examples of rampant collectivism.) Similarly, the radical left is prepared to countenance superannuation schemes of graduated contribution and benefit which represent drastic modifications of traditional forms of universalism. This seems to be as far as radicalism goes in the context of social policy and administration, where relatively frequent contact with the realities and complexities of human need quickly sobers the enthusiasm of ideologists and utopians.

In the context of democratic politics, the related concepts of relativism and proportionate justice act as a kind of catalyst, inexorably transforming universalists into reluctant selectivists and selectivists into reluctant universalists. Universalism and selectivism may therefore be seen to be alive in principle but dead in practice, just as the nineteenth-century struggle between collectivist and individualist doctrines was largely the invention of an intellectual minority. The conflict that breaks out from time to time is largely a battle between ideological ghosts, but the echoes of their gunfire serve as necessary reminders to policy-makers that issues of principle are involved. In different metaphorical terms, the ideological skeletons may hang in separate cupboards, but the same political wind rattles both sets of bones.

Paradoxically, the concept of relative poverty gathered popularity in the nineteen-sixties because of its normative implications. It seemed to offer a new ideological impetus to the overdue reform of Britain's social services.[1] There were two aspects to the notion of relative poverty. Firstly, it offered a challenge to traditional universalist doctrines by emphasizing subjective definitions of need, that is, definitions made by the poor about themselves rather than 'objective' definitions of 'subsistence' as developed by social scientists or administrators. Secondly, relative definitions of poverty—and other forms of deprivation—served as critiques of traditional universalist approaches to equality. The persistence of gross inequalities made it necessary to allocate *extra* resources for deprived individuals and groups if even a measure of equality was to be achieved. The policy device which would permit such differentiation without stigmatizing recipients came to be known, later

---

[1] See Peter Townsend, 'The Meaning of Poverty', pp. 210–27

in the nineteen-sixties, as 'positive discrimination'.[1] In this sense, Titmuss's 'infrastructure' of universalist services maintains a degree of qualitative difference from the selectivist alternative. The difference is, however, one of degree. It represents both the survival of a principle and the institution of administrative practices which place that principle in even greater jeopardy.

In administrative terms, subjective definitions of need and models of relative deprivation can heighten the awareness of policy-makers and agencies to the varieties of human need. The aim is usually to secure more generous and sensitive forms of welfare for the poor. Problems arise, however, when we seek to establish practical relationships between these relativist perspectives on poverty and actual forms of provision. As we have already argued, the more we take account of subjective definitions of need, the more complex allocation procedures must become. Relative definitions of poverty render it mandatory that justice should very clearly be seen to be done, but it is exactly this kind of definition which makes it so difficult to invent simple and easily understood procedures of allocation. Even the criteria of allocation governing positive discrimination programmes in education will soon be beyond the ready comprehension of all but a minority of experts. The more social policies take account of subjective definitions of need, the more must individual tests of means proliferate. It seems increasingly likely that such schemes will soon become not only unduly expensive to operate but impossibly difficult to explain and justify to the general public.

A further problem for those who wish to use relative definitions of need as a technique for increasing welfare provision is that relativity is a game which everyone has an equal right to play. The right to claim consideration of his subjective definition of needs is available to the marginally affluent as well as the marginally poor person. It is a mistake to identify the concept of relative deprivation exclusively with the collectivist left. The concept first appeared in English social administration in its negative form as the deterrent policy of 'less eligibility' whereby the pauper recipient of welfare was made more conscious of the

---

[1] See ch. 5, below, for a more extended analysis of the concept of positive discrimination.

relative advantage to be gained by remaining even the poorest-paid independent labourer.

Despite these objections the relative definition of social needs can be seen as an ideological attempt to provide the kind of empirical evidence which will justify radical social reform. It will be ideological in so far as the claims and definitions of one social group are valued more highly than those of others. One of the most valuable contributions of social theory to the study of social welfare might be that of improving our understanding of public attitudes towards social services. We need better maps of the current levels of satisfaction and discontent and more convincing explanations of why people hold the range of attitudes and expectations they do. One of the most impressive attempts at such a study in recent years is Runciman's *Relative Deprivation and Social Justice*, which was conducted on a national scale in the early nineteen-sixties.[1] It is the only major study of its kind, and it achieves a considerable measure of success in relating the disciplines of social theory, political philosophy and social administration. The conclusions of the study have not been seriously or damagingly challenged and have great relevance to the debate between universalism and selectivity. Significantly, the findings of the study have been largely ignored.[2]

Runciman is concerned with identifying the most socially just principles by which resources can be allocated in a society. He attempts to do this by applying 'to the notion of relative deprivation the contractual model of justice as it has been modified and developed . . . by John Rawls'.[3] The principle of allocation appealed to in the name of justice is one which should be acceptable to any reasonable man 'in a state of primordial equality'[4] before he knows whether or not he will be a loser or a gainer. It is recognized that all inequalities need to be justified, and the criteria of justification are those of need, merit and the common good. The criterion of need which is

---

[1] W. G. Runciman, *Relative Deprivation and Social Justice*, Institute of Community Studies, Routledge and Kegan Paul, 1966

[2] In a succinct and otherwise comprehensive review of 'Inequality and Exploitation in Britain', Robin Blackburn refers once to Runciman's study, in a footnote. See *New Left Review*, No. 42, March-April 1967, p. 15 fn.

[3] Runciman, *op. cit.*, p. 252 *passim*   [4] ibid.

related to inequalities of class takes precedence over the other two, because 'the right to claim more than subsistence if [we] should turn out to be at the bottom will outweight the right to keep more of what [we] earn if [we] turn out to be at the top'.[1] Thus, inequalities will be accepted if they are of a kind and for reasons which we would have agreed as being just 'under the conditions of hypothetical contract'.[2]

In summary, Runciman is arguing that 'the test of inequalities is whether they can be justified to the losers; and for the winners to be able to do this, they must be prepared, in principle, to change places'.[3]

The second criterion, of merit, is dealt with by Runciman as follows. He distinguishes between *praise* and *respect* when referring to inequalities of status. He argues that in a just society it is legitimate to recognize inequalities of status based on inequalities of praise, that is, inequalities deriving from differences of skill or attainment. Inequalities of respect are not compatible with the notion of justice. If placed in a situation of hypothetical contract an individual will be likely to accept inequalities based on differentials of praise even if he does not know in advance whether he will be highly skilled or not. He will not be disposed to accept differentials based on inequalities of respect, because these will be based on ascribed rather than achieved qualities, and these are not reasonable grounds for discrimination. Educational inequalities will be justifiable if they are accorded in terms of praise—they will not be justifiable if they derive from social rather than educational criteria. The key distinction that Runciman wishes to draw seems to be between inequalities arising from qualities of achievement and those arising from qualities of ascription.

Runciman makes little explicit reference to the common good, implying that if the criteria of need and merit are met then the common good will be realized. Runciman's idea of reasonable men in a state of nature entering into a hypothetical contract before they have grounds for vested interest, that is, before knowing whether they will be winners or losers, does have approximate parallels in the real world of social policy. The principle of social insurance and its relationship to the practice of private insurance in civilized societies comes most readily to

[1] ibid. p. 266   [2] ibid., p. 268   [3] ibid., p. 273

mind. Most of us will accept as a just restriction on our future freedom of spending contractual obligations which reduce our potentially highest levels of personal affluence in order to ensure that we never sink to an intolerable level of poverty. We also accept an obligation to preserve anyone from starvation even though he may have broken or failed to fulfil, for any reason, his part of the contract.

In this sense the principle of justice has less to do with altruism than with the deliberations of reluctant gamblers reducing, as far as possible, the dimensions of individual risk in the interests of self-preservation. The most relevant point about this implied relationship between human nature and social contract is that contracts are necessary at all. Men must be made to feel obliged and bound by contract because their altruism is not to be relied upon once they have secured relative advantage or prestige.

Furthermore, as individuals in the real world, we cannot be trusted to enter these contracts voluntarily. In most forms of collective social insurance we are compelled to join and suffer penalties if we do not. In societies where private insurance is relied upon, individuals who fail voluntarily to insure and subsequently fall on hard times are penalised by stigmatizing and parsimonious forms of relief. Nearly all industrial societies express their respect for the sanctity of human life by guaranteeing its survival wherever possible. The subsistence levels of provision represent imposed limits upon the degree of physical sanction. None the less, by giving the relief in a humiliating and stigmatizing form, greater scope and intensity is given to psychological forms of sanction. If men may legitimately praise and reward others, they may also legitimately blame and punish them without infringing the principle of justice. Justice may be equated with fairness but not necessarily with compassion and love. It is often forgotten that in the context of social welfare the principle of justice seeks to ensure not only an acceptable allocation of rewards but also of punishments in the interest of the common good.

Runciman allows that his theory of justice can 'only yield the test which any system must pass if it is not to be categorically discussed as unjust'. He recognizes the difficulties that arise as soon as we seek to continue re-allocation above the level of subsistence. At what stage, we may ask, do the claims of the relatively deprived stem from envy rather than felt injustice? Runciman's answer is that 'the search is always for a principle, not a formula'[1] and the principle should be based on the assumption that 'the right to claim more than subsistence: if [we] should turn out to be at the bottom will outweigh the right to keep more of what [we] earn if [we] turn out to be at the top'. In other words, the argument that the state should guarantee something more than subsistence rests on the argument that 'standards of need must change in some approximate ratio to rising prosperity . . .'[2]

The explicit value-bias in Runciman's argument is that reasons must always be given 'why the richest man's income should not be transferred direct to the poorest old-age pensioner'.[3] This egalitarian bias is justified on the grounds that hypothetically rational men will always prefer to insure themselves against the risk of poverty and need than to gamble on the prospect of becoming rich, when they have no means of predicting or knowing their eventual social position. Similarly the distribution of power will be ordered so that no individual has 'more power over others than he would have agreed to allow if he had had to envisage that his enemy might be set in the equivalent position of power over himself'.[4]

The explicit value-bias of Runciman's model of social justice is towards equality, albeit within the modest dimensions of bourgeois philosophy. Despite the modesty of these criteria, they were clearly beyond the expectations of the poorest respondents to Runciman's survey, who 'appear to be entitled to a greater measure of relative deprivation than the evidence shows them to feel'.[5] Amongst the old and the poor, Runciman found very little interest in achieving that 'constant regression towards the mean' in social welfare which should occur in the absence of special claims for unequal treatment.[6] His conclusion is that 'if the respondents to the survey had given answers dictated by the claims of justice, they would have been very different from those which I have reported'.[7]

Runciman is not surprised that social justice plays 'little part in the feelings even of those whose unformulated claims it would

---

[1] ibid., p. 266   [2] ibid.   [3] ibid., p. 268   [4] ibid., p. 290
[5] ibid., p. 273   [6] ibid., p. 268   [7] ibid., p. 293

vindicate'.[1] He suggests that 'most people's lives are governed more by the resentment of narrow inequalities, the cultivation of modest ambitions and the preservation of small differentials than by attitudes to public policy or the structure of society as such'.[2] We must be cautious in accepting conclusions of this nature, for there is relatively little material of a similar kind with which they can be compared. What little research has been undertaken into public attitudes towards social welfare and equality tends, however, to support Runciman's conclusions. The most significant findings of the survey conducted by the Institute of Economic Affairs—which might be said to have a contrary ideological bias—were that few respondents were disposed to make an unequivocal choice between *either* public *or* private forms of welfare provision, and that amongst this national sample of married men there was a disturbingly widespread lack of knowledge about the costs of social services.[3] Other investigations into the welfare expectations and evaluations of the general public indicate complacency, and a general disposition to be easily satisfied with relatively modest levels of social provision.[4]

It seems possible, therefore, that most of those groups in the community who are diagnosed as 'under-privileged' or 'deprived' are far less aware of their condition, and far less ideologically motivated by it than those who undertake the diagnoses. Even Runciman's modest criteria are not part of the subjective realities of everyday life for the poor. Further theoretical studies of the subjective realities that motivate users of social services may confirm the hypothesis that if the cause of social justice is to be advanced and the allocation of social resources made more equitable, it would be better left to Dicey's small group of informed citizens than to the gentle ebb and flow of public opinion.

Once normative theory and subjective evaluations of need

[1] ibid., p. 285   [2] ibid.

[3] R. Harris and A. Seldon, *Choice in Welfare, 1965*, Institute of Economic Affairs, 1965

[4] See P.E.P., *Family Needs and the Social Services*, Allen and Unwin, London, 1961; A. Cartwright, *Patients and their Doctors*, Routledge and Kegan Paul, 1967; and Office of Health Economics, *The Consumer and the Health Service*, Proceedings of a Symposium held at the Royal College of General Practitioners, London, 27 January 1968, ed. John McKenzie

are employed to indicate something more commonplace than the attitudes and values of social scientists, the policy implications become conservative rather than radical. The collection of empirical data on the subjective states of consciousness and expectations of the poor is necessary, however, if the concept of relative poverty is to have any meaning at all. But the initial yields of such surveys suggest that data of this kind are not going to provide the ideological crock of gold that some prospectors are hoping to discover. Gold there may be, but of a sociological kind not easily convertible into the appropriate ideological currency.

It is these brute facts of relative social contentment or indifference to even modestly bourgeois criteria of social justice that deprive the concept of relative deprivation of its radical significance. None the less, normative social theory may yet effect the necessary conversion or reinterpretation of the evidence. It is always possible to argue that the evidence is not what it seems to be, even if the exercise involves finding out what meaning and purpose ordinary people give to their own lives, only in order to advise them that they are wrong. The concept of alienation and its current usage demonstrates, *par excellence*, such misapplications of old-fashioned and once reputable value judgments to social evidence—a misapplication which carried to excess will make sociology into an exclusively normative discipline, or simply a rhetorical and distorting echo of the truth.

Social Criticism and the Use of Evidence

It would seem, therefore, that a more accurate knowledge of the subjective realities of social need provides little encouragement as yet to those who wish to show that the poor are highly conscious of their deprivation. Runciman's criteria of social justice are modestly drawn but appear to stand some way beyond the experience and expectations of his respondents. As a metaphor for radical criticism, the concept of relative poverty fails in the very court of public opinion to which it appeals. If we were eager to discover symptoms of serious discontent, it would be tempting to conclude that the worker's propensity for happiness is his greatest handicap.

One resolution of this dilemma might be to construct, or rediscover, a more general theory which demonstrates that the citizens of advanced industrial society are so repressed that they are incapable of recognizing the extent of their own deprivation. In his own time, Marx was able to point to extensive evidence, of an objective kind, regarding the high incidence of extreme poverty in wealthy capitalist societies. Such evidence is no longer available, even when more account is taken of subjective definitions of need. Marcuse's approach to this problem is to question the nature of the available evidence on 'affluence'. He modifies the normative theory of Marx and questions the very reality of affluence. In doing so, Marcuse also elaborates Marx's critique of ameliorative programmes of social welfare and attributes to social policies a more positive role in the repression of freedom.[1]

In his analysis of advanced industrial societies, Marcuse equates affluence with 'hell' and the affluent worker's enjoyment of material well-being with alienation in a 'repressed society'.[2] He refers to 'The slaves of developed industrial civilisation' as 'sublimated slaves, but they are slaves, for slavery is determined "neither by obedience nor by hardness of labour, but by the status of being a mere instrument, and the reduction of man to the status of a thing". This is the pure form of servitude . . . and this mode of existence is not abrogated if the thing . . . does not feel its being-a-thing, if it is a pretty, clean, mobile thing.'[3] Modern social services are typified as a central element in the framework of repression under which men live in market-dominated societies.

The 'Welfare State' is a part of a 'universe of administration in which depressions are controlled and conflicts stabilized by the beneficial effects of growing productivity and threatening nuclear war'.[4] Further developments in automation will create a demand for more welfare services. Marcuse's indictment of the Welfare State rests on the claim that for all its efficiency it is 'a state of unfreedom' and weakens the desire 'to insist on self-determination if the administered life is the comfortable and even the "good" life'.[5] The Welfare State is dismissed as

---

[1] Herbert Marcuse, *One-Dimensional Man*, Beacon Press, Boston, 1966
[2] ibid., p. 23   [3] ibid., pp. 32–3   [4] ibid., p. 21
[5] ibid., p. 49

'a historical freak between organized capitalism and socialism, servitude and freedom, totalitarianism and happiness'.[1] Marcuse fails, however, to explain why such an apparently effective means of repressing a society has not more readily commended itself to the oppressors. In one obscure paragraph he refers to the way in which liberals and conservatives denounced the 'oppressive capabilities' of the Welfare State as a way of protecting their own power '*prior*' to the establishment of these new services. Thereafter 'the competing institutions concur in solidifying the power of the whole over the individual'.[2] The social need for the maximization of profit under capitalism is given as a factor limiting this extension of social-welfare provision.[3] None the less, if social welfare really is such an effective opiate of the masses, it is remarkable that the capitalists have failed to provide the sedative in more liberal quantities.

In his critique of advanced industrial societies, Marcuse defines and uses social theory in a way that allows him considerable latitude in the interpretation of evidence. In one sense his approach allows him to ignore evidence. For Marcuse, 'The world of facts is, so to speak, one-dimensional', being concerned only with social phenomena as they *appear* to be. He explains that the task of 'critical' theory (a term which seems to be synonymous with normative theory) is to discover 'the historical alternatives which haunt the established society as subversive tendencies and forces',[4] and to extract the 'arrested and denied possibilities' for human development and freedom from the given social situation. In this exercise, the sociologist must refuse to accept 'the given universe of facts as the final context of validation'.[5]

Most of this 'given universe of facts' is nothing more than a manifestation of 'false consciousness'. In advanced industrial societies, the forces of domination exercise intellectual as well as physical control over the population, for they manipulate and create the very processes of thought and social perception. Consequently, ordinary people are unreliable judges of the true nature of their own social condition. In a recent discussion, Marcuse makes the same point by agreeing that an 'affluent' worker may well believe that he is ' "fulfilling" himself... again in

[1] ibid., p. 52   [2] ibid., p. 50   [3] ibid., p. 53
[4] ibid., pp. xi–xii   [5] ibid.

his gadgets, his car and television set'. He goes on to ask, 'But on the other hand, does false subjectivity dispose of the objective state of affairs?'[1]

The 'objective state of affairs' is revealed by critical theory that distinguishes between 'true' and 'false' consciousness, and 'true' and 'false' needs. Truth lies in the realm of possibility and the range of historical alternatives facing mankind. Marcuse refers to a process of 'transcendence', which describes 'tendencies in theory and practice which, in a given society, "overshoot" the established universe of discourse and action towards its historical alternatives (real possibilities)'.[2] 'False' needs are those which are superimposed upon the individual 'by paricular social interests in his repressions': and they include 'most of the prevailing needs to relax, to have fun, to behave and consume in accordance with the advertisements, to love and hate what others love and hate . . .'[3] Individuals must 'in the last analysis' make such distinctions for themselves, but not until 'they are free to give their own answer'.[4]

Marcuse is not very explicit about the way in which this initial freedom is to be attained. In his latest study, *An Essay on Liberation*, he reposes a measure of hope in students as an educational and revolutionary force. As in *One-Dimensional Man*, Marcuse does succeed in making explicit the affinities that concepts such as 'alienation' and 'false-consciousness' have always had with élitist theories of social change. Marcuse also exaggerates the general availability and efficiency of modern social services, although he ends his critique of 'one-dimensional' societies with a reference to social groups who are still denied these services. He writes of 'the sub-stratum of outcasts and outsiders, the exploited and persecuted of other races and other colours . . .' who may yet realize their revolutionary potential.[5]

In a perceptive review of the Cambridge 'Affluent Worker' studies, Halsey refers to 'some paradoxical shifts in the theoretical perspectives' of left- and right-wing social critics.[6] He

---

[1] Herbert Marcuse, 'The Question of Revolution', *New Left Review*, Number 45, September-October 1967, p. 6
[2] Marcuse, *One-Dimensional Man*, p. xi
[3] ibid., pp. 4–5   [4] ibid., p. 6   [5] ibid., p. 256
[6] A. H. Halsey, 'Drawing a Social Map of Ideologies', *Encounter*, Vol. XXXIV, No. 3, March 1970, pp. 83–4

observes that 'neo-Marxists have been led towards laying increasing emphasis on "super-structural forces" rather than the "material basis" of society'.[1] Halsey goes on to point out that 'the essential debate has now come to turn not so much on the changes in incomes, standards of life, conditions of work and patterns of residence, about which there is widespread agreement, but on the meaning of these events for the participants and their interpretation by the intellectuals. The central issue, then, is taken to be the setting of the Cambridge research findings against (on the one hand) the neo-Marxist theory of alienation and (on the other hand) the liberal theory of progressive 'embourgeoisement'.[2]

In neo-Marxist terms, research into subjective states of consciousness is of value only in so far as it reveals the true nature and extent of the worker's alienation and repression under capitalism. Workers enjoy and desire more mass-produced commodities, but they are capable of desiring nobler things and ought to be encouraged to do so. What men desire is the product of their social situation, and these situations can be changed. Propositions of this order are, however, no more provable or disprovable than those that underlie the procedures of psychoanalysis, where the therapist's diagnosis is vindicated as much by the patient's denial as by his acceptance of its validity.

In such debates, the concepts and theories of 'bourgeois' philosophy are poor weapons indeed. In the last resort, bourgeois philosophy permits us only to set one principle against another. It does not offer absolute and final answers to moral issues, or the possibility that one interpretation or claim will be totally vindicated at the expense of another. There are good reasons why Marxists stubbornly insist upon treating alienation as a sociological rather than a philosophical concept.

The normative social theory of Marxism bases its claim to authority, not on philosophical criteria, but an appeal to science. This indeed is what much normative social theory amounts to—an attempt to pass off value judgments as scientific methodology. But the concept of alienation has a further use. It offers us means whereby the standards of validation required in bourgeois scientific procedure can also

[1] ibid.   [2] ibid., p. 84

be dismissed as irrelevant to the task in hand. The concept of 'alienation' is used to metamorphose any set of social facts from what they actually describe into what they *ought* to mean.

In attacking this 'liberal approach' to the social sciences, Stedman-Jones remarks that 'Those who tried to create theory out of facts never understood that it was only theory that could constitute them as facts in the first place'.[1] It does, however, remain open to other theorists to question the way in which a given body of facts is selected and interpreted. It simply will not do to attribute an apparent disposition of human beings to love themselves and their creature comforts to the diabolical machinations of a capitalist social order. It is incumbent on social theorists, who place so great a reliance upon un-substantiated inferences about human psychology, either to provide better causal explanations about the nature of human personality and motivation or to recognize the hypothetical status of their claims.

The critical theory of Marcuse is a dramatic attempt to 'transcend' the confines of evidence. At a more mundane level, specialists in social-welfare problems carry on assembling evidence about the persistence of poverty in 'affluent societies'. The empirical traditions of social criticism continue to enrich the subject-matter of social policy and administration. At this level also the self-elected task of social criticism is practised with energy and conviction. There remains, however, some basis for questioning the nature of that 'widespread agreement' about the main trends in income redistribution and life chances to which Halsey refers. It is necessary to ask why some trends receive closer attention than others, and what implications this has for objectivity in the applied social sciences.

It is, for example, undeniable that despite the growth of redistributive social policies, a very small proportion of our total population continues to own a disproportionately large amount of private wealth. Inequalities of a similar scale char-acterize the distribution of income.[2] The English system of

[1] Gareth Stedman-Jones, 'The Pathology of English History', *New Left Review*, Number 46, November-December 1967, p. 42

[2] The literature on this subject is extensive, but the key studies include H. F. Lydall and D. G. Tipping, 'The Distribution of Personal Wealth in Britain', *Oxford Bulletin of Statistics*, February 1961; 'Still no Property-

taxation deals relatively generously with the better-off sections of the public and has failed to effect any significant increase in the amount of vertical redistribution since the end of the Second World War. It is also undeniable that the 1964–70 Labour government 'has abandoned any policy which threatened to produce a significant redistributive effect'.[1]

Another series of major empirical investigations has established that sizeable minorities of the population are still living in poverty, whether defined in objective or subjective terms. These minorities are composed of the elderly, the disabled, the sick, the unemployed and between 150,000 and 250,000 families whose *earned* income falls below official definitions of poverty.[2] Abel-Smith and Townsend concluded that in 1960 'Approximately 18 per cent of the households and 14·2 per cent of the persons in the United Kingdom, representing nearly 7,500,000 persons, were living below a defined "national assistance" level of living'.[3] Subsequent research in the nineteen-sixties reveals no significant change in this situation.[4] On ethical grounds, these empirical data add up to an appalling indictment of the way in which we order our social priorities.

The other aspect of income distribution in this country tends to be neglected, namely that approximately 85 per cent of persons in the United Kingdom are *not* living below a defined 'national assistance' level. Many of these persons have acquired only a recent or a marginal hold on affluence and many more

---

owning Democracy', *The Economist*, 15 January 1966; R. M. Titmuss, *Income Distribution and Social Change*, Allen and Unwin, 1962; G. Routh, *Occupation and Pay in Great Britain, 1906–60*, Cambridge University Press, 1965

[1] Robin Blackburn, 'Inequality and Exploitation', *New Left Review*, Number 42, March-April 1967, p. 11

[2] See B. Abel-Smith and Peter Townsend, *The Poor and the Poorest*, Bell, 1965; Peter Townsend and Dorothy Wedderburn, *The Aged in the Welfare State*, Occasional Papers in Social Administration, No. 14, Bell, 1965

[3] Abel-Smith and Townsend, *The Poor and the Poorest*, p. 49

[4] The most recent appraisals of the current situation regarding income distribution and the incidence of poverty include *Financial and Other Circumstances of Retirement Pensioners*, HMSO, 1966; A. B. Atkinson, *Poverty in Britain and the Reform of Social Security*, Cambridge University Press, 1969; A. Christopher, *et al.*, *Policy for Poverty*, Institute of Economic Affairs, 1970; and John Edmonds and Giles Radice, *Low Pay*, Fabian Research Series, 270, 1968

could be made better off through a more equitable system of taxation. It can, however, be hypothesized that the very precariousness of such affluence is likely to quicken and harden the disposition of the marginally prosperous to preserve what they have, especially against the attacks of egalitarian politicians and social researchers. It may be that there are now enough families in Britain who consider themselves affluent to discourage any prudent Chancellor from launching radical programmes of income redistribution in the foreseeable future. If this line of argument could be substantiated, we would have to conclude that the democratic progress of redistributive socialism is at an end, because there is no longer *sufficient* injustice, or awareness of injustice, to generate the necessary electoral pressures for reform. The question would remain open as to whether or not this state of affairs justified recourse to non-democratic pressures.

Some members of the New Left take the latter view. Blackburn, suggests, for example, that

> Reformist attacks on inequality tend to founder on the implacable demands of the economic system they take for granted. Moreover too gradual an assault on a capitalist economy demobilizes the only social forces which could carry it through. The morale of the working classes is weakened by the labyrinthine manoeuvres of a reformist policy.[1]

There remains a singular lack of evidence about the state of morale of the working classes of a kind that offers encouragement to revolutionaries. The assemblage of empirical evidence about poverty supports the normative views of justice already held by social reformers who undertake these surveys. But subjective states of mind of sociologists and applied social scientists are not the real battleground. Despite the intellectual hammering which Dicey has received in recent years, certain of his central propositions remain relevant today and still await rebuttal. Dicey was very cautiously hopeful that the 'power of opinion' in England allied to the 'basic goodwill of the richer classes of Englishmen towards their less prosperous neighbours' would prevent revolution.[2] This 'goodwill' has persisted and still manifests itself in a variety of ways. The capacity of the

[1] Blackburn, 'Inequality and Exploitation,' p. 15   [2] Dicey, *op. cit.*, p. lxiii

English ruling class for assimilating and adapting the ideas and proponents of reform remains as effective as ever. As Schumpeter observes, this class 'assimilated Disraeli, who elsewhere would have become another Lasalle . . .' and 'would have, if necessary, assimilated Trotsky himself or rather, as in that case he would assuredly have been, the Earl of Prinkipo, K.G.'[1]

Dicey was doubtful whether 'socialist ideals' would ever appeal to majority opinion or could ever be realized through democratic processes. He compared the intolerance and 'blindness' of experts, especially collectivist ones, with the 'ordinary man who knows something of history and has not shut his eyes to human nature as it actually exists'. Dicey put his trust in 'the love of self, whether justifiable or unjustifiable [which] is due to causes deeper than any political or social reform will ever touch'.[2] Dicey's assumptions about human nature are no more naïve than collectivist arguments based on a belief in the intrinsically compassionate and altruistic nature of human beings.

The basic conflict between socialism and democracy would not, however, become apparent 'until earnest socialists force upon the people some law which, though in conformity with socialistic principles, imposes some new burden upon the mass of the voters'.[3] Dicey reflects Spencer's anxiety that the burden of excessive taxation will be most bitterly resented by 'the large middle class of tradesmen and skilled artisans who may feel that they are being pressed down . . . into the ranks of the strictly poor . . .' It may be that there is a logic in the relationship between expanding scientific and social knowledge, the rising costs of medical care and the increasing range of statutory provision on a collectivist basis. But the issues of equalitarian distribution, and the subjective realities of social-class alignments remain as crucially important today as they were in Dicey's time. As the number of taxpayers has increased, fear of the taxpayers has become more rather than less important in the deliberations of professional politicians. To claim rising social expectations as an ally of social reform is to accept only a part of public attitudes towards individual and collective welfare—that part which approves of collective provision. But it seems that citizens also wish to realize their welfare as

---

[1] Schumpeter, *op. cit.*, p. 229   [2] Dicey, *op. cit.*, p. lxxx
[3] ibid., p. lxxiv

individuals in the private market, in terms of 'the love of self' and their own loved ones.

It is assumptions about these realities of everyday life that still constrain politicians to undertake many of their good deeds by subterfuge, not claiming them as their own until they have retrospectively been accorded public approval. The question remains whether or not the old Adam of self-love and self-interest is as much a figment of Dicey's imagination as a belief in the altruistic revolutionary proletariat is an illusion of the Left. We must also question the extent to which these assumptions are incorporated into normative theory in defiance or default of the evidence. It would be helpful if we could even begin to understand the extent to which the rational pursuit of personal advantage and self-interest is a variable product of different types of economic system, or simply a constant feature of human nature. It is always humbling for a discipline to look beyond its own boundaries for explanations of its own phenomena.

In the middle ranges of political radicalism, either of the left or the right, appeals are made to public opinion and assumptions are made about the altruistic potentialities of ordinary citizens. But such evidence as exists about public attitudes towards social welfare is seldom re-interpreted by either Fabians or Bow-Groupers, and may be wilfully misconstrued. With a subject like social administration, so closely involved in the world of practical politics, an element of rhetoric is a necessary part of intellectual discourse. Most reformers in democracies sustain their hopes for a better future with the belief that there is a tide in the affairs of men which flows at least for part of the time in their favour.[1] What little evidence we have suggests that it scarcely flows at all. Rhetoric becomes an increasingly important element in the debate about social welfare as the prospects for radical social reform seem to recede.

The failure of the New Left to influence any states of social consciousness outside minorities in the universities inevitably leads to frustration and disappointment. They are driven to make still more radical critiques of the existing social order or

[1] See for example the essays by Brian Abel-Smith and Peter Townsend in Norman MacKenzie (ed.), *Conviction*, MacGibbon and Kee, London, 1958

'system'. We are told that the map of social consciousness cannot be expected to delineate the true profiles of human discontent and frustration, for it is in the nature of capitalism that the masses do not know the difference between true and false consciousness. These fervent young ideologues, however, soon tire of squatting over the damp sticks of the English proletariat with their two-pennyworth of 'Young Marx' and a tinder-box. The rage of these social critics is thus displaced from the object of their utopian fantasies—the urban poor— onto a corrupt capitalist system which can only be overthrown by revolution. The practice of politics ceases to be the art of seeking justice in a pluralist society, and becomes the practice of seeking to impose on the community a minority group's definition of what justice ought to be. By confusing normative theory with ideology and rhetoric, and through the misuse of concepts like alienation, a tenuous, but bogus, relationship is maintained with both democracy and scientific procedure.

From a reformist perspective, there seems to be little evidence as yet relating to either subjective or objective definitions of need to suggest that the dominant criteria of the economic market are likely to be seriously challenged at any significant level of social life. From a revolutionary perspective, the only hope for effecting radical change lies in rejecting a whole body of empirical knowledge on the grounds that it is a manifestation of corrupted thought, and adopting unparliamentary procedures to attain 'truly' democratic ends. Yet it still remains to be shown that the persistence of residual poverty is a more causally important phenomenon than the process of 'embourgeoisement' in predicting the most likely course of development in the field of social welfare.

DEMOCRACY AND SOCIAL JUSTICE

Problems of social justice are of central concern to most forms of normative theory. This is not to argue that sociology is inescapably committed to being a normative discipline, but certain areas of its subject-matter—and social welfare is one of these—do generate very powerful degrees of value commitment. Irrespective of the degree of normative commitment, it is the nature of the relationship which holds between theory and evidence that remains the index of academic integrity. It is this relationship which we must now consider.

Philosophers, political scientists and sociologists may, as citizens, have a concern for the creation, preservation and extension of social justice, and to that extent can all be said to display value commitment from the start. Philosophy offers a variety of models and theories of social justice, and we have considered some of the implications of one such model. Within Runciman's model there remains scope for disagreement over the ordering of criteria of allocation, for example, the relative priorities which ought to be accorded to need and merit. There can be many different models of justice and as many related programmes of political action, from which a variety of social consequences follow. Those who are collectivistically inclined will stress the criterion of need, while individualists will emphasize the claims of merit.

None of these models can be proved correct or incorrect, but each can be more or less intelligently defended or criticized. The social ends postulated as desirable may be shown to be less desirable than originally supposed, or to have additional and unintended consequences which most people would wish to avoid. The difference between rational debate and dogmatic exchange of views is the criterion by which the participants can be expected to change their minds.

One role of the social scientist in the procedures of rational debate is the collection and interpretation of evidence. The evidence collected may simply describe a given situation, or be related to theories which seek to explain why such a situation exists; what are the likely consequences of leaving matters as they are, or of implementing a variety of remedies. New evidence may lead to an existing sociological theory or set of hypotheses being modified or abandoned. The new facts may no longer fit the theory, and if the facts seem to be incontrovertibly correct then the theory is abandoned. Men may, however, hold so strongly to a principle that they will not change it despite evidence which proves that putting it into practice has undesirable consequences. Those who uphold the inviolability of marriage vows might be indifferent to evidence which challenges the validity of their principles. They can ignore the evidence without weakening their ethical position, but if they distort or deny the evidence then they do weaken their ethical position in another way. We can only claim the status of rationality for our moral beliefs if we abide by the rules of rational discourse and enquiry.

Sociological theory can be applied to problems which evoke varying degrees of value commitment and concern amongst social scientists. The extent to which sociological theory is normative is determined by the extent to which the sociologist feels personally concerned that one relationship between variables should pertain rather than any other, or that one social end should be pursued rather than any other. A profile of normative social theory is also a profile of the areas of greatest moral concern to sociologists.

A normative theory tells us what will happen if we do x rather than y, but it also states explicitly or implicitly which end of action we ought to prefer when there is a choice of ends. Bowlby's theory of maternal care and deprivation is a good example of the way in which scientific enquiry in the social sciences is inspired rather than bedevilled by value factors.[1] Even limited acceptance of this theory has changed professional practice and legislation in the field of child care. As a result, certain forms of emotional distress and damage to children have been alleviated. If, as now seems likely, the causal relationships postulated in the theory do generally hold, then this addition to our knowledge could equally well have been used to inflict distress, had this been a desired end of social policy. Similarly, if we can understand more clearly how stigma is imposed and experienced, we can use this knowledge for 'good' or 'ill', according to how we define these qualities. The ends for which we use our knowledge do not invalidate the causal relationship postulated by the theory. But this is not the only kind and use of normative theory that we can encounter.

There is normative theory that seeks 'to change or to maintain the world, not to describe it'.[2] Normative theory may also describe areas of thought and possible relationships between

[1] John Bowlby, *Maternal Care and Mental Health*, W.H.O., HMSO, London, 1951

[2] Horton, p. 713

thought and action. In non-normative theory, the form of the theory is always susceptible to the nature of the evidence. The scientific credentials of normative theory must always be relatively suspect, for it is exposed to two kinds of temptation. The first temptation is to distort or suppress evidence that does not fit the normative content of the theoretical proposition. The second temptation is to make the theory one of the variables in the phenomena one is seeking to explain. If the facts in a given situation do not fit, there is always the possibility of making them fit by changing them. The sociologist can undertake certain kinds of committed social action, or aid and abet the action of others in order to create the necessary but missing evidence.

Various forms of action research can personally involve the sociologist in the behaviour he is studying. On a more general and formidable scale this has been a characteristic of Marxist social theory, which is also the ideology of major political movements. It can be postulated that a relationship exists between the declining living standards of the poor and their propensity for revolution, and that these living standards are in the process of being inexorably lowered. The available evidence may, however, indicate that such 'immiseration' is not taking place, and is unlikely to do so in the foreseeable future. The possibility remains that the normative component of such a theory will be incorporated into programmes of political persuasion and propaganda designed to create conditions of disaffection and disorder so that living standards do fall, and the postulated causal relationship is shown to be true.

This is not to imply that the authenticity of a theory matters much to revolutionaries, only that certain kinds of theory can be made to advance something other than knowledge and truth. Perhaps this is what Horton means when he suggests that 'whenever there is genuine conflict between groups and interpretations, correctness clearly becomes a practical matter of power and political persuasion'.[1] Or as Marx put the problem, more bluntly, 'The philosophers have only *interpreted* the world in different ways; the point is to change it'.[2] In Marx's time, the evidence did point to a probable increase in misery and a consequent heightening of class consciousness.

[1] ibid.   [2] Bottomore and Rubels, *op. cit.*, p. 84

Marxist theory did not rule out the possibility that better social-welfare provision could reduce or postpone the likelihood of revolution. But Marx considered this to be an undesirable development because the normative orientation of his theory prescribed, not a particular kind of welfare, but a particular kind of society, and if necessary a particular use of scientific procedure to achieve that end.

Recent improvements in standards of living require Marxists today to be more anxiously concerned with changing the facts of social consciousness so that terms like 'alienation' become central rather than marginal features of their social theory. Concepts like 'relative poverty' can also be used to engender not only discontent amongst the poor but guilt and misgivings amongst the better off. The constant temptation in these exercises is to confuse what the poor *ought* to feel about their condition with what they actually do feel. Translated into political action, normative theory often becomes little more than a euphemism for the ideology of intellectuals seeking to use ideas as forces of social change. There is nothing intrinsically reprehensible about such activity so long as it is clearly recognized that it has to do with political life and has no relationship to scientific procedure, social or otherwise.

We have already given some attention to the role of the social scientist in the making of social policy, and the honourable tradition of 'blue-book' sociology in this country. The problem of scientific objectivity has also been considered in relation to Weber's dispute with the Association for Social Policy. It is pointed out by Simey that Weber never claimed that social science could be 'entirely divorced from value judgments'[1] or that the claims of scientific objectivity precluded moral commitment. Weber was, however, very concerned to draw a distinction between 'special pleading' on behalf of interest groups and a concern for the truth.[2] It is perhaps an index of Weber's heightened moral sensibilities that he could anticipate so clearly the kinds of value problem which beset the applied social scientist today.

It would be misleading to assume, however, that those sociologists closest to policy-makers show the most marked

---

[1] Simey, p. 75, quoted from Fred H. Blum, 'Max Weber's Postulate of "Freedom"', *The American Journal of Sociology*, 1944-5   [2] ibid., p. 76

tendency to distort or ignore inconvenient evidence. Of all social scientists today, specialists in social policy and administration have enjoyed one of the longest and closest relationships with government departments and other groups supporting special interests. The preservation of scientific integrity in such relationships is contingent upon a dutiful observance of Weber's basic tenet that the researcher should make his values absolutely explicit to himself and others. The detection of any subsequent and unintentional bias in the selection and presentation of evidence can be and has been left to ordinary common sense.

We have argued that such theory as the discipline of social policy and administration possesses has derived in the main from moral rather than social sciences. The disadvantage of this relationship has been a consequent failure to develop models and theories that permit explanations of welfare phenomena. The discipline is strangely bifurcated between an impressive body of empirical explanations on the one hand and powerful rhetoric and moral exhortations on the other. The advantage of this relationship has been that the difference is nearly always clearly and unambiguously evident. Social policy and administration remains relatively free of those ambivalences of feeling which inhere in the very notion of 'normative theory', and from temptations to use sociological theory for inappropriate purposes. The first function of any kind of scientific theory is not to criticize what exists, or to 'transcend' what exists, but to help us distinguish correct from incorrect knowledge. Sociological theory does not enable us to distinguish 'goodness' from 'badness', although it may provide new forms of knowledge and insight which can be used for a variety of moral purposes. As it finds new applications in the field of social welfare, it may indicate new possibilities for social change and improvement.

There have been some criticisms of Dicey's view that trends in social legislation are closely related to and influenced by trends in the informed opinion of an influential minority.[1] None the less, many social scientists who wish to influence

[1] See for example John Goldthorpe, 'The Development of Social Policy in England, 1800–1914, Notes on a Sociological Approach to a Problem in Historical Explanation', *Transactions of the Fifth World Congress of Sociology*, Washington, D.C., Vol. IV, International Sociological Association, 1964

legislation undertake research on the assumption that new forms of knowledge revealed by specialists may crucially affect the course of events in policy-making. It remains an open question whether or not reforms such as the move towards comprehensive education, the abolition of capital punishment, the access of immigrants to welfare benefits, and the payment of grants to students in higher education would be features of today's social legislation without the lobbying, advice and research of small, specialist minorities. The point is that such ameliorations and modifications of past practices are often in advance of public opinion, but not so far removed that they evoke positive or generalized hostility. What has happened is that some sociologists have been gradually integrated into a relatively small élite once reserved to economists, political scientists, philosophers and other more traditional and less easily defined disciplines.

There is another way in which sociologists can help to make decision-taking and policy-making more open to democratic influence. They can concern themselves more systematically and theoretically with providing evidence about public attitudes towards issues of social policy and justice, and also with providing explanations of variations in public response to welfare legislation. A further role may be that of seeking to inform or change public opinion, and to help to create consciousness of problems where this consciousness is absent. There is no reason why sociologists should impose a self-denying ordinance on themselves any more than doctors should desist from warning the public of the dangers of smoking or advising on better ways of staying fit. Democracy is nothing if not an educative process, and education is nothing if it lacks a moral purpose.

The study of subjective states of social consciousness is, as we have seen, especially prone to misuse of scientific procedure, partly because of the methodological difficulties involved, and partly because of the dangers of ideological bias. Preserving the integrity of sociology as a humane discipline is contingent upon a continuing respect for evidence. It is legitimate for sociologists to resort to social action in order to create those states of social consciousness likely to make their theoretical predictions come true—even though this involves them in the delicate task of treating themselves as one of the relevant variables in the explanation! That is why they must be constantly on guard against ignoring, denying or distorting evidence when it inconveniently challenges the value assumptions which underpin their normative theory. The problem is specially acute when questions of social welfare are the subject of investigation. It can be a lonely and distressing experience for any humane person to study and acquire special knowledge of the varieties of human distress.

None of us is required to accept the *status quo* with regard to the allocation of rewards and privileges in society. If, however, we profess an attachment to democratic principles we are compelled to accept and respect the many different definitions of justice that have to co-exist in a pluralistic society. The variety of these definitions is an index of what we mean by plurality. We must also recognize that heightened awareness of these definitions appears to be restricted to small minorities of relatively politically conscious people. The central feature of ideology in advanced industrial societies would seem to be not whether it is alive or dead, but that anxiety about its condition concerns such a small minority of the general public.

There has been a long tradition of social criticism in both English sociology and social administration. Why sociologists formulate the kinds of critical normative theory that they do ought to be high on the agenda of any programme of research into the sociology of knowledge. The critical tradition of social policy and administration has been of a more moderate and pragmatic order. Marcuse's exhortation that sociology is morally bound to adopt a critical stance towards its subject-matter is only an exaggerated version of a more general trend towards social misanthropy in theoretical sociology. There is, perhaps, an almost obsessive preoccupation today with the 'sickness' of western industrial societies, and it must be rare in the history of scholarship for so many practitioners of a discipline to show so little approval of their own subject-matter.

There comes a time when normative theories must also be judged in terms of their own contribution to social progress, and that time has come for Marxist and neo-Marxist normative theory. So far these theories have helped to produce societies in which political brutality and incompetence have reached such dimensions that it is necessary to build brick walls and impose stringent controls on movement in order to preserve a social membership at all. The most charitable thing we can say about Lenin and Stalin is that had they each lived a little longer they might have grown bored with the slaughter. It simply will not do to argue that Marxist ideals have been perverted in practice, for the perversion has occurred in every known instance. Perhaps communist societies come nearest of all to being political systems in which improved welfare institutions are used as part of a regime of repression and 'un-freedom'. They exemplify the point that the enhancement of social welfare is not the only desirable end of political action.

At the other ideological extreme there seem to be no good reasons why we ought to demolish the foundations of our hard-won system of collective welfare in order that more people should have the chance to find their just deserts in a truly competitive private market. We need, instead, new types of normative theories about social welfare, which are orientated towards the middle ranges of sentiment and expectation and take account of psychological as well as social variables in seeking to explain why injustices and miseries persist.

Summary

We have argued that democracy remains the only political system in which conflicting definitions of social justice can hope to find provisional degrees of reconciliation. It is the safest context in which reasonable people can give up any claim to or prospect of being absolute winners and, in return, be guaranteed that they will never be absolute losers. The tolerable degrees of gain and loss can be agreed, unmade and remade without prejudice to social continuity and the maintenance of that balanced relationship between equality and freedom which in the last resort is the only guarantee of a modicum of justice.

The preservation of an academic discipline from the wilder reaches of ideology also plays a part in the maintenance of democratic values, because the undermining of intellectual integrity and of political freedom are virtually synonymous processes. In summary, there are certain aspects of the problem of value and bias in sociology which are relatively peripheral. Dahrendorf includes amongst these minor problems the influence of values on choice of subject, the selective formulation of theories, and the study of values as social phenomena.[1] Dahrendorf takes much more seriously the problems of ideological distortion and the confusion of untestable propositions such as 'alienation' with scientific propositions. He recognizes that sociological responsibility 'does not end when we complete the process of scientific enquiry, indeed it may begin at that very point'.[2]

We have argued that in seeking to validate normative theory by intervening in social affairs, the process of scientific enquiry can be placed in jeopardy and even denied completion. Short-run political advantages may be gained, but must be set against the damage done to sociology as a humane and scientific discipline, and to the wider aims of social justice.

This is not to argue that preserving the scientific status and integrity of a discipline is more important than, say, improving the lives of the poor. The social sciences have been able to make an increasingly useful contribution to the enhancement of social welfare, because policy-makers and sections of the public have come increasingly to trust evidence from sociologically reputable sources. In more general terms, the application of the social sciences to the analysis and remedying of social ills has widened and enriched the area of rational discourse in policy-making and public debate. Any intended or unintended subversion of the academic reputation of a discipline can only weaken the role of reason and respect for evidence in civil affairs.

The 'rules of the game' that govern the practice of civilized discourse in democracies protect us, not only from the radical onslaughts of unreason that are directed at enhancing social welfare, but also those tides of unreason that can with equal ease drive public opinion in the opposite direction. The morally outraged who use the vocabulary and tactics of the gutter in the cause of social justice pose the same threat to human well-being as racial bigots in Alabama and Russian bullies in Prague. In a subtler way, the sociologist who wilfully confuses normative theory with old-fashioned ideology damages rather than enhances the aims of social welfare and justice.

[1] Ralf Dahrendorf, *Essays in the Theory of Society*, Routledge and Kegan Paul, 1968, pp. 6 *passim*   [2] ibid., p. 18

4

Exchange and Stigma

SOCIAL SERVICES AS EXCHANGE SYSTEMS

All studies of social-welfare institutions ought to include an exploration of human sensibilities. The purpose of this chapter is to examine social services as systems of exchange and to offer a provisional classification of these services in terms of their status-enhancing and stigmatizing propensities. Social services represent a compromise between compassion and indifference, just as they reflect our dispositions both to remember and to forget our social obligations.

Titmuss draws a distinction between 'the grant, or the gift or unilateral transfer . . .', which is the 'mark of the social', and 'exchange or bilateral transfer', which is the mark of the 'economic' market.[1] The 'social market' is concerned with 'different types of moral transactions, embodying notions of gift exchange, of reciprocal obligations'.[2] The problem we face is that of establishing the extent to which these notions of reciprocity are also shared by the community. Consequently, we cannot assume that the legal imposition (or preservation) of an 'infrastructure of universalist services' will 'provide a framework of values and opportunity bases' that are most likely to minimize stigma.[3] In short, we know much more about the sentiments of philosophers and social scientists than those of ordinary people in everyday life.

We need, therefore, to construct different kinds of model and theory, which will complement those we already have by taking account of the diverse sentiments of ordinary people. This exercise is worth undertaking for its own sake in so far as

[1] R. M. Titmuss, *Commitment to Welfare*, p. 22
[2] ibid., p. 20
[3] ibid., p. 135

it seeks to widen our knowledge of social reality *as it is*. It is also necessary if we wish to change that reality into something more akin to a particular normative model or ideal type.

It may be true that the dominant value-orientations of our society are such that the forms of unilateral exchange are considered to be less stigmatizing than those of bilateral exchange. Alternatively, men and women socialized in a capitalist society, and competitively motivated for economic survival, may well experience humiliation in all forms of unilateral exchange when they are the recipients. Residualists work on this second assumption when they refer to the 'debilitating' effects of 'free' social services on the morale of the public. Briefly, we do not know how or why people are elevated or debased in exchange situations. Our present models of social welfare are largely normative ones, which include the moral prescriptions of their authors but exclude, or take for granted, the subjective perceptions of ordinary people. Titmuss's great contribution has been to identify stigma as the central issue, and to define the main practical task of social policy as that of finding ways to differentiate welfare provisions without stigmatizing recipients.

The resolution of this problem may be brought about by gaining a better understanding of why stigma is experienced, and what are the conditions of provision and usage under which it is most likely to be encountered. This aim requires the construction of a welfare model based more generally upon the normative dispositions of users rather than those of experts, or for that matter, the objective facts of social structure and organization. Such a model would have an enhanced predictive potential. The value premise of the exercise is that stigma ought to be reduced, although the model should take account of the relevant variables in such a way that it can be used for the opposite end. We share the view of Miller and Rein, however, that 'the most biting criticism of many of our social services is that they fail to reach those in greatest need'.[1] In theory at least most residualists would share that view.

We have already referred to some of the useful research that has been undertaken into the subjective aspects of human need. The concept of relative poverty has been developed and ex-

[1] S. M. Miller and Martin Rein, 'Poverty, Inequality and Policy', in H. S. Becker (ed.), *Social Problems: A Modern Approach*, Wiley, p. 515

plored by both Townsend[1] and Runciman,[2] and in the work of the latter we come nearest to a theoretical analysis of the relationship between the structural determinants of inequality in a society and the feelings of grievance and stigma that are generated by inequality. Runciman analyses in some depth the effect of means tests on applicants and the reasons for the unpopularity of such tests.[3] He refers pointedly to 'the long process of habituation to inequality without which society would be forever in a state of civil war'.[4]

None the less, we still need to know more about why people feel as they do about dependency, and whether it is true that under even the most open and universalist of social services stigma and deference still operate to inhibit usage.

When Titmuss draws his distinction between the 'social' and the 'economic' market it is important to remind ourselves that individuals in industrial societies have to live in both contexts at the same time. In the process of socialization, we have to reconcile what may be felt at times to be antipathetic ideals and practices. If our social life were exclusively dominated by either a 'welfare' or an 'economic' ethos, it would be easier for each person to know and comprehend his social world as a consistent whole.

Berger and Luckman describe how 'the transmission of the meaning of a social institution is based on the social recognition of that institution as a "permanent" solution to a "permanent" problem of the given collectivity.[5] As part of the social order, social services are humanly produced and their meaning is learned by each member of the society so that the well-socialised individual 'knows' that his social world is a consistent whole.[6] In this ideal form we can say that there is 'a high degree of symmetry between objective and subjective reality'.[7] Unfortunately, this outcome is most unlikely when the institution in question is a social service, because the 'problems' referred to frequently happen to be the people using

[1] Peter Townsend, 'The Meaning of Poverty', *British Journal of Sociology*
[2] W. G. Runciman, *Relative Deprivation and Social Justice*
[3] ibid., p. 222–6
[4] ibid., p. 294
[5] Peter L. Berger and Thomas Luckman, *The Social Construction of Reality*, Allen Lane, The Penguin Press, London, 1967, p. 87
[6] ibid., p. 83   [7] ibid., p. 183

the service. And social services, by their very nature, frequently affect people whose socialization has been far from perfect and whose hold on civic status is most tenuous.

It is possible to use social services as a device for restoring and compensating those individuals who have been stigmatized by their experience of the economic market. But this 'institutional' view of the aims of social welfare cannot be commonly and consistently shared throughout pluralistic industrial societies. The aims of social welfare are one of the main phenomena over which differences of value arise. If this were not so there would be only one normative model of social welfare to discuss. In pluralistic societies men learn to value themselves by different criteria in different situations. For the moment we will assume that in all known industrial societies, at some stage or level in economic development, social-welfare objectives are subordinated to market imperatives. At the present time this assumption seems both reasonable and modest. Even socialist communities do not hesitate to impose restrictions on welfare aims in the interests of economic or military objectives. The inevitable claims that the long-term aim of such measures is to achieve more welfare is irrelevant. This is so partly because we are concerned with the past and present reality of everyday experience, and partly because 'in the long run we are all dead anyway'.

Thus all known industrial societies at the present time impose limits on welfare objectives in the interest of immediate economic goals. In seeking to maintain and legitimate their institutional order, societies ensure that their children are taught the virtues of work and self-help as well as those of mutual aid. This process is a part of what Berger and Luckman describe as the problem of 'universe maintenance' in social life, that is, the problem of making a society meaningful and acceptable to its members.[1] This process is intended to be systematic and pervasive, and its effects are meant to endure in human consciousness. Unfortunately,

> since human beings are frequently sluggish and forgetful, there must also be procedures by which these meanings can be reimpressed and rememorised, if necessary by coercive and generally unpleasant means. Furthermore, since human beings

---

[1] ibid., pp. 120–3

are frequently stupid, institutional meanings tend to become simplified in the process of transmission . . . the meanings become sedimented.[1]

The social services are one of the major contexts in which this problem of 'universe maintenance' or legitimation is always present. It may sometimes be defined as the central function of certain or even all of the social services. This is especially apparent in the more remedial forms of social work and in those selectivist social services that are governed by the principle of negative discrimination, where the service is itself seen by users as the sanctioning agent. The clientele of such services may be defined as those who ' "inhabit" the transmitted universe [less] definitely than others'.[2] In societies where the ethos of the market predominates, social services must often combine their welfare aims with sanctioning functions. Under these circumstances the welfare practitioners must also face the problem of making their universe meaningful and consistent.

If we suppose for a moment that as a result of radical political change all deterrent sanctions were removed from a welfare service, the meaning of that service to its clientele— its place in their subjective reality—would not change markedly without their systematic social re-education. An exception to this statement would be in the unlikely event of the clientele having been the main agents of change. More usually such changes represent an alteration in the aims of ruling minorities, sometimes partially influenced by the normative models of sociologists.

The relationship between social welfare and citizenship is therefore a highly ambiguous one. Social services are used to transmit skills and a variety of goods and services designed to enhance the freedom and independence of individuals. They are also used to impose sanctions, and therefore stigma, upon individuals. Various forms of rationalization are employed to reconcile these ends. The practice and language of therapy is one such device encountered in social service. Social workers may, for example, be used as therapists to resocialize the 'deviant' so that he is able to accept the objective reality of his society and his social position in it.[3] Therapy can be seen as

[1] ibid., p. 87   [2] ibid., p. 124
[3] ibid., p. 132

one of the gentler forms of control exercised in welfare contexts.

More drastic types of sanction range from conceptual and physical forms of stigma to actual murder. These processes of 'nihilation' commonly begin in the context of social services. The outsiders, or minority group in question, may experience conceptual liquidation by being accorded the inferior status of 'paupers' or 'vagrants'. In extreme forms the status of the individual or group in question is made so inferior that programmes of physical liquidation are begun. Various forms of euthanasia, eugenic control and compulsory sterilization are more common examples than, say, the mass extermination of whole social groups stigmatized as 'sub-human', which occurred in Nazi Germany.[1]

In our society the institutional equivalent of therapy at a personal level is the attempt to incorporate deviant groups through programmes of positive discrimination. Systematic efforts are made to raise the living standards and social expectations of deprived and previously stigmatized groups so that they are in effect re-socialized into the dominant value-system of the society. Although much lip-service is paid to preserving what is best in working-class culture, very often by specialists who have subjectively left that culture, positive discrimination may be more accurately seen as a way of accelerating the embourgeoisement process, in areas where it fails to gather natural volition. It is the sociological equivalent of 'pump-priming'.

As societies become more complex and a social distribution of knowledge occurs, prospective users of social services become more dependent upon specialists who can advise them as to which of the many special forms of knowledge and help they require.[2] Social services are a key context in which this process of referral occurs, and it is here that we see most dramatically the division that can arise between what is 'part of the generally

---

[1] ibid., p. 133. As Podhoretz reminds us, 'Most societies throughout history have simply been unable to suffer the presence of distinctive minority groups among them; and the fate of minorities has generally been to disappear, either through being assimilated into the majority, or through being expelled, or through being murdered'. Quoted by Horton, 'Order and Conflict Theories of Social Problems as Competing Ideologies', p. 709

[2] Unofficial and voluntary organizations are increasingly taking on this role. An excellent example of such work is *Welfare Benefits, a Guide for*

relevant and accessible stock of knowledge' and what constitutes 'expertise'.[1]

In all industrial societies, for this reason, citizenship is a range of skills rather than a status transmitted from generation to generation. The enjoyment of citizenship is synonymous with its exercise. An extensive mastery of specialized forms of language and skills is required, including the ability to obtain 'not only the advice of experts, but the prior advice of experts on experts'.[2] The most important definitions of citizenship are subjective ones. The extent to which we exercise civic rights and responsibilities is determined by our levels of civic competence, but more profoundly so by the extent to which we believe in the authenticity of our citizenship. Such authenticity is the product of experience and socialization, which is in turn related to the objective facts of class structure. Each user of a social service brings the subjective facts of his personal biography to the experience. These facts will be more authentic to him than the officially defined aims or traditions of the service.

The relationship between social services and citizenship is thus largely determined by subjective evaluations of the purpose of the service. For some citizenship is enhanced while for others it is debased by reliance upon social services. Perceptions of status vary according to service and category of need, and it is no more true to say that all universalist services always endow status than it is to claim that selectivist services always stigmatize. Indeed, these two forms of conceptualization have done much to confuse our understanding of the process of stigmatization.

The formation of individual and public attitudes towards social services needs to be viewed as a process separate, in some respects, from legislative procedures. As we grow up, the most authentic rights we acquire and exercise are those we use in the roles of buyers and sellers in the market-place. We do not have to be persuaded that we have rights to what we buy.[3]

Welfare Workers in York, published by the York Branch of the Child Poverty Action Group, York, 1969.

[1] Berger and Luckman, *op. cit.*, p. 96   [2] ibid., p. 60

[3] This is not to suggest that consumers are always sufficiently informed to exercise these rights when claiming redress for bad service. See Molony Committee on Consumer Problems: *Final Report*, Cmnd 1781, 1962, HMSO, para. 401

The idea of paying through taxes or holding authentic claims by virtue of citizenship remains largely an intellectual conceit of the social scientist and the socialist. For the majority the idea of participant citizenship in distributive processes outside the market-place has very little meaning. Consequently most applicants for social services remain paupers at heart.[1] Such is the process of socialization in industrial societies that to feel otherwise requires a conscious effort of will. The rationale of participation campaigns in the field of social welfare is to create in the minds of citizens a natural and vivid awareness of the right to certain goods and services outside a cash nexus.[2] The present vogue for such campaigns confirms that the prevalent view of the relationship between citizenship and social services is one which sees them as incompatible. If ordinary people *do* still think of many social services as mainly sanctioning and stigmatizing agencies, then it is these subjective constructions of reality that matter. Although 'less eligibility' and 'deterrence' have officially vanished from the statute book, their ghosts still haunt the social consciousness of the British people.

The dilemma of the poor is compounded by the fact that even those rights in the private market of which they are most conscious are in practice often denied them. The poor lack the money to claim parity in the private market. Normatively and relationally they learn to define themselves as inferior persons, subordinate in terms of both money and knowledge. Thus many of the clientele of social services come to the welfare agency already stigmatized. Any request for expert service expresses a further condition of dependency. In the market situation, parity of status is maintained between layman and expert by a pay-

---

[1] U. Cormack, 'The Seebohm Report—A Great State Paper', in *Social and Economic Administration*, Vol. 3, No. 1, January 1969. ' . . . in England the persistent tendency of formal community provision has historically been to disfranchise and depersonalize, to be, in current parlance, socially divisive . . . The public provision tends to become inferior to the private: the public servant to forget to serve the public . . .,' p. 57.

[2] See T. Lynes, *Welfare Rights*, Fabian Tract 395, 1969; B. Abel-Smith, *Freedom in the Welfare State*, Fabian Tract 353, 1964; Ben Whitaker, *Participation and Poverty*, Fabian Research Series 272, 1968; Adrian Sinfield, *Which Way for Social Work*, Fabian Tract 393, 1969; Society of Labour Lawyers Report, *Justice for All*, Fabian Research Series 273, 1968

ment. Removing the need to pay, in a welfare context, does not in itself remove the stigma.

The stigmatizing experience of the market may thus be carried over into non-market situations. At the same time, certain kinds of goods and services may be of such a nature that they create marked inequalities of status between providers and users in any kind of exchange situation. This is especially likely to occur when one party has a monopoly, or near monopoly, of expert knowledge.

Medical care offers a relevant example of this unequal distribution of knowledge. In addition to the factor of expertise, so great are the uncertainties regarding the outcome and duration of treatment that the market in many cases cannot make effective provision. As Arrow suggests, 'where there is uncertainty, information or knowledge becomes a commodity'.[1] In medical care, as in many other social services, this kind of information is intrinsically not marketable. The patient must 'trust' the doctor and in such a situation 'the very word "profit" is a signal that denies the trust relations'.[2] Thus in practice 'the patient must delegate to the physician much of his freedom of choice' and thereby place himself in a subordinate relationship.[3]

One further obstacle to the establishment of parity in social-welfare relationships even within the market context is noted by Arrow. Insurance is the traditional mechanism for maintaining such parity. In medical care the ideal insurance is one which insures 'against a failure to benefit from medical care . . .'[4] Such insurance is, again, not marketable.

These arguments can be construed as a case for removing medical care and similar services from the private market on the grounds that the price mechanism cannot do what it claims to do. It does not, however, follow that, because the public sector can continue its care where the private market ceases to provide, the recipient will feel any less stigmatized. In a society where self-help and independence are powerfully sanctioned values, the subjective facts of social consciousness still impose inferior status on the dependent. These problems, which

[1] Kenneth J. Arrow, 'Uncertainty and the Welfare Economics of Medical Care', in *American Economic Review*, Vol. LIII, No. 5, December 1963, p. 946
[2] ibid., p. 965   [3] ibid.   [4] ibid., p. 964

are so explicit in medical care, may highlight a more general principle—that in the long run the risk of helplessness becomes a probability for us all, and with such probability goes the certainty of stigma. Social-welfare systems may be intended to alter the citizens' subjective frame of reference. So long as they do not do this they will merely reflect the dominant ethos of a competitive society in which dependency means inferior status. The attitudes towards, and the forms of usage which characterize, a social service are all functions of the socialization processes experienced by the clientele. In our time the objective reality of the Welfare State is subjectively meaningless to those who have not achieved citizenship in a conscious and authentic form, and whose experience of the market has already given them an enduring sense of inferiority.

PUBLIC SERVICES AS EXCHANGE SYSTEMS

'Public utility' is one of the least inviting terms with which to start a chapter; like 'gas and water socialism' it evokes little enthusiasm and still less passion. The main theme of this chapter is, however, to explore the neglected topic of 'public services' and to argue that they are enterprises that contain a great potential for new forms of social magnanimity. 'Social services' are used to impose sanctions as well as to confer benefits upon their clientele. Apart from the police, public services can only dispense benefits to their users. The sanction of a fine is incidental to the function of a library or a park.

In the private market the ultimate sanction of the buyer of a service such as education resides not in his participation as a customer but his ability to withdraw his custom altogether. So long as a consensus of values and aims exists between paying parents and private schools, active participation is irrelevant. The acts of choice and purchase are the beginning and end of the matter. If consensus later gives way to conflict, the contract can be broken off. Unfortunately there are no such easy resolutions to be found in the public sector. This model of parity and choice, however, should be the aim of public servants and of the users of public services. The only possible substitute for economic sanctions is the concept of citizenship more actively engendered and developed in the consciousness of the people.

However, there has been a long tradition in our collectively financed and universally available social services which is implicitly hostile to any notion of participant citizenship. The Webbs, as we have noted, were opposed even to free choice of doctor in the first National Insurance scheme, on the grounds that 'the average sensual man' was not fit to make such choices. Even today the most commonly advanced argument in favour of compulsion and universality is the claim that, left to themselves, too large a minority of the population would be unable to choose wisely, or alternatively would be unwilling to choose at all.

In a recent critique of voucher systems in education and medical care, Collard argues that 'a "wrong" choice is so important here that we cannot agree that bad choosers "can learn to choose wisely by being allowed to choose and at first by choosing wrongly".'[1] It may well be reasonable to insist upon an initial act of compulsion and to reject the kinds of participation offered by the free market on wider grounds of social justice. The poorest and most needy citizens would be least free to participate in market situations. It is also possible to reject the panacea of the market on the grounds that too many citizens cannot safely be trusted to make wise choices. The collectivist who uses the second argument, however, cannot then proceed to support more consumer-participation in the statutory social services unless he is prepared to help dispel the ignorance that has made compulsion necessary in the first instance.

The central point of the debate between universalists and selectivists should be concerned not only with simplifying the complexities of social-service bureaucracies, but with raising the levels of civic competence and knowledge of those who use the services. Both major parties are now committed to a greater degree of reliance upon the practice of selectivity in welfare. Rigorous school programmes designed to raise levels of social competence and change the attitudes of the young towards such services would offer some consolation to the universalists, test the good intentions of the selectivists (do they really want to increase the flow of goods and services to the most needy?) and

[1] David Collard, *The New Right: A Critique*, Fabian Tract 387, 1968, p. 6

at the same time alleviate or prevent much future suffering. In the past the neglect of this educational role has arisen from a naïve view of the relationship between social legislation and the public's consciousness of their rights and obligations expressed in law.

The supporters of a return to a free market in welfare also show inconsistencies in their arguments. They appear willing to trust the public as consumers in a private enterprise context. They are not prepared to trust them as free and participating users of statutory social services. Citizens, they appear to argue, can only be trusted with freedom if there are market sanctions against unwise spending in the private sector and public sanctions in what is left of statutory services.[1] This rump of selectivist social services is often defined as a 'concentration of help where it is most needed'. Its other purpose, however, must logically tend towards encouraging the others to continue to think and act wisely in the private sector.

In this way selectivists are prepared to allow the public to educate themselves in the ways of consumer participation, confident that the market will educate, reward and punish with justice. Collectivists hardly think about education in this sense, assuming that citizenship is a natural and self-evident right and that natural rights will be naturally exercised.

In both the collectivist and the individualist approaches to social welfare we can detect a marked lack of trust in human nature and a tendency to rationalize in defence of vested interests. Individualists rely on the market to regulate the desires and indulgences of the citizenry. But the supply of social services is also regulated and supervised by public servants such as administrators, social workers, teachers and voluntary workers. Collectivists show the same disposition to supervise, albeit for therapeutic ends.

Most definitions of social policy and administration preserve the convention of excluding public utilities and services. Since the publication of Titmuss's major essay on The Social Division of Welfare, it has been customary to include fiscal welfare as a

---

[1] As one critic of the radical right argues, ' . . . the "social purpose" of pricing is to make you think twice before using scarce resources and denying them to other uses that may be more urgent or productive'. Arthur Seldon, 'Crisis in the Welfare State', *Encounter*, December 1967, p. 58

form of social service in company with social welfare and occupational welfare. This approach is now common to both right- and left-wing social scientists, and some authorities argue strongly in favour of a greater reliance upon fiscal welfare provision in the form of negative income-tax schemes.[1] None the less, there has always been a general reluctance to include public services such as public health amenities, libraries, museums, parks and other freely available services, which are classed instead as public utilities. If we are consistently to define collectively provided services in terms of their aims, and if the aim of a social service is the enhancement of individual or collective welfare, then such a distinction is untenable.

For many years students have been advised by Penelope Hall, in her *vade mecum*, to distinguish between 'environmental services' of the kind already referred to, and 'personal' social services 'in which the aim is to provide the individual, *as an individual*, with the precise form of assistance he needs'.[2] Hall goes on to explain that

> these services which have as their objective the enhancement of the wellbeing of the individual citizen, and which in some measure at any rate, recognise his uniqueness, and deal with him as an individual, even when meeting the needs he has in common with others, are the services described in this book.[3]

The same distinction is made by Brown,[4] who justifies including retirement pensions as a social service on the grounds that they benefit 'the individual in a highly particular manner: he does not share collectively in the benefit but receives it personally for his peculiar use. This concept of collective provision to meet individual need is the hallmark of

[1] See Anthony Christopher, *et al.*, *Policy for Poverty*, Institute of Economic Affairs, 1970; and Milton Friedman, *Capitalism and Freedom*, University of Chicago Press, 1968, ch. XII

[2] See Penelope Hall, *The Social Services of Modern England*, Routledge and Kegan Paul, 5th Rev. Ed., 1962, p. 5. The quotation is taken from T. S. Simey, *Principles of Social Administration*, p. 4, and italicized by Hall

[3] ibid., p. 5. Hall's phrasing is based on the definition of a 'social service' given in Political and Economic Planning, *Report on the British Social Services*, 1937, p. 10

[4] Muriel Brown, *Introduction to Social Administration*, Hutchinson University Library, 1969, p. 11

a social service'.[1] In an earlier paper, the author also defined a social service in an almost identical way, stating that 'although many needs may be generally shared, the essence of a social service lies in its regard for the individual'.[2]

On reflection, however, this distinction seems to be illogical and misleading. The fact that we receive pensions for personal use does not exclude our treating pensions as a collective benefit at the same time, except in the case of schemes administered according to the strictest actuarial principles. Even in the latter case allowance must be made for a voluntary pooling of risks. In the same way, roads and public transport are a collective provision, but we enjoy them as persons, for our peculiar use. Pensioners taking part in a subsidized charabanc mystery tour still enjoy the collective venture *as persons*.

In a very useful analysis of this definitional problem, Slack concludes that 'Objections could be raised to some of the inclusions or exclusions' from her own list, but that 'it is neither profitable nor interesting to continue the discussion *ad nauseam*'.[3] It is significant, however, that debate has centred around the criterion of 'individual' attention and personal concern. There is a general reluctance amongst authorities to move very far away from this position. The distinction between social and public services derives partly from a tendency to confuse social welfare with social work, and partly from a disposition to confuse the normative expectations of social workers with those of the general public. These confusions are related to the belief, embedded in the practice of even libertarian forms of social service, that most individuals in need can best be helped to look after their individual interests under the personal supervision of others who possess special skills in managing social relationships.

One of the advantages of social services is that they allow greater account to be taken of individual needs and enable the necessary aid to be provided more speedily. One of Titmuss's main criticisms of Houghton's standard income tax means-test

---

[1] ibid.

[2] R. A. Pinker, 'Social Service', *Chambers's Encyclopaedia*, New Revised Edition, Vol. XII, Pergamon Press, 1967, pp. 662–5

[3] Kathleen M. Slack, *Social Administration and the Citizen*, Michael Joseph, 1966, p. 13

proposal, and of other forms of negative tax relief, is that 'computer solutions' of this kind fail to take account of the complex variety of human needs in terms of their causes, duration and urgency, and the characteristics of consumers.[1] He indicts such proposals for their naïvety, and his indictment is formidable in so far as it focuses on services traditionally defined as 'social'.

There is, however, another though neglected approach to the enhancement of individual welfare, which may commend itself on the grounds of its simplicity. We have implied that the traditional distinction between social and public services lacks logical validity. Fiscal forms of welfare are now readily accepted as social services in both collective and personal terms. Family budgets are indivisible to their owners in the sense that the relief of financial hardships in one area of expenditure makes resources available for other uses at the discretion of the persons concerned. If public libraries and parks were to charge admission fees, there might be less money available for theatres and cinemas, or less use of libraries and parks.

In defiance of economic orthodoxy, we already subsidize or pay the total cost of many public services through taxation. There is no economic reason why householders ought not to pay a fee for service for refuse collection. We recognize, however, that there might be hidden social costs and additional administrative costs in making direct charges for this service.

All but a few ideological extremists agree that valid grounds often exist for interfering with the free play of market forces to ensure equal accessibility to a range of public services. Similarly, only a minority argue that the price mechanism has no useful role whatever in the national economy. Although significant differences of view remain regarding the proper limits of state intervention, the arguments are over questions of degree rather than principle. In the context of social services, only a marked shift towards residualist or universalist policies would raise issues of principle.

Thirty years ago the nationalization of the means of production and distribution was the central point of ideological difference between parties of the political left and right. But even in its brief moments of ideological fervour, the British

[1] Titmuss, *Commitment to Welfare*, pp. 116–17

Labour Party was never committed to nationalization in order to provide 'free' transport, electricity, gas or telephones. There was a general willingness to entertain the idea of partial subsidies in the public interest. In recent years, however, the Labour Party has competed with the Conservatives in seeking to make nationalized industries 'pay their way' according to the criteria of the private market. Yet there are no more convincing economic arguments against providing a free public transport system than a free health service. A free national health service does as much violence to the workings of the price mechanism as would be the case with a free public transport system. Convention seems to prescribe what is and is not a fit subject for the suspension of the price mechanism, but it is a convention based on traditional anxieties about the unregulated abuse of freely available goods and services.

The question we need to ask ourselves is whether the introduction of a completely 'free' public service, such as transport, might do more for personal welfare and community relations than, say, sizeable increases in the allocation of social workers to local authorities, or even a generous increase in social security benefits. An adequate answer would have to take into account those indirect savings in social costs accruing from a decrease in the use of private transport—reductions in the incidence of air pollution, traffic congestion and accident rates, and savings in the costs of fare-collection and prosecutions, for example. Other possible savings might be measured in relation to the costs of alternative forms of extra welfare provision. Any increase in the quality and quantity of traditional forms of social service usually entails expensive and lengthy courses of professional training. But citizens do not need more social workers, teachers or doctors to help them decide whether or not to travel to Putney or Highgate.

A further reason for exploring the possible advantages of a free public service such as transport is that use of this kind of facility does not involve any feelings of stigmatizing dependency on the part of the beneficiaries. A free public service of this type is also unaffected by any considerations of social distance (except in terms of invidious comparisons between bus passengers and private car users) or any significant differences in terms of knowledge or skill. Nearly everyone has equal competence to look up a time-table, find a station or bus-stop and sit in a vehicle. The scope for mediating officials and experts appears to be advantageously reduced to a minimum. If such a service were paid for directly out of taxation, there is scarcely a poor family in the country that would fail to experience a marked and immediate benefit in their standard of living. Any user of a free service of this kind would enjoy an increase in disposable income without any risk of stigma and without any danger that ignorance or apathy might exclude them from maximum benefit. The introduction of such a scheme would simply complement existing arrangements by which we already pay for roads, except that vehicles as well as the permanent way would be included and a more equitable form of levy might have to be devised.

The aim of personalizing a welfare-exchange relationship is supposedly to identify more accurately the needs of the applicant, but by so heightening the sensibilities of 'giver' and 'receiver' we also risk making one party more acutely aware of his dependency. The great advantage of public services as instruments of social welfare is in their generality of application and the simplicity with which prospective users can avail themselves of the required service. If we are genuinely concerned to reduce the incidence of stigma in social welfare, we ought to give much more serious consideration to the proposition that the most anonymous forms of social provision tend to be the least stigmatizing, and the most personal forms of social service are likely to be the most humiliating for the beneficiary.

There may be valid economic arguments against such a proposal. Other and equally strong objections might be made on social grounds. We can reduce this second category of objections to a perhaps over-simplified common denominator and find that they amount to an anxiety or unwillingness to countenance the public enhancing their own welfare without let or hindrance, advice or assistance, qualification or control by others. This anxiety and reluctance derives, however, from experiences of welfare-exchange relationships in which it is conceptually possible to distinguish between a category of 'givers' and a category of 'receivers'.[1] Clearly any 'free' public

---

[1] The argument for assuming that such a dichotomy exists will be developed in Section 4 below

service which is paid for out of taxation will have a redistributive effect so that some users (and non-users) will be
indirectly 'paying' more for the service than others. But the
very nature of a public service precludes the likelihood that
personal attention or concern on the part of a professional
intermediary will intentionally or unintentionally make clear
the basic pattern of inequality that still prevails amongst users.
The inequalities between types of user will no longer be
identifiable.

Social services in complex industrial societies are strongly
orientated towards meeting individual needs on a personal
basis. Yet there is another recurring feature in the structure
and function of social services—they always allow for the
possibility of an expert having access to a layman. This access
ensures that a social service can fulfil *both* therapeutic and
sanctioning functions, and there is no other easy way of ensuring
that both functions can be discharged.

The characteristic features of public services such as libraries,
parks and museums have been freedom of access and un-
mediated opportunity for enjoyment. The origins and intentions
of those who established these services in a private capacity,
or who campaigned for their public provision, is a relatively
unresearched subject. It is worth noting, however, that few
public services have been significantly associated with the
private market. During the nineteenth century, a once flourish-
ing private-library market gave way to a more efficient public
service. Very few museums and parks have been run for profit.
Public services or utilities are a neglected area of effective
community provision that we might usefully seek to extend.
We have limited this provisional enquiry to the example of
public transport, which has the advantage of being very generally and regularly used by the whole population. Arguments
that such a service would do nothing for the non-ambulant and
various other handicapped or deprived groups have as little
logic as the observation that free health services do nothing for
the fit, or that universities are not used by the educationally
sub-normal.

Buying a ticket to sit on a bus is as much of a convention as
not buying a ticket to sit on a park bench. The economic
arguments in favour of paying or not paying for both services

can be elaborated with equal effect. The social argument against our proposal leads to the conclusion that 'free' social services ought to be kept on a mainly personal basis so that a distinction can always be maintained between 'rights' and 'privileges', and rewards and sanctions, in civic life. In the last resort this argument is an economic one. The traditional distinction between social and public services has been drawn by those members of the public who believe, rightly or wrongly, that they tend to pay more for all forms of collective provision than they receive in return. Social workers and administrators develop their own professional ideologies in order to make their apparently contradictory roles complement each other.

DEPENDENCY, COMPASSION AND STIGMA

All social services are systems of exchange. Their central problem regarding conflict and discord is the problem of equivalency, because the relationship between a giver and a receiver is always inherently an unstable and unequal one. While a minority of people go so far as to make vocations out of either service or dependency, most of us prefer a measure of equivalency in our social relationships.

Simmel writes of gratitude as the 'supplement' which seeks to restore the balance where equivalence is not legally enforceable. 'Gratitude' he goes on to describe as 'the moral memory of mankind'[1] in the sense that 'its thousandfold ramifications throughout society make it one of the most powerful means of social cohesion'.[2] At the same time the forms of gratitude which reside in exchanges are a source of obligation and discord, because

> once we have received something good from another person, once he has preceded us with his action, we no longer can make up for it completely . . . The reason is that his gift, because it was the first, has a voluntary character which no return gift can have . . . we operate under a coercion . . .[3]

As we are socialized into the economic ethos of an industrial

[1] Kurt H. Wolff (ed.), *The Sociology of George Simmel*, Free Press, London, 1964, pp. 388–9   [2] ibid., p. 389

[3] ibid., p. 392. See also Marcel Mauss, *The Gift*, Cohen and West, London, 1954

society, we learn to equate money with the protection of individual autonomy. Money gives both buyer and seller a sense of instant equivalence. Borrowing money itself at a rate of interest is the hire-purchase of such equivalency. None the less, the desire for immediate equivalency is so profoundly a part of our subjective reality that we treat our bank managers and building society secretaries with deference even when we are paying them usurious rates of interest. The social function of interest is that it publicly displays a mutual recognition that the state of dependency is only a temporary one. In ordinary social-welfare systems outside the delicate convention of the market, the very nature of human consciousness leaves us permanently exposed to the stigmas of dependency and obligation. In market situations a lack of money has the same effect. Whether or not we describe this perception of social reality as a form of 'false consciousness' or 'alienation' is largely irrelevant.[1]

The experience of exchange expresses a range of attitudes such as generosity or self-aggrandisement on the part of the giver and gratitude or resentment on the part of the receiver, accompanied by feelings of prestige or stigma, which are constant and central human experiences. In order to understand better how such sentiments have become institutionalized it may be illuminating to make broader comparisons than are usually made in the study of social policy. So far we have looked at these phenomena in industrial societies. Comparison with so-called primitive societies in which kinship ties play a more important role than class relations may provide further insights.

Lévi-Strauss defends such comparisons for certain purposes, not because they purport 'to explain contemporary customs by means of archaic institutions, but to help the reader, a member of contemporary society, to rediscover in his own experience and on the basis of either vestigial or embryonic practices,

---

[1] It is sufficient to note for the moment how the term 'alienation' is used by intellectuals as a conceptual technique for 'annihilating' opposition. 'Alienation' has become the molotov cocktail in the armoury of all normative theorists, primed and ready for instant use on their critics. Were it possible to design something like a Geneva Convention laying down rules for the conduct of academic warfare, we might be able to ban the use of the term 'alienation' on the grounds that it does indiscriminate harm to users and victims alike.

institutions that would otherwise remain unintelligible to him'.[1] Conversely, we may find that such practices which remain vestigial and embryonic in modern forms of social service are related to the contemporary attitudes towards such services. This relevance may be seen more clearly if we explore some key features of the exchange systems of pre-industrial societies.

In some simple societies based on horticulture or hunting, systems of 'total prestation' fulfilled functions akin to those of modern social-welfare systems. In systems of total prestation, social groups carry on reciprocal exchanges of goods and services, and even of persons. Marcel Mauss observes that these prestations 'are in essence strictly obligatory and their sanction is private or open warfare'.[2] In all such transactions the pattern of obligations entails giving, receiving and repaying gifts.

Radcliffe-Brown studying the same phenomenon in the Andaman Islands remarks that, in so far as the groups involved were economically self-sufficient 'the exchange of presents did not serve the same purpose as trade or barter in more developed countries. The purpose that it did serve was a moral one.'[3] A common feature of such exchanges was that the 'objects are never completely separated from the men who exchange them; the communion and alliance they establish are well-nigh indissoluble'.[4]

The development of even rudimentary forms of stratification destroys the egalitarian basis of reciprocity found in ordinary systems of prestation. Those who become wealthy may either destroy their surpluses with much public display or ostentatiously give them away in an 'agonistic' form of prestation known as 'potlach'.[5] The function of potlach is, however, not to equalize statuses but to enhance the status of the most extravagant givers. Failure to accept and participate betrays fear of having to repay, and the essence of potlach is that repayment shall be made with massive interest. 'The obligation of worthy return is imperative' in potlach.[6] Mauss concludes that 'what we call total prestation—prestation between clan and clan in which individuals and groups exchange everything

---

[1] Claude Lévi-Strauss, *Structural Anthropology*, Allen Lane, The Penguin Press, London, 1968, p. 338

[2] Mauss, *The Gift*, p. 3   [3] ibid., quoted by Mauss, pp. 17–18
[4] ibid., p. 31   [5] ibid., pp. 4–5   [6] ibid., p. 41

between them—constitutes the oldest economic system we know'.[1]

The point is made by Lenski that in simple societies where most material necessities are readily available to all, but capital goods are relatively scarce, the means of gaining prestige are very limited. Potlach 'represents a shrewd and well-calculated pursuit of self-interest designed to maximise an individual's return on his investment of time, energy and other resources' in societies where there are few forms of capital goods, where the marginal utility of most consumer goods is relatively low, and where the norms of exchange and reciprocity are strongly sanctioned.[2]

We have therefore two types of exchange—prestations and potlach—to take into account. The latter is one in which differentiation is occurring and personal advantage being sought. Even in less agonistic forms of prestation, to give was to show one's superiority while 'to accept without returning or repaying more (was) to face subordination'.[3] All the same, so long as a measure of economic reciprocity survived, sub-ordinations would be relatively uncommon and shortlived.

Mauss however also places great emphasis on the non-economic nature of these exchanges. He is especially concerned with the extent to which in pre-monetary economies the gift remains spiritually a part of the donor.[4] He concludes, there-fore, by drawing a somewhat unconvincing comparison between these ancient forms of exchange and modern forms of collective provision such as social insurance.[5] Such activities are described as a 're-emergence of a group morality'[6] so that 'the theme of the gift, of freedom and obligation in the gift, of generosity and

[1] ibid., p. 68

[2] Gerhard E. Lenski, *Power and Privilege: A Theory of Social Stratification*, McGraw-Hill, New York, 1966, pp. 134–5. See also for comparison, Thorstein Veblen, *The Theory of the Leisure Class*, Mentor, 1953

[3] Mauss, *The Gift*, p. 72

[4] Ibid. 'We may then consider that the spirit of gift-exchange is char-acteristic of societies which have passed the phase of "total prestation" (between clan and clan, family and family) but have not yet reached the stage of pure individual contract, the money market, sale proper, fixed price, and weighed and coined money.' (p. 45)

[5] ibid., p. 75

[6] ibid., p. 65

self-interest in giving, reappear in our society like the resur-
rection of a dominant motif long forgotten'.[1]

Although Mauss avoids idealizing archaic forms of exchange
(he does note the unforgotten motif of self-interest) it can be
argued that he misleadingly eulogizes contemporary forms of
collective social provision. Mauss acknowledges the uncon-
sciously harmful patronage of modern charity. He does not
recognize that forms of statutory provision such as social
insurance may be equally stigmatizing under certain conditions, and as we have argued above, typify economic rather
than social criteria of human worth.

If an analogy is to be drawn, modern welfare systems may
be seen to generate the forms of stigma and subordination that
were experienced by recipients in potlach systems. Furthermore,
modern welfare systems may be intrinsically more likely to
impose stigma than to enhance the status of either donor or
recipient. An alternative to the conscious pursuit of prestige
(especially to the majority who in industrial societies are denied
access to effective positions of power) is the imposition of stigma
on others. So long as Britain was a colonial power, 'lesser breeds
without the law' were part of the subjective reality of its poor.
Advanced industrial societies are also normatively characterized by a high degree of achievement-orientation. In such
societies, the imposition of stigma can serve as a particularly
wounding sanction. As we have seen already, social services are
one of the most likely contexts in which economic failure will
be penalized.

Systems of prestation and potlach will be effective in relatively
simple societies where to be aware of kinship obligation is
almost the same as being aware of one's total social obligations.
Where kinship is one's social universe and the norms of
reciprocity pertain, almost perfect congruence will exist between
a man's consciousness of his expectations and obligations in
daily life.

In complex societies, by contrast, the meaning of kinship
obligations for most people will have narrowed from the scope
of clan loyalty to the 'privatized' nuclear family. The survival,
or revival, of extended kinship networks in poor urban areas
during the nineteenth century might be seen as an attempt to

[1] ibid., p. 66

develop forms of mutual aid in a hostile environment.[1] The
almost uniform poverty of the sub-units of these extended
family systems prevented the development of exaggerated forms
of nepotism. Some forms of occupational ascription occurred,
with fathers 'speaking for' sons to prospective employers. It
would be argued, however, that the kinds of extended family
system described by Willmot and Young provided a sufficiently
total social environment for their children to be denied the
opportunity of acquiring those social skills needed to make
effective use of formal welfare organizations. Any significant
shift in patterns of dependence towards these outside agencies
weakened the authority and influence of the older females in
the kin-group. Whether these traditional extended family
systems retain any functional relevance to industrial societies
remains open to question, despite Townsend's claim that their
value and incidence has been underestimated.[2]

Family structures also generate and institutionalize their own
forms of dependency. Litwak identifies four family types in
advanced industrial societies, which exemplify different patterns
of dependency.[3] In the traditional extended family each nuclear
sub-family is potentially obliged to and dependent upon the
others for a wide range of goods and services. So long as the
norms of reciprocity are maintained a measure of exchange
equivalency is preserved. These family structures tend, however,
to produce a single hierarchical system in which the younger
and poorer members gravitate to positions of total dependency.
Since these familial status positions are based largely on
ascription, their legitimacy is always open to question in
achievement-orientated societies. Where these traditional family
systems prevail, bureaucratic welfare agencies are often able to

[1] M. Young and P. Willmott, *Family and Kinship in East London*, Penguin
Books, London, 1962, pp. 188–91. There is a growing body of evidence to
suggest that the 'extended family' with three generations and two or more
married couples in a single large household was not a universal pre-
industrial phenomenon. See E. A. Wrigley, *Population and History*, Weidenfeld
and Nicolson, London, 1969, p. 13

[2] Peter Townsend, *The Family Life of Old People*, Penguin Books, pp. 236
passim

[3] Eugene Litwak, 'Extended Kin Relations in a Democratic Industrial
Society', in Ethel Shanas and Gordon F. Streib (eds), *Social Structure and
the Family: Generational Relations*, Prentice-Hall Inc, 1965, pp. 290–1

limit their own range of obligations by making aid to applicants conditional upon family means tests. Such practices were common in both Britain and the U.S.A. during the Depression years. Their effect was often to weaken the authority of elderly kin when their children or grandchildren were deemed to have a prior responsibility for their maintenance. Conversely, younger kin could be driven to dependency upon their elders. In all such cases, individual members of traditional extended families are exposed to the risk of finding themselves totally dependent upon their kin.

In modified extended families we find a 'coalition of nuclear families', none of whom are obliged to be more than partially dependent upon each other. At the same time each nuclear family is in a better position to make partial use of welfare bureaucracies. In this situation the nuclear family's exchange relationships with either its wider kin or outside welfare agencies are more likely to be characterized by equality. As Litwak observes, 'Where the giver is never in a position to provide the entire service, then he is not in a position to ask for complete subservience'.[1] The modified extended family 'has a greater pool of resources to draw on than the nuclear family'[2] but not such large resources that the autonomy of any individual is jeopardized. Litwak describes such systems as arrangements of 'partial aid' or 'competitive aid'.[3]

Litwak constructs a model of exchange relationships between families and between family systems and bureaucratic welfare organizations. He notes certain antithetical features of these relationships. Welfare organizations represent public values, and can apply expertise to the solving of complex but uniform problems that require specialist knowledge. Families, because of their smaller size and the proximity of their members to one another, can define much more uniquely what is to be valued and can act with greater speed to alleviate idiosyncratic or non-uniform problems without recourse to specialized knowledge. Litwak proceeds to formulate a theory of shared functions which takes account of the fact that 'in almost any area where we have been able to reduce the idiosyncratic to a predictable event, we have at the same time opened up entirely new areas

[1] ibid., p. 310
[2] ibid., p. 309.   [3] ibid., p. 310

of the unknown and the idiosyncratic'.[1] Litwak goes on to conclude that families and welfare organizations operate at maximum efficiency if they recognize their respective areas of competence. In the case of education, formal organizations are most effective in carrying out the uniform processes of schooling with the aid of specialists. Growing recognition of the importance of the family in fulfilling related but non-uniform functions has led to a re-appraisal of home-school relationships and attempts to achieve better co-ordination between the 'power of the family' and 'the powers of the schools'.[2] Litwak suggests therefore that 'If society seeks to maximize its goal achievement, it must employ both formal organizations and primary groups such as the family'.[3]

Our concern is to draw attention to the place of the family in exchange situations in advanced industrial societies. The norms of equivalency and reciprocity are most likely to pertain when the individual is totally dependent upon neither primary groups nor formal organizations. Dependencies of a stigmatizing or humiliating nature are most likely to be avoided when the individual receives aid of a partial nature from a number of providers. Since individuals require aid from both familial and organizational sources in order to enhance their life-chances, recipients are most likely to prosper when there is an element of competition between donors. Members of 'dissolving' or nuclear family structures are placed in the least advantageous position because they are most likely to find themselves completely dependent on formal welfare organizations. Fatherless families quickly become heavily stigmatized primary groups when they are dependent on welfare agencies, irrespective of the cause of fatherlessness. Bastardy has never carried an implicit stigma except when it has resulted in dependency upon welfare agencies for relief.[4] Widowhood is a respected status, but this status has never protected widows from humiliation

---

[1] ibid., p. 303   [2] ibid., p. 305   [3] ibid., p. 307
[4] I am indebted to Professor O. R. McGregor for pointing out that during the nineteenth century the illegitimate children of the poor were often stigmatized because they were so often dependent upon poor relief. In an unpublished study of admissions to the maternity ward of a London workhouse we found that during a period of ten years over 80 per cent of the mothers were unmarried. Robert Pinker, 'The Use of Maternity Wards in a London Workhouse Between 1900 and 1910' (unpublished).

and stigma once they have become dependent upon public aid. To a lesser extent, isolated nuclear families in crises may receive help from formal welfare organizations, and in the absence of complementary support from extended kin, will be exposed to the risks of total dependence upon the welfare agencies. Their members are, for example, more prone to institutionalization, which often brings them into contact with the most inferior and stigmatized forms of welfare provision and personal service. By contrast, members of modified extended families have the best chance of using both primary-group and formal organizational forms of aid, while avoiding both nepotic and bureaucratic forms of dominance.

The growth of social inequalities and class consciousness will sharpen these structural and cultural divisions in complex societies. As the size of the economic surplus in a society increases, its distribution is more likely to be ordered by reference to the criterion of power rather than social need.[1] Prestige becomes a function of power and privilege. Capital accumulation and a wider choice of consumer goods become more satisfying alternatives to public giving. Prestation loses much of its appeal as a way of gaining prestige, although voluntary societies still offer scope for the prestation activities of one class towards another in the twentieth century.

The size of the surplus and the range of inequalities greatly affect the intensity and incidence of social conflict. Social services reflect in their levels of provision and their criteria of allocation the balance of power and the quality of the relationship between deprived and privileged groups at any one point in time. In so far as they exist at all, social services represent a disposition towards compromise rather than intransigence. Their existence must modify any tendency to characterize the society of which they are a part as being dominated by conflict. Equally, the history of social policy is always a record of conflict between social groups. We may define social-welfare

---

[1] Lenski, *op. cit.*, p. 313 *passim*. Lenski notes that 'the decline in political and economic inequality associated with the emergence of industrial societies is extremely important' and 'constitutes a reversal in a major historical trend'. The economically redistributive policies which occur in industrial societies are however of a concessionary nature and bring other benefits in terms of power to élites.

relationships as reciprocal ones based on mutual aid, but the facts of social inequality make this kind of consensus improbable.

We would argue, therefore, that the dynamics of social-welfare systems in industrial societies can best be understood if we take account of those structural and cultural factors which influence men's propensity for compassion and greed, enhancement and humiliation. Exclusively altruistic acts occur so rarely that they cannot serve as a viable basis for social policies. Men are most disposed to give in the expectation of a return. Even when there is a willingness to give, the spontaneous dictates of compassion will be insufficient to meet the volume of needs. The record of human philanthropy might be used as evidence against this proposition. Although this record is an impressive one, so is the story of unmet and ignored human needs. All industrial societies seem to have made some form of compulsory social provision. The fact that it has had to be compulsory suggests that the definitions of welfare shared by ruling minorities have not been universally shared in society.

Changes in kinship and class structure make it imperative for industrial societies to develop some kinds of compulsory social provision. In certain situations, welfare services may provide new bases of social solidarity and loyalty. In the first instance, however, social services are developed to meet individual needs which other people no longer feel obliged to meet. As Wilensky and Lebeaux point out, 'modern social welfare really has to be thought of as help given to the stranger, not to the person who by reason of personal bond commands it without asking'.[1]

Self-interest and greed may be human constants. In complex industrial societies, however, distance from the potential object of compassion becomes a problem and influences the form that social welfare takes. This variable of distance can be measured in various ways. Victorian England, for example, was an intensely hierarchical and class-conscious society. As Peter Laslett explains, the very ease with which terms like 'servant *keeping* class' and 'lower orders' were used, shows what a width of social distance existed between Victorians in different walks of life.[2] Paupers were outside the social hierarchy altogether

[1] Wilensky and Lebeaux, *Industrial Society and Social Welfare*, p. 141
[2] P. Laslett, 'The Solid Middle Class', in *The Listener*, 4th January 1962

and their social remoteness made their sufferings seem less real. And even the English pauper was better treated than his Irish counterpart.

In the complex urban societies of our time, men stand in a great variety of insubstantial relationships one to another. As Simmel observes, if in large cities 'so many inner reactions were responses to the continuous external contacts with innumerable people as are those in the small town, where one knows almost everybody one meets and where one has a positive relation to almost everyone, one would be completely atomized internally and come to an unimaginable psychic state'.[1] Large cities, by virtue of being intense numerical concentrations of people, also bring together large numbers of deprived and needy individuals. Yet only a very small minority of citizens appear to possess a limitless capacity to bear unremitting acquaintance with human suffering or to conceptualize the enormity of these sufferings in their imaginations. Even the various pressure-groups on behalf of the needy appear to be growing increasingly specialized. But the greater the total flow of information and appeals on behalf of the deprived, the more selective and detached is public response likely to become.

In terms of social welfare, and certainly of international social service, the world is still very far from becoming MacLuhan's 'global village'. The great majority of the British people were able to go on eating three substantial meals a day throughout the regular television portrayals of child starvation during the Nigerian war. There seems little danger that many of us will reach Simmel's 'unimaginable psychic state' through a surfeit of empathy and compassion for the less fortunate. It may be that 'If we had a keener vision and feeling of all ordinary human life, it would be like hearing the grass grow and the squirrel's heart beat, and we should die of that roar which lies on the other side of silence'.[2] The primary aim of every philanthropic agency working on behalf of the underprivileged is to engender in the public imagination an awareness of that 'other side' of human need. But the defences of social distance seem to be maintained by psychological imperatives of an

[1] Kurt H. Wolff (ed.), *The Sociology of George Simmel*, Free Press, Glencoe, 1964, p. 415

[2] Eliot, *Middlemarch*, Vol. II, p. 171

enduring kind, as if closer contact with the distress and dying of others threatened our own survival.

In the context of social welfare, our constructions of social reality are determined by the time and space of everyday life. The aim of normative models of social welfare is to alter these dimensions, to present a counter-reality and convince us of its truth. At one level these models present a different kind of reality from that lived by ordinary people. At the same time they may also represent some aspects of everyday sentiments and values. In a pluralistic society these conceptualizations of welfare represent the ideological positions and interests of different social groups. The models are both intellectual constructs and programmes for political action. In both senses they compete with each other to change not only 'the traditional definitions of reality, but also the ways in which these are held in the consciousness of individuals'.[1]

At the same time, stigmatized and underprivileged groups in pluralistic societies can also erect conceptual defences 'against the stigmatic identity assigned to [them]'.[2] These 'counter-realities' can offer new cultural bases of group esteem and lead eventually to a radical re-ordering of social priorities. Just as blackness becomes a sign of superiority rather than inferiority, so the poor may in a Marxian sense challenge both the dominant value-system and the existing distribution of wealth.

In capitalist societies it may be argued that those who construct institutional models of social welfare are unlikely to be part of the dominant value-system. Neither, for that matter, are the outright residualists. Both groups of specialists, however, will use what influence they have as 'counter-expert[s] in the business of defining reality . . .' even though their expertise remains, in the main, 'not wanted by the society at large.'[3]

Thus, the differences which we meaningfully feel to exist between our expectations and obligations will vary over time and place. For the reasons we have discussed, some imbalance will probably always exist, an imbalance which can be described as a kind of 'compassion gap'. Despite the varieties of stigma, the expectation of services will always exceed the willingness to supply. Increases in national prosperity will tend to widen

[1] Berger and Luckman, *The Social Construction of Reality*, p. 143
[2] ibid., p. 185   [3] ibid., p. 143

this compassion gap even if the extra wealth is more widely distributed. One neglected aspect of the process of 'embourgeoisement' is the propensity of the upwardly mobile to define themselves as givers rather than receivers of social welfare. Thus it is not surprising that the most negative forms of discrimination in social policy, such as the New Poor Law, usually gain their greatest support in periods of rapid economic growth or sharp recessions following boom periods. The experience of recent gain and the fear of imminent loss have similarly inhibiting effects on our propensity for compassion.

It may therefore be possible to demonstrate that the dominant values of an acquisitive and capitalist society are such that stigmatization is a functionally necessary part of the system. Critics of the residualist model argue that selectivist services in such a context will always discriminate negatively and serve as the normal stigmatizing agencies. Critics of those who believe that an institutional model can co-exist with the market forces of a capitalist society attempt to show that the 'universalist infrastructure' will gradually be eroded and serve merely to deceive the poor and preserve the social order from open class conflict. There will remain a marked but manageable lack of symmetry between the official aims of welfare and the subjective reality of actually being poor.

In the context of social policy, however, there are potentially greater opportunities for these normative models both to relate with and to reflect the sentiments of ordinary people. While there is no convincing evidence that the majority of people in industrial societies are preoccupied with thoughts about fundamental issues of conflict and consensus, the social services affect nearly everyone's daily life in profound and extensive ways.

A MODEL OF SOCIAL WELFARE

In this section we will attempt to draw together some of the central themes of our enquiry and formulate a model of social welfare. The contribution of social theory to the field of social policy is too often one that begins in ideology and ends in rhetoric. The subject-matter of social policy contains many of the most urgent problems of our time. Consequently theories and models of social welfare tend to be highly normative, explaining how men ought to behave if they wish to accomplish certain results.[1]

Currently the two most influential theoretical formulations in social policy are based respectively on the 'institutional' and the 'residual' models of social welfare.[2] Both models draw on historical and sociological evidence to predict future trends in social policy. The residual model rests on moral assumptions about the self-evident virtues of competition and self-help. The institutional model rests its moral case on the ethics of co-operation and mutual aid.

In both cases psychological assumptions are made about the attitudes of individuals towards welfare provision. Their common weakness is a tendency to confuse academic perceptions of social reality with those of the ordinary users of social services. There is, however, no firm evidence as yet that sizeable sections of the community are strongly committed either to the ethic of mutual aid or to the liberties of the free market.[3] The end-result for the discipline of social policy and administration is that too much is prescribed, too much indicted and too little explained.

The central and unresolved issue in this debate has been defined by Richard Titmuss as the problem of developing socially acceptable selective services within an 'infrastructure of universalist services' in such a way that stigma is reduced to a minimum.[4] This approach correctly focuses attention upon the subjective realities of everyday life for those in need.

Our intention in this section is to set out a number of empirically testable hypotheses in the form of a model of social

[1] John Horton, 'Order and Conflict Theories of Social Problems as Competing Ideologies', p. 713

[2] See p. 99n above for references to literature on the present state of the debate about universalism and selectivity. There is also an interesting article by Mike Reddin on 'Universalism and Selectivity' in *The Political Quarterly*, Vol. 40, No. 1, January-March 1969, pp. 12–22, which has since been revised and republished in W. A. Robson and B. Crick (eds), *The Future of the Social Services*, Penguin Books, 1970

[3] See pp. 104–5 above for references to some studies of public attitudes towards social welfare. There is also some treatment of the expectations which clientele have of social workers in Barbara Rodgers's valuable study, *Portrait of Social Work*, Oxford University Press, 1960. This study is currently being repeated. See Rodgers, 'A New Portrait of Social Work', *Social and Economic Administration*, Vol. 4, No. 3, July 1970, pp. 186–93

[4] R. M. Titmuss, *Commitment to Welfare*, p. 135

welfare. If substantiated, the model could be used to classify welfare systems in terms of their stigmatizing propensities. It should then be possible to formulate a theory explaining why people are elevated or debased in exchange situations, and which conditions of provision and usage are most likely to engender stigma in industrial societies.

It is postulated that a sharp distinction exists in the consciousness of ordinary people between 'givers' and 'receivers' of social services, whose respective statuses are elevated or debased by virtue of their exchange relationship. It is self-evident that citizens are sometimes subjected to humiliation in the supposed therapeutic context of social services. This paradox arises because the values of the economic market are always reflected in social-welfare systems. The extent to which this occurs in a given society influences the degree to which welfare systems are required to impose sanctions upon users. In so far as social services also operate as agents of social control they combine both therapeutic and stigmatizing functions.[1]

In relatively simple societies, systems of exchange are more likely to be based on norms of reciprocity between equals. Awareness of kinship obligations will be almost the same as awareness of total social obligations. So long as the norms of reciprocity are maintained, there will be almost perfect congruence between the individual's consciousness of his expectations and obligations and much less likelihood of stigma.

In complex industrial societies, by contrast, consciousness of kinship obligations may not go far beyond the scope of the privatized nuclear family. The growth of social inequalities also weakens notions of social reciprocity. The relationship between givers and receivers in the welfare contexts of industrial societies is always inherently an unstable and unequal one. As we are socialized into the economic ethos of such societies we learn to equate money with the protection of individual autonomy and the postponement of dependency. We might argue that it is as blessed to receive as to give, but there seems little evidence to support this view at the level of daily life in industrial societies.

The expectation which citizens have of social services is greatly affected by their prior experience of economic situations.

[1] P. L. Berger and T. Luckman, *The Social Construction of Reality*, p. 87

A large proportion of those who use social services do so after having been stigmatized by adverse experiences in the economic market. Inequalities of knowledge and expertise also serve to reinforce feelings of inferiority and dependence, and these kinds of inequality persist in welfare relationships. Whenever self-help and independence are powerfully sanctioned values, the subjective facts of social consciousness impose inferior status on the dependent.

The relationship between class structure and social consciousness manifests itself in social policies. The agreed levels of social provision reflect both the coercion of the privileged by the deprived and the resistance of the privileged to such coercion.[1] The levels and intensities of this conflict will be determined by the way in which people learn to define their welfare roles. What matters is the extent to which individuals and groups define themselves predominantly as 'givers' or 'receivers', and the extent to which the needy believe they have the right to demand from the privileged. The privileged must also define their position in relation to the poor. The imposition of stigma by the privileged can be seen as a means of self-protection from the 'excessive' demands of the poor, while preserving their own sense of moral rectitude.

We must, however, account for the fact that expectations and demand for social welfare appear to increase in industrial societies despite the revulsion people learn to feel for stigmatizing dependency. This may be explained by the fact that although stigma does inhibit demand, biological needs frequently outweigh cultural sanctions. At the same time, other cultural factors such as rising expectations reduce tolerance of felt deprivation. The unemployed labourer would suffer the indignity of the workhouse test in Victorian England because he was starving. He would none the less endure hunger before he applied. Some did choose to starve. Today the *expectation* of hunger rather than starvation will normally cause the needy to ask for help despite their feelings of stigma.

We need to know much more about how people define their roles in welfare. It is hypothesized that, within the context of social services, much sharper contrasts are drawn between

[1] G. E. Lenski, *Power and Privilege, A Theory of Social Stratification*, pp. 313 *passim*

'givers' and 'receivers', or 'providers' and 'users', than is the case in other situations such as work or leisure. However crude these distinctions may seem to specialists, they may still be very much a part of the 'commonsense' view of both the man in the Rover 2000 and the old-age pensioner on the Clapham omnibus.

Clearly these two rules are not so easily separated. The giver, for example, is often a receiver in other situations. Men act, however, according to what they think they know, or need to know. What matters is the authenticity of the experiences on which the truths and fallacies of conventional wisdom are based. The authenticity of being in receipt of a 'free' prescription is more real to most recipients than an awareness of having paid a tax when purchasing a bar of soap in the same shop. The model, therefore, makes no reference to any kind of reciprocal 'feed-back' through taxation or rates, because it is hypothesized that such phenomena are not a significant part of ordinary social consciousness.

Two levels of administrative process are involved, namely, the major protective institutions of central and local government, and their bureaucratic sub-units staffed by various professionals and other specialists. The moral component of these welfare systems expresses the criteria of social evaluation that determine the allocation of available resources.

There can be marked variations in the degree of consistency with which these evaluative criteria are applied at different levels of action. In the Poor Law, where professional workers like Relieving Officers tended to support the deterrent ideologies of the central authority, there was always a minority of relatively lenient local Boards of Guardians. Today similar variations occur at local government level, and social workers are gaining much greater autonomy in their professional roles. Social workers are, therefore, better able to act as intermediaries between 'givers' and 'receivers'. Halmos refers to them as 'moral tutors', whose professional ideology stresses the qualities of compassion and acceptance.[1] Of equal relevance are the professional expectations and attitudes of doctors, nurses, teachers and other 'personal service' professions.

The most obvious fact of social welfare, however, still tends to be misconstrued. The existence of vast welfare bureaucracies

[1] P. Halmos, *op. cit.*

in industrial societies suggests not so much that these societies are uniquely compassionate, but is a recognition of the fact that the spontaneous dictates of compassion consistently fail to meet the volume of unmet human needs. Only by taking a simplistic view of democratic processes is it possible to describe the recognition of these needs and our compulsory levels of provision as expressions of the popular will. Few of us, given the choice, would match our present compulsory level of taxation with voluntary donations. For every one of us some group of sufferers exists so different or distant from ourselves that our compassion is not aroused in any purposive way.

Our major premise is akin to a psychological proposition, namely, that in systems of exchange it is always less prestigious to receive than to give. The main hypotheses put forward in the model are that a significant proportion of citizens draw a sharp distinction between the welfare roles of 'giver' and 'receiver'; that exchange relationships in the public welfare sector are more stigmatizing than those pertaining in the private sector; but that all such exchange relationships are inherently stigmatizing in so far as they involve common cultural and biological factors defining and relating to dependency in industrial societies.

There are, none the less, a number of important qualifications that must be added to the above statement, and these can be identified as the variables of *depth*, *time* and *distance*, to which some passing reference has already been made. The first variable of *depth* refers to the extent to which the recipient is made aware of his dependence and sense of inferiority and accepts the definition of his status as legitimate. The status of a recipient may be enhanced when what he receives is recognized as being a restitution for earlier service, or a compensation for disservice previously suffered. This principle is exemplified in many forms of social insurance provision, where war pensions and industrial injuries benefits are paid on a more generous scale than other benefits.

Secondly, the status of the recipients may be enhanced when the gift is recognized as being likely to enhance his future gift-giving potential (or his propensity for reciprocity). For this reason, education is normally provided on a more generous basis than the other social services, and when means tests are used in relation to the actual educational provision, rather than supplementing welfare provisions like food, the experience of stigma is not common.

Similarly, the medical care of the young is generally given priority over that of the aged when resources are limited. The poorer quality of medical care given to the aged, especially in institutional contexts, reinforces the feelings of stigma experienced by the recipients. In the same way, diseases and handicaps having the best prognosis for recovery will be least stigmatizing to the sufferer.

Whenever such arguments are publicly credible, voluntary associations for the handicapped stress the potential usefulness of their clientele when appealing for funds. Straightforward appeals to human compassion are normally the last resort of fund-raisers working on behalf of groups with an apparently hopeless prognosis. The less likely the recovery prospects, the more likely it is that stigma, intentionally or unintentionally, will be imposed on the group in question. The mentally subnormal, for example, suffer such marked discrimination that even their institutional diets are costed more cheaply than those of other National Health Service patients.

When the factors of incurability and age are combined, we recognize in the chronic sick a social group highly exposed to the risks of stigma. Their potentiality for restitution or reciprocity is zero. As we have seen in special cases, recognition of past service or gift ameliorates the sense of stigma. Such cases are becoming more exceptional in major fields of welfare provision like pensions. Graduated pension schemes on a national basis represent the extension of market criteria of evaluation in a major field of social provision covering the entire life-span. Despite the publicity given to the element of redistribution in this scheme, its net effect must be to legitimate the market evaluations of a person's worth. If this were not so, there would be no point in graduation. Although any element of redistribution amounts to a measure of social rather than economic recognition of worth, in any graded hierarchy of persons some group must come bottom.

The facts of ageing and mortality ensure that all men will end their days in conditions of dependency. The only exceptions to this proposition would seem to be forms of sudden death and altruistic suicide. In the first case the practice of modern medicine has the effect of frequently postponing death but increasing the likelihood of very long periods of dependency. The younger victims of traditional agents of sudden death such as war and epidemic disease are less likely to die at once. The same is true of road-injury victims.

It may be that the universal fear of death as an objective certainty for us all impels men to impose some of the most hurtful forms of stigma on the dying and even upon the dead themselves. The last page in each man's autobiography will always be written by someone else. Consequently an ability to stigmatize the dying is a sanction available to all societies. The ultimate stigma of the Poor Law—the pauper's funeral—was so effective because it symbolized a public defacement of a person's last page of life in the red ink of civic debt, overdraft and humiliation. Each pauper's funeral was intended as the public debasement of a human identity. Even today old people will go without in life in order to save money for a dignified funeral. Amongst the better-off, a traditional way of cheating the stigma of terminal dependency is to defer revealing the contents of a last will and testament.

Every dependent group in society can be seen as a threat to the autonomy of the self-supporting.[1] If the dominant human impulses were compassionate, we could expect that the greatest of human tragedies such as irretrievable loss, chronic dependency, the process of dying, and death itself, would attract a prior claim on welfare resources. This is clearly not the case.

Stigmatized people may, however, reject the dominant criteria of social evaluation. Their propensity to do so ultimately depends on the factor of power. Elderly, infirm citizens receiving the lowest graduated pension payable are unlikely to challenge effectively the low esteem in which they are held. They lack both the political and physical power to demand a greater economic reward for past services, none of which are viewed as exceptional and all of which have already been evaluated retrospectively in market terms. Over their working lifetime they have already become habituated to a place of lowly social

[1] David Matza, 'The Disreputable Poor', in Reinhard Bendix and Seymour Martin Lipset (eds), *Class, Status and Power: Social Stratification in Comparative Perspective*, 2nd Ed, Routledge and Kegan Paul, 1967, p. 296

esteem. If they failed to challenge this evaluation in their prime of life, such pensioners are unlikely to do so in their declining years. The facts of relative poverty will reinforce the sense of social distance from prospective givers, as will their high propensity for institutionalization. The physically and mentally handicapped will be still more adversely affected by these factors.

Groups exposed to short-run risks of dependency, such as redundant able-bodied workers and minority groups with a high proportion of young members, are more likely to reject or be indifferent to prevailing forms of stigma. The counterclaims of such minority groups take the form of a demand for civil rather than social rights. As Marshall suggests, the contemporary demands for power amongst black Americans express a demand for something more basic than additional social rights to better health, welfare and educational provisions.[1] One of our main arguments has been that people's estimation of themselves is not necessarily enhanced if their claims to social welfare are more liberally met. It is the status of recipient or dependent which is intrinsically humiliating.

The second major variable is that of *distance*, which may be social or spatial. We have noted that the problems relating to distance are central to an understanding of welfare provision in industrial societies. It has been suggested that the more distant the recipient is from the giver, the less is he likely to receive. Social distance, measured in terms of economic inequality or status differences, may be reinforced by powerful ideological factors. In Victorian England paupers were outside the social hierarchy altogether, and their social remoteness made their sufferings seem less real. Today, ethnic differences are identified and used in the same way.

Institutionalization reinforces the effect of distance in spatial terms. Once groups like the aged and mentally handicapped are isolated they are both more easily forgotten and made aware of their stigmatized identity, even when material amenities are relatively generous.[2] There is no clear evidence to support the

[1] T. H. Marshall, 'Reflections on Power', *Sociology*, Vol. 3, No. 2, May 1969

[2] See Peter Townsend, *The Last Refuge*, Routledge and Kegan Paul, London, 1962, especially ch. 8; Pauline Morris, *Put Away*, Routledge and

view that creating new forms of welfare provision on a smaller scale at local level will necessarily reduce stigma. The English Poor Law was, at all times, a very local service and also a very stigmatizing one. Account must be taken not only of social and spatial distance but of the ideologies that reinforce awareness of distance.

The third variable is that of *time*. The longer the period of dependency persists, the more likely the dependent is to redefine his total social life in terms of the stigma. Goffman's concept of 'spoiled identity' illustrates this phenomenon with regard to personal handicap.[1] Processes of secondary socialization and resocialization reinforce feelings of inferiority in so far as they have more time in which to take effect. Institutionalization adds the dimension of intensity to that of time. Stigmas deriving from ascribed forms of inferiority such as ethnicity or religion provide the greatest scope for reinforcement. Similarly, the process of pauperization is complete when those affected have 'adapted to their poverty' and have become 'apathetic regarding their condition'.[2] Paradoxically, the long-term effect of stigmatization is to cause the despised to accept their dependent status. In this way the therapeutic aims of those who impose stigma are defeated. The sanction of stigma fails to inspire greater efforts at self-help. The importance of chronological age has already been noted in our discussion of the variable of depth.

In the long run most of us will experience extreme dependency, a condition we are socialized to equate with stigma. This relationship is not immutable, but it will certainly not be changed by the mere rhetoric of social reformers. Concepts like 'the caring society' and the 'welfare state' are subjectively meaningless to those who have not achieved citizenship in an authentic form. It may be that effecting changes in the social consciousness of ordinary people is now becoming more important than further changes in the statute book.

Kegan Paul, London, 1969; and Erving Goffman, *Asylums*, *Essays on the Social Situation of Mental Patients and Other Inmates*, Penguin Books, London, 1968, pp. 15 *passim*

[1] E. Goffman, 'Stigma', *Notes on the Management of Spoiled Identity*, Penguin Books, 1968, pp. 11 *passim*

[2] D. Matza, *op. cit.*, p. 292

This model of social welfare can be applied to exchange situations in both the public and private sectors. Public services may have a greater propensity to stigmatize. The most profound humiliation of all, however, may be experienced in learning that only money can preserve self-respect in conditions of dependency. In both fields of welfare, the quality of compassion always appears to be in short supply.

In the public sector, however, stigma becomes an administrative technique for rationing scarce resources. It also expresses the nature of the relationship between the privileged and the underprivileged. The majority of people are disposed to give less voluntarily than they will give up under coercion. They are equally disposed to coerce others in order to retain what they believe is rightly their own. In this sense, coercion is also definable as a rationing device. And stigmatization is a most effective form of coercion.

The imposition of stigma is the commonest form of violence used in democratic societies. Stigmatization is slow, unobtrusive and genteel in its effect, so much so, that when the stigmatized hit back physically in Londonderry or Chicago they can technically be accused of being the first to resort to force. Stigmatization is a highly sophisticated form of violence in so far as it is rarely associated with physical threats or attack. It can best be compared to those forms of psychological torture in which the victim is broken psychically and physically but left to all outward appearances unmarked.

The phenomenon of stigma is therefore a central one, both for understanding the structure and aims of welfare services and the balance of power within societies where most forms of conflict have become ostensibly institutionalized.

5

Some Current Problems in Social Policy

In this concluding chapter we review some of the main developments in social welfare which appear likely to attract continuous attention and research during the coming decade. The first of these developments concerns the resolution of the debate between universalists and selectivists over the allocation of scarce resources to welfare needs. This debate is ending in defeat both for the orthodox universalists and for those selectivists who favour a return to deterrent social policies. Social research has played a very important role in resolving this debate and will continue to be of central importance in the formulation of alternative principles and policies. Positive discrimination is the most important of these policies in so far as it seeks to select and discriminate with the least possible imposition of stigma.

There are already signs of a greater willingness on the part of government to make a more systematic use of social research in order to define and cover categories of greatest need. There are, for example, the research projects of the Department of Health and Social Security, which will investigate the special problems of fatherless families and the chronic sick, as well as the more general social factors that influence the quality of family life. In education there are the area-based research projects set up after the manner recommended by Plowden.

Positive discrimination and the recognition that certain areas have prior claim over others are the policies recommended by Plowden as those most likely to improve the life-chances of deprived children. The realization of aims such as making 'schools in the most deprived areas as good as the best in the country' is in part dependent upon efficient diagnosis through research and intelligent selection on the part of administrators.[1] Any policy based on positive discrimination principles is totally dependent upon adequate research if its aims are to be recognized as being reasonable and just.

Complementing this increasing use of social research, in the past few years there has been a series of radical proposals for the simplification of administrative structures that have grown too complex. The Seebohm Report proposes the combination of a variety of family-centred social services into one department.[2] The Ministry of Health's recent Green Papers are again concerned to make medical services more accessible to the general public through simpler and more localized re-groupings.[3] Such new departments will be sufficiently well-informed from research findings to pursue active policies of seeking out need. In the field of education the process would appear to be working in the opposite direction, with a trend towards increasing size and complexity in the organization of schools.

In addition to proposals for administrative reform and a greater reliance on research, account must be taken of the present development of interest in consumer participation in the running of social services. 'Participation' as a currently fashionable term has many shades of meaning. For example, it can take the shape of extreme forms of student protest when participation becomes simply a euphemism for 'takeover'. Or it might mean the inclusion of lay members of the public in the actual decision-taking processes of social and educational services by virtue of their claim as users rather than elected or appointed representatives. Again, participation might mean nothing more than professional recognition of the right of citizens to be consulted and given reasons for policy changes before they are adopted. Peter Townsend has recently suggested that the actual users of services should, for example, sit on management committees of hospitals, children's homes or old

---

[1] Central Advisory Council for Education, *Children and their Primary Schools*, HMSO, 1967, Vol. 1, Report, para. 174 (1), p. 66

[2] Report of the Committee on Local Authority and Allied Personal Social Services, Cmnd 3703, HMSO, 1968

[3] Ministry of Health, National Health Service, *The Administrative Structure of the Medical and Related Services in England and Wales*, HMSO, 1968; and Department of Health and Social Security, *National Health Service: the Future Structure of the National Health Service*, HMSO, 1970

people's homes.[1] Young and McGeeney, amongst others, are producing schemes for the closer involvement of parents and children in the life of their schools,[2] and in the establishment of 'community schools'. These new approaches express active definitions of the concepts of citizenship and participation.

The need to engender more action notions of citizenship concerned the Royal Commission on Local Government[3] and led it to recommend the establishment of local councils, more accessible and amenable to the wishes of local populations than existing arrangements. A variety of proposals have also been made to encourage a greater involvement of the public in the work of voluntary welfare agencies.[4]

Three major trends in social policy can therefore be identified. Firstly, a greater reliance on new forms of positive discrimination in the allocation of welfare resources. This development constitutes a break with both universalist and selectivist principles in their orthodox forms. The criteria of allocation will become more sophisticated and difficult to understand, and also more dependent upon adequate research. Secondly, considerable efforts are being made to simplify welfare administration and make it more comprehensible to the public. Thirdly, the public are to be encouraged to take a more active and participant role in democratic procedures.

In our view, these trends both complement and conflict with each other, and too little attention has been given to their implicit potentialities for conflict. It cannot be assumed that the evaluative criteria of specialist research workers, administrators and professional policy-makers will be in accord with those of a more participant citizenry. Comforting assumptions about public attitudes to welfare still persist and are put forward as reasons for encouraging participation. The notion of community involvement is unquestioningly assumed to be a

[1] Peter Townsend, 'Family Welfare and Seebohm', *New Society*, 1 August 1968, No. 305, pp. 159–60
[2] M. Young and P. McGeeney, *Learning Begins at Home*, Institute of Community Studies, Routledge and Kegan Paul, 1968
[3] Royal Commission on Local Government in England: Vol. 1, Report of the Commission, Cmnd 4040, HMSO, 1969
[4] See *The Voluntary Worker in the Social Services*, Report of a Committee jointly set up by the NCSS and NISWT under the Chairmanship of Geraldine M. Aves, Allen and Unwin, 1969

'good thing' and 'public apathy' to be a 'bad thing'. The continuing dominance of the evaluative criteria of the economic market over the most meaningful areas of social life is still not seriously taken into account. Yet the implications of this dominance will not fade away as a result of social legislation by governments, followed by customary exhortations to the public and self-congratulations on the part of social reformers. If the social values of altruism and a concern for the most needy (and reprehensible) members of society are not to be learned in the economic market, and if it is considered important that these values should be acquired, then they will have to be systematically taught outside the economic market. Any such development would create value-problems of a critical order. None the less, we would argue that in the last analysis, Durkheim was right—the missing factor in the process of social reform is that of social, or moral, education.

Education, as a social service, is itself a variable of growing importance. It is becoming increasingly possible to launch systematic attempts to change our social constructions of reality.[1] Current campaigns to increase citizens' participation in welfare services may eventually succeed in increasing the willingness of the poor to use social services and lower their propensity to feel stigmatized as users. If, however, these increases in social knowledge and skill lead to a demand for more and better services, and the privileged do not change their view of welfare and its aims, the end-result of social education will be an extension of conflict rather than consensus. It is always more painful to learn in an experience of social education that we have obligations rather than rights, and the nature of that experience is determined for each of us according to the position of relative advantage or disadvantage from which we start.

The attention of social administrators and policy-makers is becoming focused, in a more sophisticated manner, upon the kinds of general social problem that preoccupied Durkheim,

---

[1] The school syllabuses of totalitarian societies often illustrate very explicit attempts to reinforce and legitimate the values and norms of the dominant political culture. See U.S. Department of Health, Education and Welfare, *Social Science in Soviet Secondary Schools*, Syllabus of the New Course, OE–14124, Washington, 1966

Spencer and Weber in their studies of industrial societies. The increasing reliance upon social research in the identification and differentiation of social needs will add greater practical significance to those problems of value and objectivity in social investigation that concerned Weber in his discussions with members of the Association for Social Policy. Of still more general significance, the issues posed by Durkheim regarding the nature of the moral relationship between the individual and his community in advanced industrial societies are now becoming of urgent concern in every area of social and educational administration. The concern to make citizenship a meaningful concept at the level of everyday life renews the debate about the actual and possible nature of 'community' in societies characterized by an increasingly complex division of labour.

The growing interest in ways of raising levels of civic competence and participation can be seen as an attempt to complement and control those processes of bureaucratization that both Spencer and Weber viewed with such misgiving. At another level, the future role of professional associations as mediators between welfare bureaucracies and as groups that must maintain an ethical coexistence between the claims of the economic and social markets has become a subject of central concern in the discipline of social administration. The influence of professions such as law and medicine on the making of social policy has already been a major subject of research in social administration. The work of Abel-Smith, Stevens and others has uncovered sufficient evidence of self-interest, as well as of altruism, to suggest that civic and professional interests are not always synonymous. Despite this evidence, necessity still seems to point in the direction that Durkheim indicated. The moral components of civic and professional education can no longer be taken for granted. The capacity for self-discipline and self-denial remain the central human qualities that societies must inculcate in their youngest members in the interests of collective survival and welfare. Human societies can still best be understood as constructs that we develop in order to preserve ourselves from the baser aspects of our own natures.

Of the four sociological theorists with whom we began this study, only Marx seems to be of declining rather than increasing importance to the discipline and practice of social policy and administration. Had Marx been endowed with more of a Weberian temperament, his attitude towards ameliorative social reformers might have been tinged with anxiety rather than contempt. Social reform rather than repression has made Marxist social theory an irrelevance in advanced industrial societies.

In this final chapter we will examine two aspects of these current developments in social policy. The first concerns the changing role of the social scientist as a research worker in the context of positive discrimination programmes. We will attempt to relate this present role to those traditions of empirical sociology that we have already analysed in earlier chapters. We will also explore the different forms that positive discrimination has taken in our society. Our thesis is that the new kinds of responsibility being placed on empirical social scientists make it even more urgent that we develop new theories of social welfare, which will enable us to bridge the division between values and evidence.

Our second concern is to outline a possible application of our model of social welfare to the problem of medical need and dependency. The essay on positive discrimination is concerned with an aspect of social policy in which progress is being made and reasonable grounds exist for cautious optimism. The final essay on dependency ends with what is an intrinsically pessimistic conclusion. We are here concerned with the practical consequences arising from those cultural processes in industrial societies that encourage an identification of dependency with loss of personal and public esteem. It is not suggested, however, that these attitudes towards dependency are immutable, although they seem unlikely to be changed either by social revolution or social legislation. The problem of moral education for social life remains a subject largely ignored by social administrators. In a later study we hope to explore more fully the relationship of moral education to social welfare. At this stage, however, it seems advisable to wait for a thorough testing of our hypothesis regarding the phenomenon of dependency.

THE CONTRIBUTION OF THE SOCIAL SCIENTIST IN POSITIVE DISCRIMINATION PROGRAMMES[1]

In this section we will be mainly concerned with the contribution that social scientists in their role as research workers can make to positive discrimination programmes. In attempting to link some of the theoretical aspects of the subject, this section has been structured around two connected themes. Firstly we have examined the changing relationship of social research to social policy and social values in a historical context. Secondly we have attempted to show how the adoption of positive discrimination programmes poses a new range of problems for social research, and why the success of such programmes is more dependent upon adequate social research than is the case with other kinds of social policy.

It is a chastening thought that almost the first contribution of the social scientist to social policy programmes was the principle of 'less eligibility'. A further cause for reflection is the failure of social scientists in our own time to predict either the American race-relations crisis or the French disturbances of the last few months.

Value judgments and evidence might be said to be the key determinants of social policy. The making of social policy is so closely involved in ongoing political processes that it is very difficult in practice to draw a clear distinction between the parts played by value judgments and research. The one informs and interpenetrates the other in the continuing political debate. Just as social research is by its nature partly a political activity, so do social researchers differ amongst themselves in their political values. It may be argued that such differences are founded on a greater degree of objectivity and a more rational appraisal of evidence than is found amongst laymen or even politicians. None the less social scientists do disagree over the interpretation of the same research findings when it comes to drawing practical conclusions for action. This implies that how-

[1] This was originally presented as a paper to the Second Conference of the Social Administration Association on 13 July 1968, and published in *Social and Economic Administration*, Vol 2, Number 4, October 1968, pp. 227–41

ever difficult it may be in practice to draw a clear distinction between values and facts, such a distinction does exist.

The relatively recent growth in the range and quality of available evidence has made it harder to make this distinction clear. The growth of our knowledge has also made it more likely that hitherto unquestioned assumptions are challenged by new evidence when policies are being re-appraised. A cynic might say that we now take longer in selecting the evidence which renders our beliefs intellectually respectable. Alternatively we might describe this process as the secularization of value elements in social policy.

In the seventeenth century men justified a stern Poor Law by reference to the will of God. By the eighteen-forties the still obscure laws of political economy were beginning to take over from God. Today the tablets of the law are more usually handed down to us in the secularized form of punched cards and computer tapes. Values, like the poor, have always been with us. Social research has only recently come of age.

The changing quality of the relationship between values and evidence largely determines the nature of social policy and the extent to which the social scientist is able to make an effective contribution in the formulation of policy. Variations in this relationship between value judgments and evidence have been used in earlier chapters as an index for comparing key periods in the development of English social policy.

The new Poor Law of 1834 was essentially a programme of relief based on discrimination. Within a structure of deterrence and stigma, problems such as the ordering of social priorities and diagnosis of need were largely self-resolving. Willingness to enter a workhouse was in itself proof of need. The process of selection and discrimination was a process of moral judgment on the part of the community and of self-judgment on the part of the individual, in which the workhouse test was meant to operate as a kind of moral computer, largely taking the place of social research as an instrument of social diagnosis. The social scientist or whoever filled that role had only to enumerate and record.

The evidence collected for the Poor Law Commissioners between 1832 and 1834 was used to support Chadwick's already clearly formulated assumptions about the nature and causes of poverty, the effect of relief upon the poor and the relationship of the individual citizens to market forces in an industrializing society. The relationship of social research to these value judgments was essentially a subordinate one. That it remained so can be seen year after year in the statistical sections of the annual reports of the poor law commissions, the Poor Law Board and the Local Government Board.[1] The survey techniques of social scientists at the time were of course severely limited. The crucial point, however, is that the evidence of experts simply was not considered relevant to the formulation of a policy the guiding principles of which had in any event been clearly laid down and accepted. Even experts of the eminence of Sir John Simon were carefully limited by lay administrators in their range of activities and denied any role in advising on policy.[2]

This is not to suggest that the value judgments or principles of 1834 were never challenged by the evidence of research. From the eighteen-sixties onwards there was a steady accumulation of evidence from surveys and research which pointed to the grow-

[1] The 1834 Report had paid only scant attention to the needs of the sick and the aged, giving passing reference to their need for non-punitive institutions. (See *Report from His Majesty's Commissioners for Inquiring into the Administration and Practical Operation of the Poor Laws*, p. 307, London, Fellowes, 1834.) Even the requirement that out-relief could be made available to the sick and the aged was not clarified until 1852 (*Outdoor Relief Regulation Order*, 1852). The official Poor Law statistics collected between 1834 and 1849 were virtually worthless for any classificatory purpose and were not even obtained on a nationally uniform basis. As late as 1906 Beatrice Webb was to find that the number and distribution of sick children receiving poor relief was not known, as the custom was to define the child according to the physical and mental condition of the parent. It appears that no one could inform Mrs Webb of the procedure followed when parents were differently classified. *Royal Commission on the Poor Laws and Relief of Distress, Appendix, Vol. XXV, Statistics Relating to England and Wales* (Cd. 5077), Part II, P.P. 1910, LIII, p. 70

For a further analysis of the deficiencies in Poor Law statistics in the first decade of this century see B. Abel-Smith and Robert Pinker, *Changes in the Use of Institutions in England and Wales between 1911 and 1951*, Manchester Statistical Society, 1960, pp. 20–4.

Sir John Simon's work to improve the collection of health statistics is described in Royston Lambert, *Sir John Simon 1816–1904 and English Social Administration*, MacGibbon & Kee, 1963, pp. 418–23.

[2] Royston Lambert, *Sir John Simon 1816–1904*, Ch. XXII, pp. 518 *passim*

ing needs of the sick, the infirm and the unemployed and other causes of destitution. These contributions came not only from independent sources such as the *Lancet* enquiries,[1] and later on, the work of Charles Booth and Seebohm Rowntree, but from official investigations within the Poor Law.[2] All that these and other surveys achieved was a series of grudging concessions which removed one group of needy persons after another from the full rigours of a deterrent Poor Law, the central ideology of which remained dominant. Official support for a separate Poor Law hospital service came only when such classification was recognized as a possible way of preserving a deterrent poor law for the able bodied.

The Poor Law lay administrators built their case on issues of principle when they submitted their evidence to the Royal Commission of 1905–9. Their key spokesman, Chief Inspector J. S. Davy, argued the case for selectivity and deterrence with the same ideological passion which has been manifested in some recent defences of universalism. Davy conceded that evidence concerning the growing incidence of sick paupers was incontrovertible. None the less the development of Poor Law hospitals constituted a betrayal of Poor Law principles. Therefore it was necessary that the sick should be removed from the Poor Law in order that workhouses might become once again truly deterrent institutions for the able-bodied unemployed. Davy had no interest in any causal explanation of unemployment,

[1] *Report of the Lancet Sanitary Commission for Investigating the State of the Infirmaries of Workhouses*, London, 1866

[2] H of C Sessional Paper 372, 1866, BPP, Vol. LXI, 1866 (*Report of Dr Edward Smith, Poor Law Inspector and Medical Officer to the PLB, on the Metropolitan Workhouse Infirmaries and Sick Wards*) and *Dr Smith's second report*, H of C Sessional Paper 4, 1867–8, BPP, Vol. LX, 1867–8 (*Report of Dr Edward Smith, Medical Officer to the PLB, on the Sufficiency of the Existing Arrangements for the Care and Treatment of the Sick Poor in Forty-eight Provincial Workhouses in England and Wales*) and H of C Sessional Paper 387, 1866, BPP, Vol. LXI, 1866 (*Report of H. B. Farnall, Esquire, Poor Law Inspector, on the Infirmary Wards of the Several Metropolitan Workhouses and their existing Arrangements*).

For a further analysis of these early attempts by official investigators to collect adequate statistical data on the incidence of sickness and infirmity in Poor Law institutions and Voluntary Hospitals at this time, see Robert Pinker, *English Hospital Statistics 1861–1938*, Heinemann, 1966, pp. 90–5

holding simply that 'The unemployed man must stand by his accidents' and 'suffer for the good of the body politic'.[1]

In their work for the Royal Commission the Webbs ruthlessly exposed the irrelevance of the official statistical data collected by the Poor Law. If they failed to achieve a new and continuing relationship between social research and social policy they did at least succeed in indicating how that relationship might come into being and in demonstrating the extent of the contribution to be made by research.

In one sense social science did become more directly involved in social administration. The Charity Organization Society in the late eighteen-sixties attempted to systematize the organization of voluntary social services and to make these complementary to a deterrent Poor Law, in theory still mainly concerned with the destitute. The practice of selectivity in voluntary services was slightly ameliorated by the inclusion of the deserving poor in addition to the deserving destitute.[2] Once again the critera of need were moral ones. Need was defined in relation to desert. From the eighteen-eighties onward the contribution of social workers in this role became more important, with the improvement in the quality of certain kinds of social service, notably that of medical care. The function of these workers was to help limit demand in a context of discrimination. During the nineteen-thirties the development of case-work theory was also used by some to give a semblance of objectivity and respectability to these restrictive actions. Thus it came about that these professional workers, deriving their status from social sciences, worked on in their vocations, calling sometimes on the name of God and sometimes on that of Freud.

Perhaps it is chiefly due to the impact of the Royal Commission of 1905–9, and the deadlock that followed the publication of a Majority and Minority report, that we owe the interregnum in social policy that followed between the wars. There started a dual process in which the principles of 1834 began losing their credibility as slowly and hesitatingly as the principle of universality began to be discussed as an emergent

---

[1] *Royal Commission on the Poor Laws*, 1905–9, Vol. I, Cd. 4625, para. 3290 *passim*

[2] C. L. Mowat, *The Charity Organisation Society 1869–1913*, 1961

and challenging ideology. Some would argue that this hiatus persists at the present time. The inter-war years remain a relatively unresearched period regarding the development of social policy. It was a time in which policies based on stigma and deterrence were increasingly recognized as inadequate to meet the needs of an industrial society. In at least one area, that of housing, it is possible to detect the beginning of vigorous positive discrimination programmes, although these ventures were soon to be checked by major economic crises. None the less it can be argued that the imposition of drastic cuts in social-service spending, and particularly the stringent application of means tests during the nineteen-thirties, were the products of expediency rather than principle.[1]

It is in effect easier to define a period in which 'less eligibility' was the dominant ideology of English social policy than to define a comparable period in which 'universalist' principles dominated our social services.

To what extent has universalism been a generally accepted principle of social policy in the sense in which 'less eligibility' —the most stringent form of selectivity—was accepted by policy-makers? An understanding of the role of the social scientist in the making of social policy is central to the answering of this question. It is arguable that the universalist ideology, so dramatically expounded in the work of writers like Tawney, has never developed far beyond the stage of being a passionate and emotional reaction against the excesses of the Poor Law and Public Assistance. Again, the research component of the Beveridge Report comprises little more than a rudimentary diagnosis and description of a range of needs which it was widely believed ought to be met by collective provision. There was a general failure to recognize that different ideologies carry different methodological and theoretical implications, the key differences being between exclusive and inclusive ideologies and discrimination programmes. So long as selectivity in the form of 'less eligibility' was the ruling ideology, stigma kept down demand. In the spate of legislation after the Second World War the barriers of stigma were removed, yet in an enduring context of scarcity there was hardly any adequate attempt at

[1] See T. H. Marshall, *Social Policy*, Hutchinson University Library, 1965, pp. 60–74 and especially pp. 64–5

making comparisons between the yields from different ways of spending money,[1] and there was little systematic attempt to order social priorities or even to assess the relative adequacy of levels of provision in different social services. In a range of social services suddenly committed to provide the best possible standards of provision the main consequence of this lack of basic research has been to bring universalism into disrepute.

For over twenty years universalism has been eroded by what can only be described as the free play of social forces. One result of this free play has been the remarkable growth of *ad hoc* means tests within local authorities.[2] A second result has been the monopolization of the best social services by middle-class citizens practising positive discrimination on their own behalf.[3] The contribution of the social scientist might have been to do the same on behalf of the underprivileged. The combined lack of adequate research and adequate resources has reduced universalism to the level of a slogan.

Positive discrimination is therefore open to a variety of definitions and as a practice it pre-dates Plowden and Newsom by many years. In a general sense positive discrimination is a process of diagnosis and selection, free from stigmatization in so far as it aims at raising standards to the best possible level rather than the minimum level tolerable. Such adjectives confirm that positive discrimination programmes are expressions of value as well as techniques of procedure. Under the free

---

[1] Bleddyn Davies, 'The Cost Effectiveness of Education Spending', in Mark Blaug, H. D. Hughes, and Bleddyn Davies, *Social Services for All?* Part Two: Fabian Tract 383, p. 49

[2] Mike Reddin, 'Local Authority Means-tested Services', in Peter Townsend, Mike Reddin, and Peter Kaim-Caudle, *Social Services for All?* Part One, Fabian Tract 382, pp. 7–15

[3] A. Little and J. Westergaard, 'The Trend of Class Differentials in Educational Opportunity in England and Wales', *The British Journal of Sociology*, Vol. XV, No. 4, December 1964, pp. 301–16. The consequences of such policies in which value judgements supported by circumstantial evidence do service in place of social research is described by Bleddyn Davies, *Social Needs and Researches in Local Services*, Joseph, 1968, p. 59. 'The combined effect of the differing expenditure is that total expenditure per primary school pupil is uncorrelated with low social class, while total expenditure per secondary school pupil is negatively correlated with it. In expenditure on secondary education, at any rate, what we have at the moment is negative not positive discrimination.'

play of social forces, which has filled the place of social research, the best possible services have rarely been focused on those social groups in greatest need. This is the sense in which Plowden uses the term when it writes of making 'schools in the most deprived areas as good as the best of the country'.[1] The realization of such an aim is in part dependent on diagnosis and selection.

Discrimination can therefore be practised in a number of ways. Firstly there is negative discrimination against the under-privileged, which occurred under the Poor Law and which can and does occur within our own ostensibly universalist frame-work today. As Reddin points out, the current debate over selectivity is one 'centering not on redistribution but on retrenchment and reduction in public expenditure'.[2] It is significantly a debate in which there has not been 'any realistic enquiry into the current operation of selective means-tested systems, their utilization or their value to recipients'.[3] Stigma, complexity and secrecy are the modern counterpart of the workhouse test, namely processes of exclusion depending on value judgments rather than research into their effects. Dis-crimination in this sense becomes a strategy in its own right, aimed simply at alleviating the grossest forms of inequality, with little or no concern for quality of service. The effect of stigma is to make the discrimination take a negative form. The most ruthless form of selectivity is the human psyche responding to shame and humiliation.

Secondly, as already referred to, there is positive discrimina-tion by the privileged practised on their own behalf which again can and does occur within both selectivist and universalist frameworks. This form of positive discrimination has become possible in post-war Britain, where an officially dominant ideology of universalism has removed the restricting effect of stigma but not of scarcity. In the absence of objective research, subjective self-help has ordered the pattern of priorities. Positive discrimination in this universalist context becomes the tactic of a privileged minority; it becomes increasingly

[1] Central Advisory Council for Education, *Children and their Primary Schools*, HMSO, 1967, Vol. I: Report

[2] Reddin, *op. cit.*, p. 7

[3] ibid.

dysfunctional in relation to the ostensibly universalist strategy of the wider society.

Thirdly there is positive discrimination on behalf of or by the underprivileged within a framework of universalism. As Titmuss argues, 'Some structure of universalism is an essential prerequisite' in order 'to provide a framework of value and opportunity bases within and around which can be developed socially acceptable selective services aiming to discriminate positively, with the minimum risk of stigma, in favour of those whose needs are greatest'.[1] In this sense positive discrimination becomes a tactical exercise within a wider universalist strategy. Such discrimination is the only form of selectivity compatible with the idea of a welfare society because its ultimate goal is the achievement of optimal rather than minimal standards. Discrimination becomes a process of inclusion rather than exclusion.

We can illustrate these three types of discrimination by reference to current housing policies. Local-authority accommodation for the homeless is an example of *negative discrimination against the underprivileged* as a strategy in its own right. Fathers are kept apart from their families and are constantly reminded of the degrading and temporary nature of the shelter provided. The purpose of this kind of discrimination is to minimize public expenditure.

Secondly, there is *positive discrimination by the privileged on their own behalf*. This phenomenon usually occurs when there is a marked discrepancy between professed principles and actual practices in social policy, in short, when there is no really effective strategy. Tax relief on mortgage interest repayments, which confer the greatest benefits on those borrowing the largest sums and paying the highest rates of tax, is an example of positive discrimination by the privileged. The purpose of this kind of discrimination is rarely made explicit.

An example of the third type—*positive discrimination within a universalist framework*—is the concentration of council building programmes in those local authorities which have the worst slum problems. Another relevant case is the operation of differential rent schemes within local authorities in order to

[1] Richard M. Titmuss, *Commitment to Welfare*, George Allen and Unwin Ltd, 1968, p. 135

help the larger and poorer families. The rigorous pursuit of such policies might mean placing larger tax burdens on those best able to pay, for example, by reducing tax relief on mortgage interest repayments.

The rationale of this third approach derives from our inability to distinguish between ' "faults" in the individual (moral, psychological or social) and the "faults of society".'[1] Simply because 'the causal agents of need cannot be identified or are so diffuse as to defy the wit of law' we cannot, says Titmuss, morally allow the social costs of our economy 'to lie where they fall'.[2] This argument could be taken to mean that so long as social research is unable to solve its problems of causal explanation, we must justify our universalism on grounds of sheer moral necessity. Clearly, problems of multiple deprivation do not offer the easiest context for developing adequate theories of social causation. It seems likely, therefore, that we will be depending on morality for some time to come.

This third approach poses a whole new range of problems for the social scientist, which must be solved, if the initial universalist value judgments are ever to become an empirical reality in an administrative structure that will embody and fulfil them. Positive discrimination programmes within an inclusive universalist value system make social research mandatory. The improvement in the techniques and skills of the social sciences makes such programming operationally possible and such values realistically sustainable.

In exclusive and stigmatizing forms of discrimination like the new Poor Law the initial value judgments were also able to serve as the process of diagnosis and selection, systematically eliminating all but the most indigent minority. In universally orientated forms of discrimination the problems of diagnosis and selection, of identification and presentation, are far more complex than those recognized by either Chadwick or Beveridge.

Positive discrimination is a device for 'intervening more directly at strategic points in the social structure'.[3] The initial problem is that of diagnosing the strategic areas of need in

---

[1] ibid., p. 134   [2] ibid., p. 133
[3] S. M. Miller and Martin Rein, 'Poverty, Inequality and Policy', in Howard S. Becker, *Social Problems: A Modern Approach*, Wiley, p. 516

relation to the provision of social services. Our cause for concern, argues Reddin, 'should centre on two problems which can be headed *utilization* and *evaluation*'.[1] It is, firstly, impossible to 'assess the extent of utilization of a service if we have no idea of the number of potential recipients'.[2] Secondly, we cannot adequately evaluate the effectiveness of services in reaching a group when, once again, we lack reliable indices of the numbers involved. These problems are intensified when there is uncertainty about criteria of 'eligibility'.

We have to begin by asking who needs help most, and often the answers will reflect a compromise between expediency and principle. Social research can help to clarify the possible consequences arising from different kinds of resource allocation. It cannot by itself resolve the differences of opinion and evaluation.

If, for example, we are to pursue deprivation wherever we find it we may end by giving priority to rural areas or the smaller urban areas of the North-East, thereby ruling out many of our big cities. Alternatively, we may concentrate on building up institutions such as Parent-Teacher and Housing Associations, as well as informal kinds of legal advice in very deprived areas, which will not necessarily be utilized *at first* by those in greatest need.

We have to view positive discrimination in the whole social context of an advanced industrial society. It can be argued that societies such as our own have a built-in tendency to deprive certain groups. If this is so, positive discrimination ought to be a permanent feature of social policy governing the broadest possible range of services.

The focus of research and discrimination programmes may be upon individuals, families, households, income units, or particular groups, such as large families, disability groups and groups generally defined as social deviants such as gypsies, barge families and some categories of immigrant. Alternatively attention may be concentrated upon an area. Donnison and Little argue that 'to be successful' positive discrimination 'should not be confined to particular individuals and families but must help everyone in the chosen area'.[3]

---

[1] Reddin, *op. cit.*, p. 14   [2] ibid.

[3] D. V. Donnison and A. Little, *Poverty: A Paper for the S.S.R.C.* Appendix 1, para. (b), (unpublished)

There is potential danger in the readiness with which we associate positive discrimination programmes with the 'priority area' concept, namely that such programmes are thought of as geographical rather than political exercises. The area concept has its attractions in terms of administrative and research convenience. It may also help to alleviate stigma.[1] The essence of positive discrimination lies not in where it takes effect but in what it does, namely the allocation of social resources to areas of special need and the more extensive directing and financing of local government by the central government.

The argument against restricting positive discrimination programmes to the 'area' concept is stated at length by Davies.[2] Clearly the 'area' approach would be inappropriate for research into income maintenance services because many low-income families do not live in those areas with the lowest median incomes.[3] Some of the worst poverty is found in areas which have experienced rapid economic growth and rises in *per capita* incomes. Furthermore, only a very small minority of the total number of poor families will be found living in areas where the standards of all social services are relatively low.

Davies concludes that there is 'little case for assuming that a policy of positive discrimination, applied in such a way that a small group of areas had a priority with respect to *all* services, would lead to an efficient allocation of resources in the absence of policies for favouring other areas in the allocation of resources for specific services'.[4]

These observations lead Davies to distinguish between the 'priority area' form of positive discrimination and his concept of 'territorial justice' in that 'the former is not defined in such a way that it is a necessary condition for social justice, while the latter has been so defined'.[5] Davies's definition of territorial justice is stated as 'an area distribution of provision of services

---

[1] See also Anne Corbett, 'Priority Schools', *New Society*, 30 May 1968, No. 296, pp. 785–7, in which it is suggested that positive discrimination programmes may do no more than transfer or widen the sense of stigma from individual citizens and social groups, to whole local authorities and their employees. Corbett refers to 'wide support for the view that to be classified as an E.P.A. is a slur'.

[2] Davies, *Social Needs and Resources in Local Services*, Ch. I

[3] ibid., footnote on p. 304

[4] ibid.   [5] ibid.

such that each area's standard is proportional to the total needs
for the services of its population'[1] and more briefly as 'to each
area according to the needs of the population of that area'.[2]

The difference between these two approaches is less than at
first seems to be the case. Plowden's key point was that all local
authorities—even the richest ones—should adopt positive discrimination programmes favouring their most deprived schools.[3]
Ideally such programmes would involve other services such as
housing, social work and welfare provision. Those local authorities with the largest proportion of deprived schools would
receive priority aid from central government. Plowden's concern was focused on the distribution of resources within local
authorities, while Davies seems to concentrate on the overall
distribution of services between local authorities.

Territorial justice can be measured in terms of resources
allocated, the extensiveness of provision and the intensity of
provision in relation to needs. This measurement of existing
utilization and evaluation of the effectiveness of social service
provision would form an initial and major contribution of
social scientists in programmes of positive discrimination.

Such problems of measurement and evaluation are complicated by a number of factors. Firstly, the circumstances under
which social services are made available range from those
which are universally provided to those subject to one of the
numerous means tests in force. Secondly, use of services is
differentially affected by the level of public awareness and
initiative. Lack of publicity, complexity of application procedures and the historical ill-repute of certain services affect
degrees of usage.

Thirdly, there is the factor of substitutability. Davies suggests
that there is more disagreement in both central and local
government about which services should be used to care for

[1] ibid., p. 39
[2] ibid., p. 16. The statistical definition of 'territorial justice' is given as
'a high correlation between indices of resource-use, or standards of provision, and an index measuring the relative needs of an area's population
for the service, the relative inequality of the standards indices being the same
as that of the need index'
[3] *Children and their Primary Schools*, Vol. I, p. 57, 'Every authority where
deprivation is found should be asked to adopt "positive discrimination"
within its own area . . .'

people than there is about which kind of people should be helped.[1] At the same time there is a relatively high degree of substitutability between different social services, which tend to be administered by different departments applying different criteria of eligibility. Income maintenance services for widowed mothers and welfare services for the elderly are examples of this kind of problem.

Substitutability is a key index of efficiency. The rational allocation of resources requires an ability and willingness to vary a combination of substitutable services in relation to changing patterns of need and preference. Davies shows very clearly how little response there has so far been in local government to the findings of social research or even to the financial pressures of central government in terms of making the best use of available resources.[2] This question of substitutability is central to the problems of measurement and evaluation that will be posed by positive discrimination programmes. Research projects designed to tackle this problem will require a high degree of inter-disciplinary co-ordination. They will also face conflict with other interested parties over the actual criteria of measurement and evaluation that they use. This is not to imply that social scientists are yet competent to give adequate advice on the best combination of services, or upon the causes of need, or on the best ways of measuring standards of effectiveness in our social services.[3] What Plowden argues is the imperative need for provision to be made so that social scientists can equip themselves to make such contributions.[4]

We can identify three main types of social research essential to positive discrimination programmes. Each type of research should be developed in close relationship with the others. Firstly, research is necessary for monitoring progress, measuring utilization and assessing the effectiveness of services. Thus a major function of research units will be the collection and collation of up-to-date knowledge. Most of this material should be gathered or is gathered in the form of censuses linked to Inland Revenue, Social Survey and National Census data. The social scientist's role may here be misinterpreted by public

[1] Davies, *op. cit.*   [2] ibid., pp. 214 *passim*
[3] ibid., p. 274 and pp. 284–5
[4] *Children and their Primary Schools*, Vol. I, p. 426

authorities as one of collecting facts as quickly as possible on an *ad hoc* basis. Sharpe gives a more accurate definition of this function as being 'systematic long-term research within a defined field but not directed to a specific limited exercise'.[1] As Donnison suggests, 'Research by its nature cannot be guaranteed to produce specific results to a given timetable'.[2]

This kind of material, regularly and systematically gathered, would comprise basic living standards data about income, housing, educational and health standards, with emphasis on those social groups at greatest risk. Complementary data would be required to help in the assessment of special and general problems of policy in the public services and their effects on trends in the divergence of average standards of living and the distribution and spread of income. These data would form the essential basis for an ongoing analysis of changing patterns of consumer demand, intensities of use by groups in relation to their relative needs and the evaluation of changing consumer preferences.

The development of a data-bank system for common use and secondary analysis purposes will provide the factual basis necessary for long-term planning and production. However much the extension of research facilities and expertise may raise the level of rationality and objectivity in the distribution of resources between local authorities, elements of conflict and competition will remain implicit in the allocation process.

No single local authority can at the moment hope to evaluate objectively its own needs for services and resources in relation to the needs of other local authorities. While research units at local-authority level should be concerned with helping to re-order their own social priorities, the function of central government research units should be to advise on allocating priorities between different local authorities and positive discrimination programmes.

A second and related aspect will be operational or 'action' research, which focuses on devising new solutions to existing

[1] Greater London Papers: No. 10, *Research in Local Government*, by L. J. Sharpe, London School of Economics and Political Science, 1965, p. 11

[2] D. V. Donnison, *Housing Research: Some European Impressions*, Urban Studies, May 1964. See also D. V. Donnison, *The Government of Housing*, Penguin Books, Ch. 11 *passim*

problems of resource use and testing out practical schemes at an experimental stage. Such 'development teams' might follow up attempts at achieving more effective combinations of substitutable services. This type of work is not so much research as 'systematically planned experiment and innovation'.[1]

Thirdly, there is a need for more theoretical long-range studies of such fundamental issues as the causes and consequences of poverty in advanced industrial societies. Such studies would again be interdisciplinary in character because they would seek to relate the making of social policy to the wider social structure. They might, for example, investigate the extent to which the goal of social equality can be made compatible with other desirable social goals such as economic growth and political democracy.

One reason for the lengthy and unchallenged dominance of value judgments in the formulation of social policy may be that 'We still lack a theory which provides a basis for the allocation of resources and the improvement of the operations of welfare and educational bureaucracies'.[2] As Rex points out, 'As soon as any discipline gets beyond brute empiricism it has not merely to record the co-existence of phenomena. It has to show why those things coexist as they do'.[3]

The development of an adequate body of social theory should help us to structure our values in social policy on a more coherent and rational basis and also to make the relationship between values and evidence a closer and more fruitful one. Then at least we may find it possible to be universalists or selectivists or in-betweens in response to knowledge rather than as a reaction against the defects of our social analysis and the dubious lessons of political history. In this way we can hold to our values with a little less desperation than we do today.

A further contribution of the social scientist in positive discrimination programmes can be to help in giving more reality to our democratic values. Many positive discrimination programmes are likely to invoke intense hostility from the public,

[1] Donnison, *The Government of Housing*, p. 361

[2] S. M. Miller, 'Poverty', *Transactions of the Sixth World Congress of Sociology*, Vol. II, International Sociological Association, 1967, p. 182

[3] *New Society*, 7 March 1968, No. 284, review of *Causation and Functionalism in Sociology* by Wzevolod W. Isajiw, Routledge, p. 354

especially when these programmes are focused on highly mobile groups such as gypsies and stigmatized groups such as unmarried mothers.

The social scientist is in a position to provide an effective and continuing link between citizenry, field-workers, administrators, local councillors and central government departments. One aspect of this work—carrying out periodical surveys on the changing pattern of consumer needs and demands—has already been mentioned. Another complementary aspect would be research into methods of improving techniques for the dissemination of information about social services.

Clearly the social scientist will have to hold a difficult balance between loyalty to his employing agency and the fulfilment of an innovatory role in democratic processes. As Marris and Rein found in their study of poverty projects in the U.S.A., there was 'little difficulty in evoking a response from the people they tried to serve: their most urgent and intractable problem was to satisfy the demand they raised'.[1] This will be a characteristic dilemma in the early stages of British positive discrimination programmes. Again we need to note how difficult it will be to win over the participants in practice, when resources are very limited and there is conflict between research findings and lay opinion.

Social scientists risk being typed as a corps of 'agents provocateurs' in positive discrimination programmes. None the less it is possible for the social scientist to help make a reality of Abel-Smith's plea for 'consumer sovereignty of a new kind to be exercised within the public services so as to widen the freedom of the individual'.[2] Without such a contribution local government will remain at best a potential structure for effective participant democracy, which is always available against the day when the British public might decide to use it. Authentic choice and freedom are however contingent upon knowledge, much of which is currently not available. Without such knowledge the prejudices of the ignorant masquerade as values and principles.

[1] P. Marris and M. Rein, *Dilemmas of Social Reform*, Routledge and Kegan Paul, London, 1967, p. 225

[2] Brian Abel-Smith, *Freedom in the Welfare State*, Fabian Tract 353, p. 16. Sharpe also suggests that 'It may well be that one of the reasons for the low esteem in which local government is held is derived from its reluctance to recognize the growth of consumer consciousness'. ibid., p. 14

Social research, like social work and teaching, shares many of the characteristics of a personal-service profession. As a career it offers enough personal satisfaction and involvement to foster an exaggerated notion regarding the importance and effectiveness of one's work. Few occupations are technically better qualified to guard against such dangers, for who more than social scientists have so ruthlessly dissected the pretensions and vices of other professional groups? It is always possible in these days of 'direct action' that social research will come to be seen as the true opium of the intellectuals.

The dominant value orientations of a society order the relationship of social research to policy-making. In exclusive and stigmatizing systems such as the Poor Law and much of the Victorian voluntary social services the functions of rational enquiry were pre-empted by conventional morality. Where the dominant values and aims are universalist and inclusive, positive discrimination becomes a necessary tactic in the process of allocating scarce social resources and rectifying persistent inequalities. Such a process is heavily dependent upon the contribution of social research, and the relationship between ideology and the objective pursuit of evidence becomes more of a partnership. None the less social scientists cannot subsume decision-taking roles within their research function.

When positive discrimination programmes are developed within a universalist framework, the problems of ordering social priorities become exceedingly complex. The interdisciplinary and interdepartmental nature of social research poses new problems of co-ordination and co-operation. The contribution that social scientists are able to make will be greatly affected by the way in which research units are set up and the way in which research develops as a career structure. A further consideration is the need to improve our methods of collecting and sharing research material at a national level. If the research facilities of local government can be greatly improved, there is no reason why the development of positive discrimination programmes should lead to a drastic loss of autonomy on the part of local government.

It remains to be seen whether or not the social sciences are yet competent to fulfil the crucial role required by positive discrimination programmes. The imminence of these programmes will soon provide us with an answer. Unless this research contribution can be made, positive discrimination will become yet another of those slogans which all too often pass for principles in social policy.

It may be that because we lack an adequate body of theory, much of our research in the social services lacks even the apparent coherence and clarity with which the dominant issues of value and principle have been expounded in the past. Perhaps this difference is endemic in the conflict between the necessarily sceptical nature of research and the emotive character of strongly held beliefs.

In the last analysis the place of social research in positive discrimination programmes is justified as much on the grounds of its necessity as by its objectivity. A social scientist engaged on research into the re-ordering of social priorities is concerned with issues of relative advantage and disadvantage. Ultimately these issues affect not only the quality of life but actual matters of life and death. Consequently, as the social scientist plays a more strategic role in the making of social policy, he becomes more likely to encounter situations in which he will have to question the role he is asked to play in an enterprise, or the use to which the research findings are put. If on these occasions the social scientist still feels bound to follow the dictates of his conscience, the most important problem of value will have been faced, if not always resolved according to the criteria of objectivity.

CITIZENSHIP AND DEPENDENCY

In all industrial societies citizenship is an achieved rather than an ascribed status. In totalitarian societies the absence of civic rights is an objective fact; in democracies the most important definitions of citizenship are subjective ones. The extent to which we exercise civic rights and responsibilities is determined by our levels of civic competence, but more profoundly so by the extent to which we believe in the authenticity of our citizenship. Such authenticity is the product of experience and socialization.

In democratic industrial societies characterized by mixed

economies, the relationship between citizenship and social policy is again determined by subjective evaluations. In Britain there remain deep value-conflicts regarding the proper relationship between the individual and the community. Our legally extensive range of public social services derives from collectivist ideologies. At the same time the ideology of self-help and individualism receives powerful support from the continuing dominance of market values in our lives. It is therefore still possible to demonstrate extreme definitions of the relationship between citizenship and social policy. For some, citizenship is enhanced and extended by the existence and use of social services. For others, citizenship is debased by reliance upon such aid.

This perceived relationship between citizenship and social policy can vary from one service to another. We have argued that social services can be stratified in terms of the extent to which they endow esteem or impose stigma upon users. It has also been suggested that not all universalist services endow esteem and not all selectivist services impose a stigma on their users. Few citizens appear to feel enhanced in status by recourse to family allowances, and even fewer seem to be stigmatized by the imposition of a means test when their children apply for a County Major award. The public's tendency to view social services as a taxpayers' 'burden' appears to vary according to the service and the category of need perceived.

In our present state of knowledge it is very difficult to understand the cultural processes by which social services and their users become stigmatized. It may be that some groups of users are held in such low public esteem that any service and personnel concerned mainly with their needs become stigmatized merely by association. The inferior care provided in consequence thereafter confirms and reinforces the stigma. The treatment of the mentally subnormal, the young chronic sick and the senile aged offer examples of this process of mutual reinforcement.[1] The appearance of physical normality, intelligence and the capacity to work are generally esteemed social qualities, the absence of which leads to stigma and negative discrimination. Services provided for such groups invariably

[1] Report of the Committee on Local Authority and Allied Personal Social Services, Cmnd 3703, HMSO, 1968, pp. 45–6

experience difficulty in recruiting all kinds of specialist staff and particularly personnel from high-status professions such as medicine, nursing and specialized forms of pedagogy.

In this way the standard of service provided can appear to give official approval to general community prejudices against such groups. Whilst it might be true to say that many of the staff of mental subnormality hospitals are dedicated to the welfare of their patients, quite clearly the majority of the public are not similarly inclined.[1] Yet it remains surprising how little we understand this process of social evaluation in the context of social services. For all we know, the sequence of evaluation may operate in a direction contrary to that already suggested. The public may equally well be taking its cue from the explicitly hierarchical ranking order of our social services. Clearly the priority ranking of expenditure across the full range of our public social services does express some kind of social evaluation. A minority of citizens tend to express outrage at extreme forms of negative discrimination or to seek their redress. Other members of the public may more passively conclude that those who receive, for example, the best hospital treatment or the best school places, do so on grounds of merit, while those who are left with inferior provision must have been judged by someone and found wanting.

We know almost nothing about the reasons for which citizens use services as they do, or about what attitudes lead them to feel deterred or encouraged in the search for assistance. Consequently, it remains difficult to estimate the degree of variation in the use of different but theoretically substitutable services between families[2] with similar needs and resources. We

<hr>

[1] Referring to the plight of the senile and mentally helpless, Enoch Powell writes, 'Of all the claims on any increment (of public resources), the least pressing and attractive politically is the claim of the *sans* everything. For they are in effect *sans* vote, *sans* M.P. and *sans* relatives . . . I see no likelihood . . . that the voters will start to clamour for less attention to the treatment of accident, or cancer, or mothers and children so that the quality of staff and conditions in mental and geriatric hospitals can be improved'. 'Politics of the Helpless' (Review of B. Robb, *et al.*, *Sans Everything*, Nelson, 1967), *New Society*, 13 July 1967, p. 57

[2] See Bleddyn Davies, *Social Needs and Resources in Local Services*, Joseph, 1968, pp. 32–8, and L. G. Moseley, 'Variations in Socio-medical Services for the Aged', *Social and Economic Administration*, Vol. 2, No. 3, July 1968,

have some information about the extent to which the elderly are deterred from claiming supplementary cash benefits.[1] Similar information is available on the educational preferences of parents.[2] We are largely left to speculate about the cultural origins and ideological bases of these preferences. In the immensely complicated field of personal welfare, where so much still depends on the initiative of citizens, our ignorance carries perhaps the most serious implications.[3]

Our general lack of evidence in this matter arises partly from the fact that there has been so little integration of Britain's social services between major services such as education, health, cash benefit systems, housing, and personal welfare. At another level, the world of social research has been equally divided. Sociologists, psychologists, social administrators and social workers know too little about one another's sphere of interest and derive insufficient support from one another's special area of competence.

The formation of individual and public attitudes towards social services needs to be viewed as a process separate, in some respects, from legislative procedures.

Redistributive social policies have egalitarian ends, yet even when such ends are legally attained in particular areas such as health care, the participation has not in practice taken place. It can be argued that the inception of services such as the National Health and National Insurance schemes represented a major break with the stigmas of Public Assistance and charity. In strictly legal terms, this is true, but changes in the law are not always the best indication of changes in public opinion and

---

pp. 169–83, for a study of variations in the use and provision of a particular group of services

[1] See Committee of Inquiry into the Impact of Rates on Households, Cmd 2582, HMSO, 1965, and Ministry of Pensions and National Insurance Report on Financial and Other Circumstances of Retirement Pensioners, HMSO, 1966

[2] See J. W. B. Douglas, *The Home and the School*, McGibbon and Kee, 1964; Ministry of Education, *15–18*, Central Advisory Council for Education, HMSO, 1959; and Department of Education and Science, *Children and their Primary Schools*, Vol. I, Central Advisory Council for Education, HMSO, 1967. (see also Vol. II, Appendix 3.)

[3] Cmnd 3703, especially chs XV and XVI (paras 491–4) on the need for more continuous research and consumer participation

attitude. It is now a commonplace to assume that old people, whose attitudes to social services were formed in poor law days, still feel stigmatized in the acceptance of supplementary benefit or residential care in a former workhouse. Some old people, in order to avoid stigma, do not take advantage of these benefits.

This continuing passivity of the poor in relation to social services is all the more remarkable when it is clear that market alternatives are effectively closed to them. We have yet to see the various lobbies in favour of returning the social services to private enterprise gather widespread working-class support. The market can shower its own slings and arrows of humiliation upon the heads of the poor; such humiliation forms part of the history of every working-class community. Another part of this tradition dating from pre-welfare-state times is the habit of deference and gratitude.

In a society where work and economic independence are still highly esteemed, the majority of prospective users of social services have also learned to value money for the status it bestows. Any request for expert service expresses a condition of dependency. In a market situation, parity of status is maintained between layman and expert by a payment. The client may depend on the expert for his skill, but the expert depends on his clients for a livelihood. This model role-relationship does not, however, apply equally throughout British society. The poor have lacked the money to claim any effective parity in the private market.

The aim of participation campaigns in the field of social welfare is to create in the minds of citizens a natural and vivid awareness of the right to certain goods and services outside a cash nexus.[1] The present vogue for such campaigns confirms that the prevalent view of the relationship between citizenship and social services is one which sees them as incompatible.[2]

[1] See A. Lester, *Democracy and Individual Rights*, Fabian Tract 390, in which the author outlines the case for a new Bill of Rights and more effective remedies for maladministration. Lester, however, ends this paper by stating, 'Yet if one examines situations in which individuals are already guaranteed by law, one discovers a vast gap between the rights which are written in the statute book and what is in fact enjoyed', p. 22

[2] See *Justice for All*: Society of Labour Lawyers' Report, Fabian Research Series 273, for a survey of evidence on the public's ignorance and general

Similarly, proposals such as the establishment of local legal centres staffed by salaried lawyers who advertise their services, although admirable, will not by themselves change long-established attitudes of deference and passivity. M. Zander, referring to American experience of 'neighbourhood law firms' discusses the methods of community education used to improve levels of social competence and information.[1]

By contrast, middle-class families have developed a more confident and demanding set of social expectations based on their experience of the private market. These expectations they carry over into the publicly financed social services where they vigorously practise positive discrimination on their own behalf. They also remain highly conscious of being taxpayers by virtue of their economic advantages. The professionals staffing the social services share this same life-style and reinforce these role definitions. Further study of the socialization of middle-class children would help us to understand more fully the transmission from generation to generation of these class differences in levels of social competence and expectation.

There may be equally good or better reasons for transmitting similar skills and attitudes to working-class children. Rather than working towards this end we have tended to give far more attention to a minority of poor families, who do use expensive social services as vigorously as do the middle class. Such families, however, are indicted for their incompetence rather than praised for their social expertise. The services used by such families are also generally held in low esteem and considered to stigmatize their recipients.[2]

---

apathy regarding the exercise of civic rights in both the public and private sectors. The authors describe as 'the key problem—the relative non-use of the available type of facilities by those who most need them', p. 37

[1] *Justice for All.* 'Of course these methods will not always prove successful; lectures, debates, discussions, even leaflets are fairly sophisticated means of communication . . . [and are] . . . unlikely to reach the hard core of those who are most apathetic and most alienated from society. But it is nevertheless considered to be a potentially most important adjunct to the normal functioning of the neighbourhood offices', p. 64

[2] One of the very few studies of how the public regard social workers concludes that 'Not only is there a serious lack of knowledge about social work and social workers, but in relation to particular social problems (e.g. marital conflict) a serious pessimism in the face of possible help or the

It would seem, therefore, that middle-class families who use high-status social services are esteemed for their social competence. Working-class families who follow their example share in community approval. When a minority of low-income families with multiple social problems make an equally intensive use of low-status social services, they experience social disapproval and stigma. This way of evaluating levels of social competence and incompetence is positive in so far as it measures actual usage. The categories of families that tend to be overlooked are those whose social problems arise or persist because they under-use the social services.

A truly comprehensive index of social competence must be equally concerned with measuring the extent to which some families under-use social services and the reasons why this under-usage occurs. One possible reason for the reluctance of local and central authorities to concern themselves with such problems is their difficulty in meeting present demands from current resources. A second reason may be that the services most likely to be needed by 'incompetent' families are those which rank low in public esteem. Such a list might include more subsidized housing, welfare foods, family allowances, supplementary benefits and community care. Setting out to encourage a greater use of these services might seem tantamount to subsidizing civic incompetence. The point at issue here is whether we measure competence in terms of use or non-use of social services, and whether we conceptualize social services as an extension to or a diminution of citizenship.

We have traced the development of the prolonged and often highly ideological debate between universalists and selectivists, which has been one of the central issues in social policy. Universalists tend to argue that social services are under-used when provided on a selectivist basis, because means-testing and similar procedures are felt by a significant minority of potential users to be intrinsically stigmatizing. Selectivists claim that means tests permit a more economical use of resources by directing them to where the needs are greatest in sufficient quantity and quality. Both groups agree that present forms of

feeling that one ought not to interfere'. Noel Timms, 'The Public and the Social Worker', *Social Work*, January 1962, p. 7

allocation are inefficient and that many eligible persons are not getting the services they need.

We would wish, however, to draw attention to the lack of convincing evidence about how people themselves define their relationship to social services. Our central hypothesis has been that social services can be ranked in terms of their stigmatizing potentialities, but we question the assumption that the principles governing allocation, eligibility and forms of provision play as significant a role in this process of ranking as may be inferred from the ongoing debate. From the little evidence that we have, there does not seem to be any consistency in public response and attitudes towards the use of social services that is explicable by reference solely to the principles of universality or selectivity.

If the hypotheses we have advanced in our model of social welfare should be substantiated, then it may be possible to account for some of these inconsistencies in public response. Furthermore, some doubt will be cast on the viability of alternative policies for encouraging a greater use of social services by deprived groups, policies which are based on the principle of positive discrimination and the encouragement of more 'consumer' participation.

Medical need is chosen as the best context for testing our hypothesis, because illness is a major cause of dependency, and the treatment and care of the sick usually involves the use of a wide range of non-medical services employing a variety of allocative criteria. The context of medical need is also one in which it is sometimes easier to separate physical from moral causes of dependency. Most deprived or underprivileged groups are so defined in terms of their relative social incompetence or incapacity with regard to performance in independent work-roles. Incompetence is more difficult to define than incapacity. Any measurement of social incompetence implies a degree of moral evaluation and disagreement over the question of desert. Incapacity arising from physical causes can be assessed with a greater degree of objectivity and in many instances a prognosis can be made with some certainty.

Other factors influencing our choice of medical need include the very total and personal kinds of dependency which can arise from medical causes. Even a partial loss of control over bodily functions may lead to a patient becoming dependent in very intimate ways upon the aid and good-will of both professional and lay persons. In conditions such as diabetes where capacity for self-care and work can be maintained at a normal level, the patient still depends for survival upon expert surveillance at regular intervals. Medical needs of a long-term kind are therefore likely to provide groups of people who will have relatively clearly formulated attitudes and expectations about dependency and the use of social services.

It should therefore be possible to test our hypothesis that dependency *per se* is a seriously neglected factor in the study of public attitudes towards the use of welfare services. Further study of this phenomenon might offer a more convincing explanation of the way in which people define the relationship between civic status and reliance upon social services. It may be that the nature of the dependency has a greater effect upon the user's definition of his own status than the principles governing the allocation of social services; and that this effect is greatest when the disability prevents the users from recovering independent status as workers and providers.

The hypothesis could be tested by selecting a number of dependency groups who require a wide range of social and medical services. Three suitable groups might be sufferers from diabetes, post-coronary conditions and disseminated sclerosis. Each of these groups allows consideration to be given to what appear to be the most relevant variables. These variables are:

(i)   *The nature of the illness* which affects the likely duration/recurrence of the dependency; capacity for work and self-care; and the patient's own attitude towards dependency, including the extent to which recovery is felt to be stigmatizing, and his own expectations regarding recovery;

(ii) *Age at onset of dependency,* which affects notions of 'entitlement' to social services;

(iii) *Sex,* in so far as it affects contexts of employment and work prospects and expectations;

(iv) *Marital status and household composition,* which affect the

types and range of supportive service available and
needed, and also variations in the claims of other related
dependents;

(v) *Social class,* covering the dimensions of
    (a) income, and the effect of dependency on earnings;
    (b) occupation and variations in opportunities for
        remaining in the same job;
    (c) normative/relational aspects and variations in levels
        of social skill and competence;
    (d) education and variations in capacity for retraining;

(vi) *Use of services*
    (a) services for which the patient is eligible;
    (b) services which the patient knows about;
    (c) services which the patient is using;
    (d) reasons for any discrepancies between (a), (b) and
        (c), including attitudes towards social services and
        other forms of aid.

Of these three groups, diabetes and post-coronary conditions
cover a range of recovery prospects from very poor to excellent
(when recovery is defined in terms of restoration to an independent work role). The prognosis for disseminated sclerosis
cases will be uniformly very poor, and the past work-record
of these patients will entitle them to little right to restitution
in terms of economic market criteria. This range of dependencies would allow full account to be taken of the three key
variables of time, depth and distance that we outlined in our
model of social welfare.[1]

On humanitarian grounds we would wish to see the hypotheses invalidated. If, however, they were to be sustained, the
investigation would show that the subjects define their claims
to citizenship and welfare rights, not so much in response to
the publicization of welfare rights and other incidental procedures, but through those processes of socialization that
transmit the norms and values characteristic of industrial
societies, namely, an emphasis on self-help, individual effort
and being independent. Dependency will be shown to be
culturally equated with subordinate and stigmatized status.
These definitions will also be reflected in the available social

[1] See ch. 4 above

services so that at both personal and institutional levels the most important criteria of social evaluation will remain economic ones.

Willingness to use social services will be affected by the potential user's ability to identify such usage with an eventual recovery of full or partial independence, and the capacity to make full or partial restitution for services received. When rehabilitative agencies identify 'success' with return to work and self-supporting status, they will be reinforcing the expectations and attitudes of their clientele. The consequences of using this criterion of 'success' will be to elevate the morale of those who respond to treatment and lower still further the morale of those who do not recover. Not only is it in the nature of certain medical conditions that some prognoses are hopeless, but the proportion of such patients is certain to grow as advances in medical science improve and prolong survival chances, especially in younger age-groups.

It is hypothesized, therefore, that patients with the best recovery prospects will make the most intensive use of social services. Conversely, the same value orientations, expressed at a societal level, will influence the allocation of services, so that those with the best recovery prospects will receive the better quality and greater quantity of services. Patients will also be most disposed to use those services which seem to them to have a direct and explicit bearing on the restoration of earning capacity, but so long as one such service is included to some effect in the total range of services employed, the general disposition to use social services will be positive. The reverse process and effects are hypothesized for groups with poor recovery prospects.

In summary, it is postulated that wherever the criteria of the economic market prevail, those states of dependency with the worst prognosis will receive the poorest social services. Advances in human knowledge and material wealth have helped to bring about a situation in which industrial societies can be shown to be culturally and psychologically incapable of assimilating extreme cases of dependency. Present levels of provision and effective concern for the chronic and incurably sick of all ages, but especially the young and the mentally subnormal, imply that even in the context of social welfare 'Unto everyone which hath shall be given; and from him that hath not, even that he hath shall be taken away from him'.[1]

At this stage the argument stands at a hypothetical level, but without some such set of hypotheses, formulated in terms of a model of social welfare, we are unlikely to make the best use of social research into human need, or to develop the most relevant policies.

CONCLUSION

In the last analysis, the study of social welfare is a study of human nature in a political context. It is undeniable that the history of social policy is a record of the compassion and altruism that men are capable of showing towards the unfortunate. It is this record which gives substance to the ideals and hopes of social reformers. Yet it is equally beyond dispute that the history of social policy is a chronicle of unrelieved or inadequately relieved suffering, and of the human tendency to ignore evidence of need and despair. We may point both to social progress and to the hesitant and tardy course that it has taken. Compassionate people still need to deaden their imaginations and sensibilities in order to live with a bearable conscience.

The welfare institutions of a society symbolize an unstable compromise between compassion and indifference, between altruism and self-interest. If men were predominantly altruistic, compulsory forms of social service would not be necessary; and if men were exclusively self-regarding, such compulsion would be impossible. Welfare institutions also represent a compromise between the claims of individual liberty and the need for social control. We have enough altruism to accept social restraints upon our more selfish dispositions. Social-welfare legislation ensures a modest provision for the needy and also prevents us from jeopardizing our own future welfare in the pursuit of instant gratification. But socialization is necessary to curb our desires; during infancy we require little instruction in hedonism. The spirit of altruism, far from being a natural flowering of human nature, must be seen as the product of rigorous discipline, of injuction to self-denial and the repression of the grosser forms of self-love.

[1] Luke 19:26

In our exploration of one area of social change we have observed how the process of social research and social reform have become increasingly interdependent, so that the two often seem to be synonymous. The normative theories that have inspired social criticism leave open to question the relationship between the ideals of democracy and welfare and the realities of human nature. There has been too great a readiness to assume that advances in social legislation are an expression of the democratic will and that by encouraging more participant forms of democracy we will hasten the progress of social reforms. The self-interest of the privileged has always acted as a restraint upon policies that seek to redistribute benefits to the under-privileged. Since the poor are now in a minority it might be better to reform by stealth and be grateful for the stubborn apathy of the majority.

At best, the exact relationship between changes in social consciousness and changes in social structures remains open to doubt. It can be hypothesized that greed and self-interest are constant factors in human history, and that their social manifestations vary according to changes in social organization. Social revolutions and the establishment of new political systems are unlikely to liberate any qualities in human nature that are not already known to us, or to give greater scope to those qualities we most admire. If Dicey's 'love of self . . . is due to causes deeper than any political or social reform will ever touch', we would do best to accept, as the least of evils, a democratic way of life that tolerates the persistence of self-interest but also restrains its excesses, and in so doing gives hope and substance to the claims of social welfare. The ultimate justification for seeking the enhancement of social welfare by democratic means rests on the belief that in states of greater freedom or greater control the evil that men are likely to do to one another far outweighs the good.

The tradition of social welfare is a positive expression of human altruism, albeit tempered with judicious self-regard. It is a part of that desire in human beings to become nobler than they would otherwise be in a state of nature and of their wish to avoid the greater evils of moral anarchy. It is not social theory but society itself that is a transcendental phenomenon.

Bibliography

(*Publications which were of particular value in
preparing the study)

*Abel-Smith, Brian, *The Hospitals 1800–1948, A Study in Social Administration in England and Wales*, London, 1964
Abel-Smith, Brian, *Freedom in the Welfare State*, London, 1964
Abel-Smith, B. and Pinker, R., Changes in the Use of Institutions in England and Wales between 1911 and 1951, Manchester Statistical Society, 1960
*Abel-Smith, Brian and Townsend, Peter, *The Poor and the Poorest*, London, 1965
Abel-Smith, Brian, Whose Welfare State, in MacKenzie, Norman (ed.), *Conviction*, London, 1958
Anderson, Perry, Components of the National Culture, in *New Left Review*, 1968
*Aron, Raymond, *Main Currents in Sociological Thought*, Vols I & II, London, 1968 & 1970
*Arrow, Kenneth J., Uncertainty and the Welfare Economics of Medical Care, in *American Economic Review*, Stanford, 1963
*Atkinson, A. B., *Poverty in Britain and the Reform of Social Security*, Cambridge, 1969
*Bendix, Reinhard, *Max Weber, An Intellectual Portrait*, New York, 1962
Beveridge, Janet, *An Epic of Clare Market*, London, 1960
*Berger, Peter and Luckman, Thomas, *The Social Construction of Reality*, London, 1967
Blackburn, Robin, Inequality and Exploitation in Britain, in *New Left Review*, London, 1967
Bottomore, T. B. and Rubels, Maximilien, *Karl Marx, Selected Writings in Sociology and Social Philosophy*, London, 1963
Briggs, Asa, *Seebohm Rowntree 1871–1954*, London, 1961
*Briggs, Asa, The Welfare State in Historical Perspective, *European Journal of Sociology*, Paris, 1961
Brown, Muriel, *Introduction to Social Administration*, London, 1969
*Burrow, J. W., *Evolution and Society*, Cambridge, 1970
Cartwright, Ann, *Patients and their Doctors*, London, 1967
Christopher, A. and others, *Policy for Poverty*, Institute of Economic Affairs, London, 1970

*Cohen, Percy S., *Modern Social Theory*, London, 1968
Collard, D., *The New Right*, London, 1968
Corbett, Anne, Priority Schools, in *New Society*, 30th May, 1968
Cormack, Una, The Seebohm Report—A Great State Paper, in *Social and Economic Administration*, Exeter, 1969
*Dahrendorf, Ralf, *Essays in the Theory of Society*, London, 1968
*Dahrendorf, Ralf, Out of Utopia, in Demarath III, N.J. and Peterson, Richard A. (eds), *System, Change and Conflict*, New York, 1967
Davies, Bleddyn, The Cost Effectiveness of Educational Spending, in Blaug, Mark and Others, *Social Services for All?* Part Two, London, 1968
*Davies, Bleddyn, *Social Needs and Resources in Local Services*, London, 1968
Dawson, H., *Bismarck and State Socialism*, London, 1890
*Dicey, A. V., *Law and Public Opinion in England During the Nineteenth Century*, London, 1962
Dickens, Charles, *The Old Curiosity Shop*, London
Donnison, D. V., *The Government of Housing*, London, 1967
Donnison, D. V. and Chapman, V., *Social Policy and Administration*, London, 1965
Douglas, J. W. B., *The Home and the School*, London, 1964
*Durkheim, Emile, *The Division of Labour in Society*, Glencoe, 1964
Durkheim, Emile, *Education and Sociology*, Glencoe, 1956
*Durkheim, Emile, *Moral Education*, Glencoe, 1968
*Durkheim, Emile, *Professional Ethics and Civic Morals*, London, 1957
*Durkheim, Emile, *Socialism*, New York, 1967
Durkheim, Emile, *Suicide*, Glencoe, 1951
Eliot, George, *Middlemarch*, London, 1959
Finer, S. E., *The Life and Times of Sir Edwin Chadwick*, London, 1952
*Ford, P., *Social Theory and Social Practice*, Shannon, 1969
*Friedman, Milton, *Capitalism and Freedom*, Chicago, 1968
*Gerth, H. H. and Mills, C. Wright, *From Max Weber*, London, 1961
*Ginsberg, Morris, The Growth of Social Responsibility, in Ginsberg, Morris (ed.), *Law and Opinion in England in the Twentieth Century*, London, 1959
Goffman, Erving, *Asylums, Essays on the Social Situation of Mental Patients and Other Inmates*, London, 1968
*Goffman, Erving, *Stigma: Notes on the Management of Spoiled Identity*, London, 1968
*Goldthorpe, John, The Development of Social Policy in England, 1800–1914, in *Transactions of the Fifth World Congress of Sociology*, 1962, Washington, International Sociological Association, London, 1964

Hajnal, J., European Marriage Patterns in Perspective, in Glass, D. V. and Eversley, D. E. C. (eds), *Population in History*, London, 1965

Hall, Penelope, *The Social Services of Modern England*, London, 1962

*Halmos, Paul, The Personal Service Society, in *British Journal of Sociology*, 1967

Halsey, A. H., Drawing a Map of Social Ideologies, in *Encounter*, London, 1970

*Harris, R. and Seldon, A., *Choice in Welfare*, London, 1965

Heywood, Jean S., The Public Understanding of Casework, in *Social Work*, London, 1962

*Hobbes, T., *Leviathan*, Oxford, 1946

*Homans, G. C., Structural, Functional and Psychological Theories, in Demarath III, N.J. and Peterson, Richard A. (eds), *System, Change and Conflict*, New York, 1967

*Horton, John, The Dehumanization of Anomie and Alienation: A Problem in the Ideology of Society, *The British Journal of Sociology*, London, 1964

*Horton, John, Order and Conflict Theories of Social Problems as Competing Ideologies, *American Journal of Sociology*, Chicago, 1966

*Hughes, H. Stuart, *Consciousness and Society*, London, 1959

Isajiw, W. W., *Causation and Functionalism in Sociology*, London, 1968

*Kaim-Caudle, P. R., Selectivity and the Social Services, *Lloyds Bank Review*, 1969

*Lambert, Royston, *Sir John Simon—1861-1904—and English Social Administration*, London, 1963

Lancet Sanitary Commission (Report of), London, 1866

*Lenski, Gerhard E., *Power and Privilege: A Theory of Social Stratification*, New York, 1966

*Leonard, Peter, The Application of Sociological Analysis to Social Work Training, *The British Journal of Sociology*, London, 1968

*Leonard, Peter, *Sociology in Social Work*, London, 1966

Lester, A., *Democracy and Individual Rights*, London, 1969

*Lévi-Strauss, Claude, *Structural Anthropology*, London, 1968

*Lévi-Strauss, Claude, *The Elementary Structures of Kinship*, London, 1969

Lewis, R. A., *Edwin Chadwick and the Public Health Movement, 1832-1854*, London, 1952

Lichtheim, George, *The Origins of Socialism*, London, 1969

Little, A. and Westergaard, J., The Trend of Class Differentials in Educational Opportunity in England and Wales, in *British Journal of Sociology*, 1964

*Litwak, Eugene, Extended Kin Relations in a Democratic Society, in Shanas, Ethel and Streib, Gordon F. (eds), *Social

Structure and the Family: Generational Relations, Prentice-Hall, New Jersey, 1965

*Lydall, H. F. and Tipping, D. G., The Distribution of Personal Wealth in Britain, in *Oxford Bulletin of Statistics*, London, 1961

Lynes, T., *Welfare Rights*, London, 1969

*Mack, Mary P., *Jeremy Bentham. An Odyssey of Ideas, 1748—1792*, London, 1962

*Marcuse, Herbert, *Eros and Civilization*, Boston, 1955

*Marcuse, Herbert, *One Dimensional Man*, Boston, 1966

Marcuse, Herbert, The Question of Revolution, in *New Left Review*, London, 1967

Marcuse, Herbert, *Reason and Revolution*, New York, 1941

Marsh, David C., *The Future of the Welfare State*, London, 1964

Marshall, T. H., Reflections on Power, in *Sociology*, London, 1969

*Marshall, T. H., *Social Policy*, London, 1967

*Marx, Karl, *Capital*, London, 1946

Marx, Karl, *The Civil War in France*, Peking, 1966

Marx, Karl, *The Eighteenth Brumaire of Louise Napoleon*, London, 1943

*Marx, Karl and Engels, Frederick, *Manifesto of the Communist Party*, Moscow, 1959

*Matza, David, The Disreputable Poor, in Bendix, Reinhard and Lipset, Seymour Martin, *Class, Status and Power: Social Stratification in Comparative Perspective*, London, 1967

*Mauss, Marcel, *The Gift*, London, 1954

*Mayer, J. P., *Max Weber and German Politics*, London, 1956

*McBriar, A. M., *Fabian Socialism and English Politics, 1884–1918*, Cambridge, 1962

McCallum ,R. B., The Liberal Outlook, in Ginsberg, Morris (ed.), *Law and Opinion in England in the Twentieth Century*, London, 1958

*McGregor, O. R., Social Research and Social Policy in the Nineteenth Century, *The British Journal of Sociology*, London, 1957

MacRae, Donald G., The Crisis of Sociology, in J. H. Plumb (ed.), *Crisis in the Humanities*, London, 1964

*MacRae, Donald G., *Ideology and Society*, London, 1961

*Mill, J. S., *Utilitarianism, Liberty, and Representative Government*, London, 1954

Miller, S. M., Poverty, in *Transactions of the Sixth World Congress in Sociology*, Vol. II, London, 1967

*Miller, S. M. and Rein, Martin, Poverty, Inequality and Policy, in Becker, H. S. (ed.), *Social Problems: A Modern Approach*.

Moseley, L. G., Variations in Socio-Medical Services for the Aged, in *Social and Economic Administration* (Exeter), 1968

Mowat, C. L., *The Charity Organization Society, 1869-1913, Its Ideas and Work*, London, 1961

*Nisbet, Robert A., *The Sociological Tradition*, London, 1967
*Parris, Henry, *Constitutional Bureaucracy, The Development of British Central Administration Since the Eighteenth Century*, London, 1969
*Perkin, H., *The Origins of Modern English Society, 1780–1880*, London, 1969
Pinker, Robert, *English Hospital Statistics, 1861–1938*, London, 1964
Political and Economic Planning, *Family Needs and the Social Services*, London, 1961
*Powell, Enoch, Politics of the Helpless, in *New Society*, 13 July 1967
*Poynter, J. R., *Society and Pauperism*, London, 1969
Reddin, Mike, Local Authority Means-tested Services, in Peter Townsend and others, *Social Services for All?*, Part One, London 1968
*Rex, John, *Key Problems of Sociological Theory*, London, 1961
*Roberts, David, *Victorian Origins of the British Welfare State*, New Haven, 1960
Rodgers, Barbara N., with Greve, John and Morgan, John S., *Comparative Social Administration*, London, 1968
Rumney, J., *Herbert Spencer's Sociology*, London, 1934
*Runciman, W. G., *Relative Deprivation and Social Justice*, London, 1966
*Schumpeter, J., *Capitalism, Socialism and Democracy*, London, 1961
Seldon, Arthur, Crisis in the Welfare State, *Encounter*, London, 1967
Seldon, Arthur, Which Way to Welfare?, in *Lloyds Bank Review*, London, 1966
Sharpe, L. J., *Research in Local Government*, London, 1965
Shils, Edward and Finch, Henry A. (eds), *Max Weber on the Methodology of the Social Sciences*, Glencoe, 1949
*Simey, T. S., *Social Science and Social Purpose*, London, 1968
*Sinfield, Adrian, *Which Way for Social Work*, London, 1969
*Slack, Kathleen M., *Social Administration and the Citizen*, London, 1966
Society of Labour Lawyers, *Justice for All*, London, 1968
Spencer, Herbert, *An Autobiography*, London, 1904
*Spencer, Herbert, *The Man versus the State* (ed. Donald G. MacRae), London, 1970
*Spencer, Herbert, *Principles of Sociology* (ed. Stanislav Andreski), London, 1969
*Spencer, Herbert, *The Study of Sociology*, London, 1894
Stedman-Jones, Gareth, The Pathology of English History, in *New Left Review*, London, 1967
*Tawney, R. H., *The Acquisitive Society*, London, 1946
Thoenes, Piet, *The Elite in the Welfare State*, London, 1966

Timms, Noel, The Public and the Social Worker, in *Social Work*, London, 1962

*Titmuss, Richard M., *Commitment to Welfare*, London, 1968

*Titmuss, Richard M., *Essays on the Welfare State*, London, 1958

*Titmuss, Richard M., *Income Distribution and Social Change*, London, 1962

Titmuss, Richard M., *The Irresponsible Society*, London, 1960

Titmuss, Richard M., *Problems of Social Policy*, London, 1950

Townsend, Peter, *The Family Life of Old People*, London, 1957

Townsend, Peter, *The Last Refuge*, London, 1962

*Townsend, Peter, The Meaning of Poverty, *The British Journal of Sociology*, London, 1962

Townsend, Peter, A Society for People, in MacKenzie, Norman (ed.), *Conviction*, London, 1958

Townsend, Peter and Wedderburn, Dorothy, *The Aged in the Welfare State*, London, 1965

*Webb, Beatrice, *Our Partnership*, London, 1948

Webb, Beatrice, *My Apprenticeship*, London, 1950

*Webb, Sidney and Webb, Beatrice, *English Local Government: English Poor Law History*, London, 1963

*Weber, Max, *General Economic History*, New York, 1961

*Weber, Max, *The Protestant Ethic and the Spirit of Capitalism*, New York, 1958

*Weber, Max, *Theory of Social and Economic Organization*, Glencoe, 1964

*Wedderburn, Dorothy, Facts and Theories of the Welfare State, in Miliband, R. and Saville, J., *The Socialist Register*, London, 1965

*Wilensky, H. L. and Lebeaux, C. N., *Industrial Society and Social Welfare*, Glencoe, 1965

Winter, Gibson, *Elements for a Social Ethic*, New York, 1970

*Wolff, Kurt H. (ed.), *The Sociology of George Simmel*, Glencoe, 1964

Wrigley, E. A., *Population and History*, London, 1969

Young, Michael and McGeeney, P., *Learning Begins at Home*, London, 1968

Young, Michael and Willmott, Peter, *Family and Kinship In East London*, London, 1962

*Zeitlin, Irving M., *Ideology and the Development of Sociological Theory*, New Jersey, 1968

Official Publications

Report from His Majesty's Commissioners for Inquiry into the Administration and Practical Operations of the Poor Laws, Fellowes, 1834

Report of the Royal Commission on Smallpox and Fever Hospitals, 1882, C 3314, 1882

Report of the House of Lords Select Committee on Poor Relief, 1888 (239), HMSO, 1888

Report of the Royal Commission on the Aged Poor, C 7684, London, HMSO, 1895

Report of the Royal Commission on the Poor Laws and Relief of Distress, Cd 4499, HMSO, 1909

(Beveridge Report) Social Insurance and Allied Services, Cmd 6404, HMSO, 1942

Report of the Committee of Enquiry on the Rehabilitation, Training and Resettlement of Disabled Persons, Cmd 9883, HMSO, 1956

Report of the Committee of Enquiry on the Costs of the National Health Service, Cmd 9663, HMSO, 1956

Report of a Working Party on Social Workers in the Local Authority Health and Welfare Services, HMSO, 1959

Molony Committee on Consumer Problems, Final Report, Cmnd 1781, HMSO, 1962

Ministry of Pensions and National Insurance, Report on Financial and Other Circumstances of Retirement Pensioners, HMSO, 1966

Report of the Committee on Local Authority and Allied Personal Social Services, Cmnd 3703, HMSO, 1968

Central Advisory Council for Education, Children and Their Primary Schools, HMSO, 1967

Royal Commission on Local Government in England, Cmnd 4040, London, HMSO, 1969

Ministry of Health, National Health Service, The Administrative Structure of the Medical and Related Services in England and Wales, HMSO, 1968

Department of Health and Social Security, National Health Service, The Future Structure of the National Health Service, HMSO, 1970

Index